HEY YOU – YEP, YOU!

Whether you're reading this in the bookstore or online and pondering whether to buy, or you've already taken the plunge and made the purchase, let's have a chat.

I know what you're going through. Yes, I have a 'glamorous' job on TV now, but that came to me late in life. Libby and I struggled for years with four young kids, a big mortgage and trying to build our own family business. It's a tough period of your life, juggling a relationship, children and a job – and don't even get me started on the nonstop bills. And all this at a time when wage rises are almost non-existent.

These financial pressures can take a toll on our emotional and mental wellbeing. We start being grumpy with our partner and family. The struggle to make ends meet seems endless, and life's little luxuries seem constantly out of reach. 'Money doesn't buy happiness', the old saying goes. That may be right, but gee, having enough to relieve the financial stress and enjoy a few luxuries can make you feel so much better!

So enough with feeling sorry for ourselves. Let's do something about it.

I'm here to help. But I need a commitment from you first. You have to *want* to change your life. I need you to commit to a step-by-step plan to get on top of your finances and possibly make some life-changing decisions – for the better. If you commit, *I'll commit and be there for you.* We're getting into a sort of ongoing partnership here to change your life.

This book outlines the 11 steps you need to take to get your finances under control and have a bit left over to afford the good things in life. But it doesn't end there. The problem with a book is that it's written at one point in time, but as we all know, when it comes to money there's constant change. Whether it's the economy, shares, property, interest rates, new investments, good deals – there's always something happening.

For that reason, the book also comes with a weekly email from me to keep you constantly updated on threats, opportunities, best deals and top suggestions for your money. It will basically contain the updates and information I think you need to know each week to keep your finances in shape. My promise is that the weekly email will be relevant and easy to understand, plus have a significant impact on your family finances. And it will help you sleep better at night.

This book is just the start of a unique partnership between us.

I'm excited! I hope you are too.

We advise that the information contained in this book does not negate personal responsibility on the part of the reader for their own financial management, including compliance with any legal requirements. It is recommended that individually tailored advice is sought where appropriate. The publishers and their respective employees, agents and authors are not liable for injuries or damage occasioned to any person as a result of reading or following the information contained in this book.

Kochie's 11-STEP MONEY PLAN

FOR A BETTER LIFE

DAVID KOCH

Pan Macmillan Australia

First published 2019 in Macmillan by Pan Macmillan Australia Pty Ltd
1 Market Street, Sydney, New South Wales, Australia, 2000

Copyright © David Koch 2019

The moral right of the author to be identified as the author of this work has been asserted.

All rights reserved. No part of this book may be reproduced or transmitted by any person or entity (including Google, Amazon or similar organisations), in any form or by any means, electronic or mechanical, including photocopying, recording, scanning or by any information storage and retrieval system, without prior permission in writing from the publisher.

Cataloguing-in-Publication entry is available
from the National Library of Australia
http://catalogue.nla.gov.au

Typeset in Univers 9.75/12.5 by Post Pre-press Group
Printed by McPherson's Printing Group
Pages design by Kirby Armstrong

The paper in this book is FSC® certified. FSC® promotes environmentally responsible, socially beneficial and economically viable management of the world's forests.

CONTENTS

INTRODUCTION vii

STEP 1: MAKE A LIST OF YOUR MONEY VALUES 1

This is a biggie. It's working out what you want your money to do for you as an individual, and for you as a couple if you're in a relationship. It will give you the foundation on which to develop good financial habits and set goals, and will provide the motivation you need to free yourself from any financial nasties you've fallen into.

STEP 2: DO YOUR HOUSEHOLD BUDGET, NOW 25

And while we're at it, let's have a squiz at your banking and clean up that pile of documents you've shoved down the end of the dining-room table. Trust me, you'll feel better.

STEP 3: TAKE THE NO-DEBT/LOW-DEBT PLEDGE 43

Then whip your mortgage into shape, take a scalpel to your credit card debt, and inoculate yourself against financial crisis.

STEP 4: CUT COSTS TO GROW HAPPINESS 63

And while you're there, plug the spending leaks so that you can afford the fun stuff and luxuries that really matter to you and your family.

STEP 5: GROW YOUR INCOME 93

Ask your boss for a pay rise. But if that goes south, investigate working for yourself or getting a side hustle.

STEP 6: FUTURE-PROOF YOUR EARNINGS AND ASSETS 123

Write a will, and while you're thinking long term, turbocharge your super and sort out your insurance.

STEP 7: BUY YOUR OWN HOME – OR DON'T 143

How do you make the best decision possible one way or the other? If you do buy, what's the best approach? If you don't buy, what are your options?

STEP 8: MAKE MONEY A FAMILY AFFAIR 163

Yes, you can afford a baby: draw up a baby budget. Doing this will show you how you can afford it and put your mind at ease, while also showing you strategies for minimising costs and teaching your kids about money.

STEP 9: SORT OUT YOUR TAX 191

And do it now – for peace of mind, to make sure you're paying what you should and not MORE than you should, and to avoid attracting ATO attention.

STEP 10: INVEST A THOUSAND BUCKS 207

Go on, do it. It will get you started on what's possibly the most beneficial financial activity available. If you're already an investor, read on for further tips.

STEP 11: MAINTAIN GOOD HABITS 227

Get steps one to 10 in place and then it's just a matter of maintenance.

ACKNOWLEDGEMENTS 241

INDEX 243

INTRODUCTION

Welcome – to the first page of what I hope will be a defining moment in your life.

This book provides not only an 11-step personal blueprint for getting your money and life under control, but also an ongoing relationship that will help you keep on top of the constantly changing financial environment, the economy, taxes and good deals.

But before we even start, let me ask you one question: what's your ultimate aim?

You see, the most common question I get asked is, 'Kochie, what should I do with my money?'

I just look back, thinking, 'How the hell should I know? I don't know you from a bar of soap and everyone is so different.' So my stock-standard reply to that question is, 'What do *you* want your money to do for you?'

Initially, I get a blank look . . . and then the penny drops. They realise they first have to decide what they *want* from their money.

This book is designed to help you answer that 'what' and give you a roadmap on how to get it.

This isn't a get-rich-quick book

Sorry, but it's best I tell you that right up front. Getting rich quick is usually high risk, and although it's achieved by a few, these success stories are normally counterbalanced by a lot who go broke just as quick, because the risks were just too high and the path too dodgy.

I don't want that and I'm sure you don't want that either. This book outlines a safe path where you can be comfortable at this stage of your life and set yourself up to gradually build wealth that will stay with you.

The three stages of your financial life

I find the problem with a lot of investment books is that they treat everyone the same, no matter their age or life stage. But obviously we're not all the same. I break down our life cycle of money into roughly three stages:

1. **18–35 years old:** young, having fun, building a career
2. **35–55 years old:** settled into a career, perhaps in a relationship, buying a home, having kids, trying to have a life while balancing the high expenses of children and the household
3. **55+ years old:** kids grown up – or you're close to getting rid of them (in the nicest possible way) – and more independent, while you're

transitioning to (or in) retirement, dependent on superannuation, with a lower income.

The people in each of these stages have completely different objectives for their money.

This book is aimed at the middle stage, when you're settling down and consolidating your life, money and assets.

Who should read this book?

This book is for you if:

* you've become an adult – i.e. you're 35 or older
* you've partnered up
* you haven't partnered up, but you're no longer at the young wild stage of life
* you've had kids, or you're thinking about it
* you've bought a house, or you're thinking about it
* you're carrying a little bit, or a lot, of debt
* you get a bit anxious about your finances and regularly stress about how you're going to make financial ends meet
* you have that nagging feeling that your finances are spinning out of control, and know you could do better but don't know how
* you're starting to wonder if you'll have enough super
* you're starting to wonder how you're ever going to afford a holiday, and school expenses, and the weekly expenses – and have a life
* you maybe feel a little embarrassed about your lack of financial competence
* you feel confused by the amount of financial information out there – you need one reliable, consistent source of information.

If I've just described you, imagine me sitting next to you with my hand out and saying, 'You've got this. Let's work through this as a team.'

The important thing is that you're fully committed to this process of getting your money under control. Quite simply, you have to want to do this or it's going to be like many of our ventures – full of enthusiasm early on that then wanes and eventually stops without us getting anything really important achieved.

That's not what I want for you. If your life and family are important to you – and why wouldn't they be? – then money is important. It might not be everything, but it really is vital.

INTRODUCTION

Why money is important

Here's a big statement: **I want this book to change your life forever.** Shit, I'm even nervous writing such a big claim in black and white. But there you have it. And I truly think it can – but only if *you* really want it to.

Caring for your finances is as important as caring for your kids, your house, your health or your parents, because it's an integral part of all of these things. The trouble is that many people find financial matters a little bit scary or confusing, or they're worried they'll make a mistake and get into hot water. And so they avoid looking after their finances and never make the most of the opportunities we can all take advantage of to grow our wealth and care for our loved ones.

What you'll learn

In this book, we'll go through your family finances in an easy-to-understand, entertaining, step-by-step process – think of it as your personal money makeover. You'll learn how to make a budget and stick to it; how to get your debt under control; how to cut costs and grow your income; how to invest your money wisely, including in a home if that's what you want; how to future-proof everything you've worked so hard for; how to sort out your tax obligations so you can rest easy; and how to make room in your financial life for children.

You'll find it isn't hard at all. Really. I reckon that as you read, you'll regularly say to yourself, 'That's not hard. It's really just common sense, so why haven't I done it before?'

This book is all about empowering you. Because knowledge is power – it gives you the confidence you need to get better deals, and to ensure you're doing the best you can with your money and it's doing the best it can for you.

And let me apologise in advance for all the nagging I'm going to do as you read. That's because I want to make sure it really does change your life. It's too easy to read something and then not follow through. So throughout each chapter (or 'Step'), there'll be 'Do This Now' actions and other exercises to keep you on track and ensure you reap the full benefits from this book.

Why does it feel so hard to make ends meet?

We're all being bombarded with information every day, through traditional media and social media. And so much of it seems to be negative or scary. It impacts the way we think. We get concerned for our family's safety, for the future of the country, for our jobs, for our money. And life can be so stressful anyway, as we try to balance family with work and life.

The facts are, Australia has never been safer (except, tragically, when it comes to domestic violence), our economy has never been healthier (27 consecutive years of positive economic growth) and we've never been wealthier (according to the Credit Suisse Global Wealth Index, the average Australian citizen is the richest in the world, ahead of the Swiss).

But all these positive facts are swamped by falling property prices, a roller-coaster share market and terrible scandals from the Banking Royal Commission. And while the average Australian may be wealthy from rising superannuation balances and house prices over the last 10 years, wage rises have been tiny over the last couple of years.

It's hard to make ends meet because we're asset-rich and cash-poor. You can't eat your house or superannuation, and wage rises aren't covering the increase in grocery prices.

Can you pay your bills and still live a great life?

You betcha. Of course you can! And I'm going to show you how.

Believe me, you'll find that making little adjustments in the way you manage your money every day will add up to a significant amount of surplus cash. It's then up to you to decide what to do with that extra cash – invest it, spend it, stack it away for an emergency: *the power is in your hands*.

Just to prove my point, as we go through the process we'll work out how much each change in behaviour would save you. Because I don't know each and every one of you, I'll base a lot of these calculations on the average Australian family of four, as measured by the Australian Bureau of Statistics (ABS).

WHAT DO THE FINANCES OF THE AVERAGE AUSTRALIAN FAMILY LOOK LIKE?

From all their latest data, this is what the ABS says about the average Australian family of two adults and two children:

AVERAGE HOUSEHOLD INCOME	$110,000 a year
AVERAGE HOUSEHOLD NET WORTH	$929,000
AVERAGE HOUSE VALUE	$656,000
AVERAGE HOUSEHOLD CAR VALUE	$36,500
AVERAGE AUSTRALIAN HOUSEHOLD SPENDING PER YEAR	
Housing (rent/mortgage)	$14,524
Food and non-alcoholic beverages	$12,301
Transport	$10,738
Recreation	$8966
Miscellaneous goods and services	$5039
Medical/health	$4298
Household furniture/equipment	$3038
Communication	$2445
Household services/operations	$2371
Clothing and footwear	$2297
Education	$2297
Domestic fuel and power	$2149
Alcohol	$1630
Personal care	$1482
Tobacco	$667

AVERAGE HOUSEHOLD DEBT	
Mortgage	$152,000
Consumer	$17,000
Credit card balance	$3273
Credit card balance accruing interest	$2062

This might not be anything like your own income, assets and spending, but the sorts of savings and earnings I'll outline throughout the book are genuinely possible, both for our imaginary average Aussie family and for your unique one.

Now, let's get right down to changing your financial future!

NOTES

NOTES

STEP 1: MAKE A LIST OF YOUR MONEY VALUES

This is a biggie. It's working out what you want your money to do for you as an individual, and for you as a couple if you're in a relationship. It will give you the foundation on which to develop good financial habits and set goals, and will provide the motivation you need to free yourself from any financial nasties you've fallen into.

> **DO THIS NOW**
>
> Think about your money. Is there one big dream you'd love to achieve that would change your life? Dream big, don't hold back. Write it down and refer to it every time your enthusiasm wanes.

IT'S TIME TO GET YOUR HEAD RIGHT

No one is going to make you financially well-off. Only you. It's up to you to be focused, disciplined and committed.

We have to be in the right headspace to achieve our dreams, regardless of whether we're single or in a relationship. Being in that headspace will give you the confidence you need to take control of your finances and change your financial world for the better.

That has certainly applied to Libby and me. In our relationship, I'm the primary breadwinner, and when I get a bit tired and cranky at work I come down with a bad dose of what we call the 'martyr syndrome'. You know the sort of thing:

'I earn the money and everyone else spends it! Where does it all go?'

'You don't care how hard I work for this money! You just spend it.'

'What, am I here just to feed everyone's spending habit?'

'Why are those princes and princesses [the kids] wasting *my* money?'

Whenever I get like this, Libby just smiles, ignores the comments and waits for the martyr to go back into its box and for me to get back into the right headspace.

It's not that I'm tight with our money, but sometimes I feel like everyone's enjoying the spoils except me. I reckon I work hard, and sometimes I like to buy a treat as a bit of a reward to keep me motivated. This can be a red rag to a bull with Lib.

You see, Libby is very particular about money. She:

* loves to see our savings balances grow
* is a rabid recycler, both to save the environment and save on costs
* hates paying credit card interest with a passion
* reads every label and trawls the comparison websites to find the best deals
* watches every dollar we spend.

I'm the first to admit that we wouldn't have been able to survive financially if it hadn't been for Libby's management of the family finances. But now we're on top of the mortgage, the high-expense education years are behind us and I'm earning a pretty good income, I reckon we can ease up a bit in terms of scrimping with our money.

Libby agrees. It's just that we often don't agree on the degree of easing up.

But it reminds us to keep reinforcing to each other that both of us have to be committed to making the most of our money. That we have to be completely transparent with how we spend it so neither of us can be accused of taking it for granted.

STEP 1: MAKE A LIST OF YOUR MONEY VALUES

In this chapter I'm going to give you tips on how to build a foundation for Steps 2–11 and give your relationship with your partner the support it needs to weather the inevitable financial storms.

I'm going to show you how to:

* understand and create your financial values and goals
* develop healthy financial habits
* if you're in a relationship, become a team that stays strong even under financial strain.

But first I want to show you that I'm really just like you!

Nobody's perfect: Kochie's financial weaknesses

It does amuse me at times that, just because I love talking and writing about business and finance, people think I must be perfect at managing my own money. Hey, I'm only human . . . Remember the old saying from your grandmother about the cobbler whose children had holes in their shoes?

It pays to remember that no one's perfect at everything. We're all normal, we all have strengths and weaknesses. The key to any sort of success is recognising your weaknesses, working out how to overcome them and, ultimately, turning them into strengths. Wherever that weakness might be – your personality, your career, your health or your money management – financial success is about plugging those holes.

Thankfully, Libby is very different from me and, in most cases, her financial strengths complement my weaknesses. And let me tell you, I have a few money weaknesses.

* **I'm not a details person.** My work life (co-hosting *Sunrise*, running the family business, being chairman of Port Adelaide Football Club, etc.) is pretty hectic. I love being busy. I tend to put tasks like regularly going through the credit card and bank statements to check the transactions are all correct on the backburner, which means, eventually, things can fall through the cracks. Libby, on the other hand, loves going through every item on a statement and checking its authenticity. She has this sort of 'dog with a bone' personality where she won't let anything go without fully investigating it.

* **I need to buy myself little rewards.** When I've had a particularly busy week that's turned out to be a bit of a grind, I often get tempted to buy myself something (a shirt, a music album, a book) as a personal reward for all that effort. Yes, Libby often gets annoyed with me and gives me 'the talk' about financial leakages.

* **I focus on going forward rather than pausing regularly to look back.**
  I tend to be the guy who's always looking for what's next and not spending enough time analysing what I've just done. Libby often has to remind me to look back, for example, on how we're doing with our household budget and learn from that information. I'm always looking ahead to what we need to do in the coming month.

* **I can be too embarrassed to say no and walk away.** Here's a case in point from about 20 years ago that I still think about today. I was shopping for a leather jacket at a store where I knew the owners quite well. They showed me this stunning jacket, I tried it on, it fitted like a glove, we all agreed it looked fantastic. Perfect. Got to the register and they rang up the price . . . I almost had a heart attack. You could've bought a new fridge for the price. But I knew them, I was embarrassed to say no, so I paid, sweating at the thought of telling Libby. She was very good and said something about 'learning from mistakes'. But that jacket still seems to get a mention today when the two us have robust discussions about our spending habits!

* **Some of my 'hobbies' can be pretty costly.** I once bought a share (a very small one) in a professional basketball team. Yep, every sports nut's dream. I justified it in all sorts of ways to Libby: 'I don't play golf, so this is the same as my club and greens fees', 'It could be a good investment', 'It will be great fun for the kids and a good family activity'. Yes, it turned out to be fun, but it was a terrible, terrible investment. Another time I rebuilt a 1967 Mustang Shelby GT500 car. You know, the car from the classic movie *Gone in 60 Seconds*, the Eleanor. The body shape is a work of art. I love that car, but it was, umm, a bit over budget to complete.

My point here is for you not to think that just because you've made mistakes in the past or you have 'bad' money habits, you're not cut out for financial success. In fact, quite the contrary – we all are. We just need to put in the effort and keep an eye on our weaknesses.

STEP 1: MAKE A LIST OF YOUR MONEY VALUES

DO YOU WANT TO BE RICH?

I'm guessing you're here reading this book because you want at the very least to be happy with your financial situation – you might even hope it will help you get rich. You're not alone – a recent survey found a burning desire among average Australians to be 'rich', but their definition of 'rich' varied enormously. Naturally, it depended on the lifestyle, the values and the personality of each individual. Definitions ranged from not having any money worries to being able to buy a private island!

While the average Australian may be ranked the richest in the world, for most of us it doesn't seem like that as wage growth stays low and so many people are making incredible sacrifices just to make ends meet. Financial stress seems to be rampant throughout the community. So how do you know when you're well-off and don't need to worry about money?

The truth is, there's no magic number. It's very individual. I come across people who are objectively well-off but can't see the forest for the trees, and others who don't earn much at all but are in a fantastic financial position.

What is 'rich'?

I believe that the start of every project like this has to have a goal, so here's what I ultimately want for you after you've read this book and as we work together over the years to come: our goal is to be rich – based on my nine-point definition of 'rich', outlined below.

1. The basics are sorted

Ready access to food, clean water, high-quality health and education services, plus a safe environment to live and work in, are all things we take for granted in this country. We need to remind ourselves that more than 2 billion people live on less than two dollars a day, according to the World Bank, and lack access to even the most basic services.

In Australia, many of the basics come at a financial cost. My goal is to make sure you don't have to worry about affording them.

2. You have zero debt

Truly rich people aren't drowning in debt. Their assets are paid off, while their income is used to fund their lifestyle or invest in growth assets that will continue to build their wealth.

A seemingly rich person who has everything but has paid for it through debt will be in for a rude awakening if their situation changes and they can no longer meet their repayments.

3. You can afford to be healthy

Rich people are able to invest in their health. That means they can afford regular dental check-ups and whatever doctor, specialist or hospital treatments they require, and can take advantage of other health services like visiting the physiotherapist or joining a gym.

4. Your kids are covered

Rich people can fully support their kids until they reach adulthood, including food, education and extracurricular activities. It's not about spoiling them or giving them lots of cash. It's about providing them with the opportunities they need to develop into successful adults in their own right.

5. It doesn't matter if something comes up

Whether it's marriage or divorce, having another baby, or an unfortunate illness, life events aren't going to affect a rich person's standard of living.

6. There are no financial constraints on your activities

You can do whatever you want, whenever you want, without even thinking about the costs. Within reason, of course – a Kim Kardashian jet-set lifestyle doesn't count.

A side effect of being able to live off passive income (see point 8 below) and not being crippled by debt is the ability to choose what you want to do when you wake up in the morning. While rich people may be employed, they're free to decide which opportunities they want to pursue. And they enjoy their work.

7. You make a difference for others

Being able to use your wealth to help others indicates you're rich in spirit as well as financially. To become a philanthropist, supporting organisations that make a difference in the community, or directly supporting others in need, is the ultimate virtue of being 'rich'.

It's acknowledgement that, while you've worked hard, others may not have received the same opportunities to be financially independent themselves, and you have an obligation to help.

8. You can live off your passive income, and it won't run out

Passive income is money coming in that you didn't directly earn, like share dividend payments or rental income from an investment property. Rich people are able to support themselves and maintain their standard of living using just passive income. While this might sound like a pipe dream right now, remember that we'll all have to do this at some stage when we retire and lose a regular wage.

Again, we're lucky in this country that we have a compulsory superannuation system that gives everyone a leg-up. But rich people, regardless of whether they live to 82 or 102, have organised their affairs so their money won't run out.

Much of that means spending on a lifestyle you can afford.

9. You realise that money isn't everything

This is the most important measure of being rich. Plenty of people who prioritise money over their personal relationships or morals live to regret their wealth. Truly rich people, on the other hand, are grounded, have great relationships with their family and friends, and are proud of their achievements.

So what do you think? What's your definition of being rich? Dream a little and add your own personal benchmarks that would indicate you're worry-free.

NOTES

THE HABITS OF RICH PEOPLE

In my job I get to meet a lot of people, many of them wealthy businesspeople, entrepreneurs, movie stars and famous singers. I'm fascinated with what makes them tick, and more than a little envious. I'm always curious to know what makes them different from the rest of us and what we can learn from them to help us be as successful.

Paul Sullivan, author of *The Thin Green Line: The Money Secrets of the Super Wealthy*, puts it concisely: wealthy people don't just have money, they know how to protect and grow their wealth as well. The good news is the rest of us can learn from the money habits of these super-wealthy people, incorporate them into our own lives and hopefully get there ourselves a little faster.

I think there are eight money lessons we can learn from the wealthy.

1. They create wealth

Flick through Australia's AFR Rich List or Young Rich List on any given year and you'll notice the majority of entrants are in the business of wealth creation. Maybe they started their own business, had an amazing idea or are at the pinnacle of their career.

The lesson here is that these people have given it a go and, as a result, are able to generate their own income and assets to grow their overall wealth.

2. They take smart risks

Wealthy people understand that there's no reward without risk. Of course, you could always win the lottery, but you could also get struck by lightning. It's not something you want to rely on.

So whether it's borrowing money to grow a business or investing in income-generating assets over the long term, rich people are comfortable with taking on a reasonable level of risk to generate an above-average return.

3. But they do their homework

While the wealthy are happy to take a risk, they do their homework carefully before making a move. They put in the time and effort to ensure they have every base covered, and they're not emotional about it. If a deal doesn't stack up, they'll just walk away.

4. And they're not afraid of failure

Gerry Harvey, the co-founder of retailer Harvey Norman, once said to me, 'You've never been in business until you've been to the brink, looked over the cliff, learnt the lesson and then stepped back.' Great advice. I thought he was just being dramatic until it happened to me and I realised how insightful he was. Most rich people have had plenty of failures – the key is learning from them.

5. They're frugal

This one always stumps people. Aren't rich people constantly splurging on designer watches, fancy restaurants and first-class flights? Nope. They're much more likely to be watching every dollar that goes in and out like a hawk: it's how they got so rich in the first place (and why they'll stay that way). According to research Paul Sullivan completed with financial psychologist Brad Klontz, the richest 1 per cent eats out 30 per cent less often than an average wealthy person, and also saves 30 per cent more for retirement.

Frugal and conservative decisions like these are a way of life for wealthy people and extend into all aspects of their finances.

6. They work hard (really hard) . . .

Self-made people know from experience that one of the surest ways of rising above the rest is working harder than most other people. There's no way around it. In almost any field, if you're looking for work–life balance and reasonable hours, then chances are you're not going to be striking it rich.

So if you're looking to earn lots of money, get ready to make some sacrifices.

7. And drive a hard bargain

Most wealthy people are born negotiators who want the very best deal in every situation, including pay rises and promotions, and are prepared to haggle to get it. They don't get embarrassed about pushing too hard on a purchase and are relentless in getting the best deal on everything they can, no matter how small the purchase.

8. Finally, they keep their feet on the ground

I'm a big believer that the richest people are those with a great family around them, not just a lot of money in the bank. In my experience the 'wannabes' are usually the pains in the backside, while those who've made it are by and large pretty sensible and down-to-earth people.

After all, you can always earn more money, but family, friends and values you can't buy.

YOUR FINANCIAL VALUES AND GOALS

Being a better money manager can be boring and appear pointless unless you have an enticing goal to aim for and values to uphold.

Values are something we all have. They're the principles, standards, morals and ideals we live by. They're the backbone of our day-to-day decisions. They're those intangible things we hold most dear in life. They're the core of our being – and doing.

There's nothing better than a relationship where values and goals are shared. Successful couples come up with goals together, based on their values, and check in frequently to make sure they're on the same page. They break them down into short-, medium- and long-term goals, and constantly refine them. Do you want to purchase a home together? Are you saving up for kids? Do you want to make extra superannuation contributions? Or plan a big trip? Successful couples talk about where every dollar is being spent and reset their goals regularly.

You just rolled your eyes, didn't you? Come on, admit it. I know it sounds airy-fairy, but formulating your values and goals can have a huge impact, motivating you to develop and implement an action plan to change your financial life.

If it makes it any easier, a trick Libby and I use is to sit down with a bottle of wine and a cheese plate (our personal preferences) when we assess our values and goals. I must admit, after a couple of glasses our goal setting becomes a lot more fun. So set aside some time to talk things through, and have something good to eat and drink while you do it.

Let's go through the process.

How to set your values and goals

As a family, Libby and I are pretty big on living with strict values – we see them as the core of our lives. Values come first – and we then align them with our goals. Although you may not realise it, this is the process your mind works through too.

'Values' can be our need for security, health, happiness, providing for our loved ones – the list is endless. As you can see in the table opposite, it's possible to agree on the fundamental values of a relationship, but how to achieve that for each individual can be very different. The key is each partner understanding the other's goals and working together to achieve them.

STEP 1: MAKE A LIST OF YOUR MONEY VALUES

WHAT MIGHT VALUES AND GOALS LOOK LIKE?

Let's take these three core values – security, health and happiness – and add goals from two different people: Libby and me. As you can see below, although our values are the same, our goals are different.

VALUE	LIBBY'S GOALS	DAVID'S GOALS
SECURITY	Owning a house	Having a stable job
HEALTH	Eating well	Going to the gym
HAPPINESS	Helping others	Fulfilling dreams

If both partners can achieve their own individual goals to meet their common values, there should be close to financial harmony in the relationship. If things are working as they should, then those goals will be intertwined. For example, my goal of a stable job should lead to Lib's goal of us owning our house and, as a result, we both meet our 'security' value.

Lib's always been a stickler for us eating well, while I've become a bit of a gym junkie. Keeping fit has been an important part of the way I cope with the strange hours I work, while Libby reckons it's a reflection of my midlife crisis. But in recent times she's started going to a different gym and enjoying the benefits of improved fitness. So it's nice when shared values can lead to the same goal.

It's similar with happiness. I love fulfilling my personal dreams, which are often travelling to different countries and enjoying their unique experiences. East Timor is a passion of mine, after visiting that struggling neighbour and understanding what we should be doing to help it move from poverty to self-sufficiency. Libby has caught that passion and now helps an orphanage there, which fulfils her goal of helping others.

DO THIS NOW

Sit down – with your partner if you're in a relationship or with a close friend – and work out what your money goals and values are. Make it enjoyable by turning it into a social occasion, with a drink and some nibbles.

HEALTHY FINANCIAL HABITS

Of all the couples we know, the ones who manage their finances the most successfully have these 10 important traits, all of which you'll develop as you work through this book.

1. They have no money secrets

As soon as a money-wise couple is in a committed relationship they declare their entire financial world to each other. That means coming clean about salaries, credit card debt, university debt, credit scores, betting accounts and anything else that might affect their financial future as a couple.

It can be tough to confess all your money secrets, but it's crucial. It really is the first step in starting to build a household budget (see Step 2) and set financial goals.

You don't want any financial skeletons in the closet.

2. They talk a lot about money

> **DO THIS NOW**
>
> Get out your diaries and schedule a regular money meeting with your partner or a close friend; I recommend setting aside at least 15 minutes a month just to talk about your money. I don't mean paying bills or checking credit card statements, but talking about the parameters of managing your finances.
>
> Be open and be honest and don't be afraid to disagree. Just as each relationship is unique, so are each couple's financial affairs. It's a time to look at your big-picture financial situation and discuss whether you're comfortable with where you're at.

It doesn't matter so much *what* couples do with their cash, but that they make decisions together and respect each other's opinions.

STEP 1: MAKE A LIST OF YOUR MONEY VALUES

WHAT DOES A 15-MINUTE MONTHLY MEETING LOOK LIKE?

Your agenda should be tailored to you. Here's an example to help you put your own agenda together.

Amy and Linda have two children and a mortgage. Linda is a freelancer and is concerned her superannuation is underfunded, while Amy dreams of taking the kids to Disneyland. Their agenda for their 15-minute monthly catch-up might be:

* Is the family budget working to plan?
* Are we adding $50 a week to the Disneyland account and $40 a week in extra superannuation contributions?
* Are we happy with the Disneyland and superannuation priority or do we want to add or change priorities?
* Do we need to reassess our wills to cover the two children?
* Are any unforeseen costs emerging?

3. They set specific goals

Successful couples come up with goals together and check in frequently to make sure they're in synch and on track – as part of their monthly 15-minute catch-ups. They break them down into short-, medium- and long-term goals and refine them constantly.

Do you want to purchase a home together (see Step 7)? Are you saving up for kids (see Step 8)? Do you want to make extra superannuation contributions (see Step 6)? Or plan a big trip (see Step 4)? Successful couples talk about where every dollar is being spent and reset their goals regularly.

4. They divide up responsibilities

One partner should never have sole responsibility for a couple's finances. That's a recipe for relationship disaster that can lead to financial infidelity (see page 17) and abuse of power.

Whether it's opening joint accounts, paying the rent or mortgage, the power bill, superannuation contributions or other expenses, your financial commitments are the responsibility of both parties. Successful couples don't assume their partner will take care of certain aspects; they work together to divvy up the responsibilities.

There's no right answer on who looks after what, but it's important to be on the same page and not let it default to one person without having a conversation about it. Partners should discuss joint bank accounts, who's paying which bill, and how they want to use any discretionary income as a team. At the end of the day, it's all about clear communication. That's why I recommend the monthly 15-minute catch-up.

HOW COULD WE DIVIDE UP THE FINANCIAL TASKS?

Everyone's responsibilities will fall differently, but here's an example of how it could work.

Ingrid and Faruk both work full time and have agreed to divide their joint financial responsibilities as follows:

* **Ingrid:** investments, superannuation, dealing with the bank (checking statements, loans, credit cards etc.).
* **Faruk:** paying bills, monitoring expenses against the budget, looking after insurance.

They make sure they discuss these with each other, so they're always on the same page.

5. They protect what they have

When couples bind their lives together, it doesn't just create an emotional bond but a financial one as well. If something were to happen to either spouse, it's better to be safe than sorry and know the other person is taken care of.

That means ensuring you have adequate insurance cover (see Step 6). The greater the financial responsibilities (home loan, consumer debt, children, expenses), the larger the cover required to protect against losing an income stream from a partner. Life, income and trauma insurance are essential, depending on your circumstances, along with adequate coverage for major assets such as the house, cars and valuables.

6. They plan for the unthinkable

Though often overlooked, estate planning – such as writing wills – is a key factor in a successful financial future (see Step 6). As soon as they start a serious, long-term relationship, couples should think about naming beneficiaries, executors and powers of attorney. When kids come into play, it's important to name guardians for them as well.

Not only that, but couples should update these documents at least every five years, as goals and circumstances can change drastically over time.

7. They accept they are different and never judge

Everyone has different priorities, and part of operating within a partnership is to respect your partner's choices. That includes keeping an open mind, for example, if your spouse's spending habits differ from your own. If you truly think your partner has a spending (or thrift) problem, then it's time to have an honest and loving conversation with them. If you're just annoyed that they spent money on something you'd never spend money on, give your partner the benefit of the doubt.

And pick your battles. A small purchase that doesn't impact on your financial goals and plans is nothing to get annoyed about. If you or your partner want to make a bigger purchase, your first step should be to talk it through together.

8. They live within their means

Spend less than you think you need to, or than you earn. It's that simple.

It all starts with that good-old family budget, which tracks expenses and income to make sure the former don't exceed the latter (see Step 2). Then it's about maintaining the personal discipline you need to stick to it – to forgo non-essentials when necessary and cut back when it's right (see Step 4).

The reward is having money left over to achieve a goal like investing (see Step 10) or taking that dream holiday.

9. They set strong ground rules

Once you're in a long-term relationship, your spending habits are no longer purely your own – they affect someone else as well. That's why it's crucial to decide together how and when you'll spend, and create a set of ground rules for handling money that works for both you and your partner.

Don't forget, every relationship needs a bit of individual independence to flourish – and that includes money. Each person needs a level of discretionary spending for which they're unaccountable, to support hobbies, gifts and passions.

10. They have fun!

Saving or investing just for the sake of making more money is boring. Life is for living, and a good financial relationship will help you to live better – and have fun. Money can be a point of contention, but successful couples don't let it ruin their relationship. They don't make it the ultimate goal, they use it to fuel other goals.

None of this is rocket science but, believe me, it will make a huge difference to your relationship and reduce financial stress. If you and your partner can talk openly about money and agree to develop similar habits, you'll be able to solve any financial crisis quickly and calmly.

KEEPING YOUR RELATIONSHIP SOLID IN A CRISIS

I saw a sticker on the back of a van recently that made me laugh out loud: 'Driver carries no money – married with kids.'

Stress over finances can put enormous pressure on any relationship. The way money is managed and who has the power and control is obviously an important issue that couples need to sort out fairly early in their relationship. If there's conflict in this area, it can create a personal financial crisis (PFC – more about those on page 58).

Sometimes problems arise because one partner hands money matters over to the other and then isn't happy with how things are being handled. It's just one example of how a couple might not effectively delegate to each other so that the necessary financial responsibilities are fulfilled. What they're not doing as a team is agreeing on ways that certain things will be done in order to meet both their needs. In other words, they're not honouring their financial values and goals. Sometimes arguments over money come about because there are no agreed-upon goals, rather than because of how the money is handled.

In a small business, it's best for the partners to have a business or strategic plan that they review along the way, particularly with regard to the various responsibilities of each partner. Relationships are similar. You need to have a common vision of where you're going with your money and what your goals are – whether it's to travel or purchase a home or something else. Once the parameters or vision are agreed upon, then certain responsibilities can be allocated. So not only does there need to be agreement on financial goals, but there also needs to be a level of planning in order to achieve those goals.

One reason money can create problems is that for many people it does have a notion of power attached to it. Like it or not, money is the single most obvious sign of power in our society, and the ability to get money is valued very highly. So in a relationship, the partner who gets more money can feel entitled to wield power over how the money is managed – and that can present all sorts of problems. Money problems can also be a symptom of other difficulties. If things aren't going well with the relationship, then they're unlikely to be going well with the money either.

Resolving your differences

Sure, strains are going to be put on a relationship when there's simply not enough money to make ends meet. And there are obviously going to be problems if a penny-pinching miser gets together with a credit-bingeing shopaholic. And if a couple of spendthrifts get together they might walk hand in hand into bankruptcy.

If these issues aren't sorted out, there can also be unforeseen, long-term consequences. For example, when two people are both conservative with their money, and reinforce this conservatism in each other, they'll probably avoid taking on investment risk. The danger is that they could miss out on returns from their investments and fall behind in their savings, perhaps leaving them short of money in their retirement.

Psychologists say that the way we view money is largely determined by how we were brought up. For example, some people come from families in which love and appreciation is shown by buying gifts, while others only buy the necessities and see too much gift-giving as frivolous and materialistic.

Given opposites attract, it's possible you and your partner have come from very different backgrounds. Let's face it, that, and a bit of the old midnight magic is probably what brought you together in the first place. And while all the other things might be working, it's actually quite rare for a couple to come together with exactly the same attitudes to money and spending. Usually one partner is more restrained in their spending and the other more spontaneous.

Some of the tips below for dealing with much worse problems apply here, but the most important thing is to talk to your partner, establish your values and priorities, and figure out a way to ensure you can work together to achieve your goals without coming into regular conflict. Letting a financial issue silently fester can destroy a relationship.

When your partner cheats on you – financial infidelity

It's that feeling in your gut, that intuition that something isn't quite right. Things just don't add up financially. Infidelity in a relationship isn't necessarily sexual – it can be financial as well, and equally devastating.

I know of one couple where the wife had that intuition that something was awry, did nothing about it and one day was confronted by the sheriff evicting her from the family home. Her partner had bet everything they had on a dodgy investment that went bad, and they lost everything.

Financial infidelity comes in many guises. Hiding a new clothing purchase ('this old thing'), having a small secret betting account to make the occasional punt, or secretly splurging on a good night out with friends is one level of financial infidelity. But then there's operating secret credit cards, taking out loans to make risky investments and hiding sources of income. This is a much more serious and damaging level of financial infidelity.

Yes, individuals need their own financial space. It allows you to breathe and spoil yourself with little pick-me-ups, which are so important to keeping life in perspective. Maintaining your financial sanity with little indulgences keeps you motivated and on top of things.

But there's a limit. When financial infidelity gets to a stage where large amounts of money are involved, either earned or spent, without a partner's knowledge, then that 'cheating' becomes a serious breach of trust.

TAKE THIS QUIZ: Is there financial infidelity going on?

When I talk to friends who come to us with concerns of suspected financial infidelity, I use this very simple quiz as a starting point.

1. Do you have online access to all bank accounts?   Y / N
2. Do you have access to all the insurance papers, land title deeds, investment documents and wills?   Y / N
3. Do you know your partner's salary and superannuation fund?   Y / N

If the answer to any of these three questions is no, then you could have a problem and need to dig deeper.

The warning signs of financial infidelity

You could well have a serious problem with your partner if:

* **Your money questions are met with evasive or defensive responses that leave you none the wiser.** Answers like 'No need to worry', 'Don't you trust me?' or 'I'll check on it but it's under control'. Even more worrying is an angry reaction out of proportion with the question asked.
* **Your partner refuses to have regular sit-down meetings to go through your finances.** Even when you explain it's for your own peace of mind in case they get hit by a bus, you're still never included in managing the finances.
* **Financial statements start to disappear.** You can't find recent credit card or bank statements, or investment files are missing from the filing cabinet. Even worse, your partner won't produce them or denies anything to do with them.
* **There are unexpected cash withdrawals or transfers from accounts.** When you ask your partner about them there's tension, nervousness or weird explanations.
* **Your partner asks you to sign documents without explanation or a chance to review.** When you ask to read the documents you're told there isn't time or you wouldn't understand.

- **There are strange phone calls or letters and emails demanding payment that you know nothing about.** And your partner is evasive when you ask them to explain.
- **You discover a secret account or credit card you never knew existed and your partner doesn't explain it properly.**

If a couple of these red flags start to appear together, you must confront the situation immediately. Often the guilty partner will be relieved to unburden their secret, which could have been tearing them apart.

How to fix it

Most financial infidelity originates from a mistake a partner has been too embarrassed to admit to that has then festered and spiralled out of control.
To sort the mess out:

- **Agree on financial goals and a budget.** If your goals and desires are significantly different, talk about how you'll set priorities and compromise. Try to come to an understanding about what's important to both of you.
- **Discuss your money styles.** If you have different styles of spending, consider creating separate accounts so that each of you has control over a reasonable amount of discretionary cash.
- **Forgive and forget – within reason.** Weigh the situation rationally, but ensure your partner makes some financial sacrifices, such as delaying other purchases, to get the family budget back on track.
- **Have regular financial conversations.** Follow my rule of setting aside 15 minutes a month to sit down with your partner to talk about money and your financial goals and priorities.

Avoiding sexually transmitted debt

STD . . . no, it's not a social disease, but it can be just as worrying – sexually transmitted debt. It's where one partner in a relationship is lumbered with the debts of the other. You'd be amazed just how common this problem is.

None of us is so smart that we could turn around and say we've never made a mistake where money is concerned. It worries me though that women tend to be more trusting than men, so a higher proportion of them get taken for a ride financially.

It seems a sad fact of my stage of life that so many of our family friends are separating at the moment, and I'm shocked at how many wives are left so financially vulnerable.

How to keep on top of money matters

* **Base financial decisions on economics, not emotions.** When the flowers fade the socks still have to be washed. If you trust each other, you should have no problem formalising that trust by keeping each other informed about financial decisions.
* **Don't dismiss it, read it.** When you have to sign papers it's better to be one day late than to lose everything in five years' time just because you were too busy to read the small print. This is as relevant for simple matters, such as reading the guarantee documents on a newly purchased electrical appliance, as it is for familiarising yourself with the conditions of use on a credit card or opening a bank account.
* **Agree on a financial plan.** That way both partners have common goals and know where they're heading.

Courts can be unsympathetic to the cry, 'I didn't know'. Ignorance is no defence, so insist on knowing what's going on with your finances.

Danger zones

* **Going guarantor.** If the bank doesn't have confidence in the principal applicant, why should you? Remember, when you sign as guarantor, you're indicating that you're prepared to take over the debt if the borrower defaults.
* **Not knowing where the money is coming from and where it's going.** Each partner should know how much the other is earning and what the bills are. Money should have a source. If it doesn't then there may be something underhand going on.
* **Not having joint consent on joint accounts.** If you have a joint account with your spouse, make sure the bank doesn't allow payments above a certain amount unless there's joint consent.
* **Look carefully at how you buy assets.** Whose name are they in – just one of you or both of you? It could all be extremely relevant, both for tax purposes and if the relationship breaks up.

STEP 1: MAKE A LIST OF YOUR MONEY VALUES

Family matters

* **If you're asked to sign something, make sure you understand what it is.** You might, for example, be agreeing to put the family home up as collateral for a loan. The price of loyalty can be your own and your children's wellbeing. When you think about it, why should one spouse have the responsibility of worrying about the family home? A marriage is a partnership.
* **If you've signed documents as part of a business agreement with your partner, make sure you receive duplicate copies of any correspondence sent to other directors of the company.** Insist on the bank doing this – account statements, letters, copies of contracts, everything.
* **Keep your lender informed about your activities if running a family business.** A meeting of all directors (you and your partner) and the bank manager should take place at least once a year.
* **Don't define a marriage or de facto relationship as just a romantic liaison.** It's also a business and should be run like a partnership. In a successful small business everyone should know what's going on. If you don't, it's a recipe for disaster.
* **If you're a director of a family company you have a right to see the books.** Insist on the accountant showing them to you. If stopped from doing so, you can take action under the Companies Code.

NOTES

WHAT HAVE WE LEARNT?

The biggest takeaway message from this chapter is that you need to *talk financial matters through with your partner*, both at the beginning to establish your values, priorities and goals, and then regularly to ensure your goals are being met and you're both well informed and on track.

You need to share financial responsibilities and keep your partner informed of your transactions. If there's a big financial decision or purchase to be made, talk it through first, to ensure you're both happy with going in that direction. But make sure there's still room for fun – you both need to have a small fund of your own so that you can make discretionary purchases to stay happy and motivated.

If you suspect there are financial problems your partner isn't sharing with you, you need to find out as soon as you can what's going on, so that you can work together on a solution that will save you both from possible financial disaster.

If you don't have a partner, it's still crucial that you get your financial head right: think about your values and goals, track your progress and keep yourself informed. I still recommend having a monthly meeting: pick a close friend to be your 'finances buddy' and help and support each other.

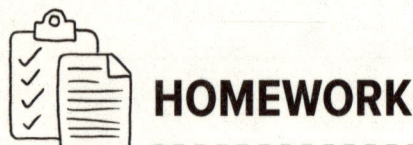

HOMEWORK

KEY POINTS

- Structure is crucial to financial planning and communication

- Set goals to save

- Be realistic about your money habits

HOMEWORK

- ☐ Set aside a regular time – at least 15 minutes a month – to talk finances

- ☐ Make a plan for short-, medium- and long-term financial goals

- ☐ Be honest with yourself and with your partner about your spending habits

STEP 1: MAKE A LIST OF YOUR MONEY VALUES

NOTES

STEP 2: DO YOUR HOUSEHOLD BUDGET, NOW

And while we're at it, let's have a squiz at your banking and clean up that pile of documents you've shoved down the end of the dining-room table. Trust me, you'll feel better.

> **DO THIS NOW**
>
> Before you start this chapter, grab a pen and paper and write down what you think your five biggest weekly costs are. (Is it the mortgage? Groceries? Power? Or your daily coffee?) By the end of this chapter, you'll find out just how well you know where your money is going!

IT'S TIME TO GET ORGANISED

A friend of ours took a week off work recently and we were excited to hear what she'd done, where she'd been and the highlights of her break.

'I just relaxed at home and focused on my life admin.'

'What?'

'You know, all those things you never get around to but can reduce stress and make your life function so much more smoothly.'

We knew what she meant and it inspired us to spend a weekend getting our own financial foundations right – and that's what I want you to do right now.

In this chapter we'll sort out the three key areas that are the foundation of any sound financial system – and a great place to start when trying to wrangle control of your finances:

1. your budget
2. your documentation
3. your banking.

If you don't really know where your money goes, you have no hope of getting it under control and seeing it grow. Creating your household budget (in writing) is the absolute cornerstone of your entire financial wellbeing – it's that important.

STEP 2: DO YOUR HOUSEHOLD BUDGET, NOW

WHERE'S YOUR MONEY GOING?

Too many families just meander along with a bit of budget here, a quick decision on how to spend a bit of extra cash there, a holiday because they deserve it, and suddenly the credit cards are at their limit and the family finances are way off track.

Sit down and set your family budget for the year. If you've done a budget before, don't skip this thinking you're done – use this time to update it. Things like child care and education expenses, for example, will change regularly as your children grow, so it's important to work from a budget that's as up to date as possible.

WHAT DOES THE AVERAGE FAMILY BUDGET LOOK LIKE?

According to the ABS the average family of two parents and two children has a monthly budget that looks like this.

Housing (rent and mortgage)	$1209
Food and non-alcoholic beverages	$1023
Transport	$867
Recreation	$745
Miscellaneous goods and services	$416
Medical/health	$355
Household furniture/equipment	$251
Communication	$204
Household services/operations	$195
Clothing and footwear	$191
Education	$191
Domestic fuel and power	$178
Alcohol	$134
Personal care	$121
Tobacco	$56
TOTAL	**$6136**

How to prepare your own budget

1. Get organised

Get together all your bank account and credit card statements, pay slips, big bills and any old budgets. Block out some time, with your partner if you have one, when you won't be interrupted, and clear the dining-room table.

The easiest way to keep track of your budget and update it is to do it on your computer, tablet or mobile. If you want help with formatting you can use one of the online budget planners from a bank or ASIC, or use the template on page 30 (which might also help you make sure you cover all the necessary categories).

2. List your income

This is usually the easy bit. List all the money you receive each month: wages, pensions and Centrelink benefits, child support, investment income such as bank interest, rent or dividends, everything. Remember to adjust each income component so you're noting down the *monthly* amount you receive – if you're paid fortnightly, for example, multiply it by 26 then divide it by 12.

Total your income.

3. List your expenses

List all your essential expenses, the things that are unavoidable. I'm talking mortgage repayments, rent, loan and credit card repayments, transport, utilities, phone and internet, car rego, insurance premiums, and basic groceries. For an expense that comes once a year, such as rego for example, you'll need to divide the figure by 12. Now comes the tricky bit. How much are you spending on things that aren't essential? Bought lunches, magazines, alcohol, cigarettes, dinners out, entertainment and so on. These expenses are usually harder to estimate because they may be irregular and you don't have official bills filed away.

When you're doing your budget, you have to be ruthless and honest with yourself. If you overestimate or underestimate your expenses you'll never be able to stick to your budget. Go through your bills and bank and credit card statements to get exact figures for purchases like groceries and clothes. Again, don't forget to adjust them into monthly figures.

Total your expenses.

4. Balance your budget

With any luck, your income covers your expenses and you're left with a little bit to save. Some family budgets, however, may end up with a deficit. That doesn't mean putting the shortfall on credit. Instead, work out how to increase your income (see Step 5) or decrease your expenses (see Step 4).

What can you live without while you get your finances under control and build some savings? Can you put off buying new clothes, eat in on date night, or go camping for your next holiday? When you're at the supermarket, look for cheaper home-brand products on the things where it doesn't matter as much, buy in bulk when you spot a good special, and plan meals for the weekend so you don't have to order in.

If you can't balance your budget, earning more income – if you have the time – can be just as good as cutting expenses. Can you volunteer for overtime or extra shifts at work? Does your field allow you to do a bit of freelance work outside your regular job? What about getting a second job in the evenings or on the weekend? Look out for ads for everything from bar work to stacking shelves at the local supermarket. I know for many of you it might sound like I'm asking the impossible, but there are loads of creative ways to generate extra income these days: I'll go through some options in detail in Step 5. The point I'm making is that if your financial crisis is serious or your financial dream is compelling, it could be worth sacrificing lifestyle in the short term to achieve success.

5. Set savings targets

If we only saved what was left at the end of each month we'd have a tough battle ever getting ahead. Decide how much you can afford to save each pay period and treat it like an expense in your budget, a bill that has to be paid. Never withdraw it from the bank and treat it like a slush fund.

To motivate you to save, give your savings a purpose. It could be a regular contribution to your emergency fund or that monthly amount you put towards the Disneyland trip. Now, revise your budget by adding a line in the expenses for the amount you've calculated you can save regularly each month. Libby and I transfer a set amount at the start of the month when our wages are paid. Our monthly savings target is put away before we start spending, and we're now used to thinking of what's left over as our salary.

> **DO THIS NOW**
>
> **No more putting it off, you should now have all the information you need: create your own weekly or monthly budget, one that takes into account yearly costs too! Use a bank budget calculator or the template over the page.**

We'll be reviewing each aspect of your financial life as the book goes on, so make sure you update your budget as you go and as your circumstances change.

WHAT MIGHT MY BUDGET LOOK LIKE?

INCOME	Amount per month
Salary	
Bonuses	
Investment income (bank interest, property, shares, bonds, etc.)	
Allowances	
Other income	
TOTAL INCOME	**(A)**

EXPENSES	Amount per month
Living expenses	
Rent	
Rates (council, water, etc.)	
Utilities (electricity, gas, etc.)	
Phones and internet	
Home maintenance	
Groceries	
Medical and pharmaceutical (doctors visits, prescriptions, etc.)	
Personal care (cosmetics, haircuts, salon services, etc.)	
Clothes and shoes	
Education (fees, child care, etc.)	
Pets (food, litter, pest treatments, vet expenses, etc.)	
Donations	
Other expenses	
Total living expenses	(a)
Insurance and superannuation	
Life insurance	
Income protection insurance	
Health insurance	
Superannuation (voluntary contributions)	
Home and contents insurance	

STEP 2: DO YOUR HOUSEHOLD BUDGET, NOW

Car insurance	
Business insurance	
Other insurance (boat, caravan, trailer)	
Total insurance and superannuation	(b)
Loans and credit cards	
Mortgage	
Personal loan repayments	
Credit card #1 repayments	
Credit card #2 repayments	
Credit card #3 repayments	
Store card repayments	
Other loan repayments (car loans, etc.)	
Total loans and credit cards	(c)
Transport	
Rego	
Maintenance (hardware, etc.)	
Petrol	
Parking	
Public transport/taxis/Uber	
Other transport	
Total transport	(d)
Leisure and entertainment	
Holidays	
Restaurants and takeaway	
Sport, hobbies and memberships	
Events (sports, movies, concerts etc.)	
TV and music subscription services	
Newspapers, magazines and books	
Gifts (Christmas, birthdays, etc.)	
Total leisure and entertainment	(e)
TOTAL EXPENSES (a + b + c + d + e)	**(B)**
SURPLUS/DEFICIT (A − B)	

SORT YOUR IMPORTANT DOCUMENTS

How hard was it to pull all your documents together when you were doing your budget? Wouldn't life be easier if they were all in one place and you could put your hands on everything straight away? If you died suddenly, would your loved ones be able to quickly find all the important documents – investment details, insurance policies, will, title deeds, banking, etc.? If your answer is 'They couldn't', then do something about it – now!

A key a part of managing your money is bringing some order and process to your financial life so you're prepared for any eventualities. As our grandparents would tell us, 'A tidy desk shows a tidy mind'. I was always a bit of a disappointment in this area, but I can see the logic – if an unexpected financial problem arises, you're armed with the information you need to deal with it calmly and positively.

I know there are all these apps for scanning and storing important documents but, call me old-fashioned, I still prefer the good old expandable file from a stationery shop. Mark the different sections clearly – will, life and income protection policies, house and contents insurance, title deeds for the house, employment contract, tax returns, investment documents – you get the gist. Then, make sure you keep filing everything away. Maybe use your monthly financial catch-up meeting as a trigger to clear up all the latest documents.

Once you're finished, tell your loved ones where to find it. It's so important that those closest to you know where it all is. You'll feel an enormous sense of relief, and you and your loved ones will sleep better at night.

NOTES

STEP 2: DO YOUR HOUSEHOLD BUDGET, NOW

ORGANISE YOUR BANKING

Your most important financial relationship is with your bank (or credit union or building society). Just think about it. A great relationship with your bank can make life so much easier. That's why choosing the right one is critical – and then it's about maintaining a good relationship.

So much of your life is wrapped up in that home loan, those credit cards and, maybe, insurance and investments as well. There's a deep connection, but it can come at a cost. You need to make sure you're paying the lowest possible fees and getting the best interest rates. You need to strike a balance between having a close relationship and working that relationship to get the best deals.

Before reading one more word about how to get your banking under control, I have a task for you.

DO THIS NOW

> If you have a home loan, I want you to ring your bank/lender and ask for a discount on your interest rate. Do it right now. If applicable, don't forget to mention all the other products you use from them – credit cards, insurance, other loans and accounts, investments and superannuation. It reinforces your loyalty and reminds them what a great customer you are.
>
> This is what you say: 'Hi, I have a home loan with you and I was just wondering whether I was getting the best interest rate on that loan. I have a lot of other banking services from you and I've heard I might be eligible for a discount on my rate.'
>
> Do it now – it's a simple phone call. Even if you don't have other banking products, still give it a go. What have you got to lose? The worst they can do is say no – and they might not.
>
> Do it right now. I'll wait.

How was that? I'll guarantee 90 per cent of you snagged a discount. Are you amazed at how easy it is? I wanted you to do this exercise right at the start to prove how simple it is for you to take control of your banking.

I don't know about you, but I'm a bit intimidated by my bank. The power they have over my financial life is huge. Naturally, you should be respectful when dealing with your bank, but there's actually no need to be intimidated by it. There's plenty of competition out there for your business, so make it work in your favour.

Let's step through the process of assessing and choosing the right bank, with the right products, so you can build the right relationship.

Don't assume the bigger banks are better

In Australia, the Big Four banks – CBA, ANZ, Westpac and NAB – account for about 80 per cent of all loans made. Despite all the competition from credit unions, building societies, second-tier banks (for example, regional banks), and new online financiers (see page 50), they still dominate.

One of the reasons for this is that most Australians think they're safer. So let me put this myth to bed. The entire financial and banking system is regulated by the same authorities – the Australian Securities and Investments Commission (ASIC) and the Australian Prudential Regulatory Authority (APRA). They impose the same rules, demand the same reporting and monitor all companies in the financial sector with the same scrutiny. So your local credit union must abide by the same rules as a Big Four bank and is monitored by the same authorities.

The bottom line is, when you're comparing financial providers, don't be influenced by the supposed safety of size.

How to find the right bank for you

Why are we so loyal to our banks? Is it because we have one of the strongest and safest banking systems in the world and we've become complacent? Is it because our finances are so complicated and we're so entwined with our banks that we think it's too hard, and we couldn't be bothered, to look at alternatives and actually change?

It's probably a combination of reasons, but the stories that came out of the Banking Royal Commission showed that it's worth undergoing an audit of your personal banking, assessing the alternatives and switching if necessary. Yes, it will take a bit of effort, but if you get it right, the rewards could be significant.

Despite the horrifying findings of the last Banking Royal Commission, a huge range of alternatives and new entrants, Australians are still generally more likely to get divorced than change their bank. Okay, so it's not a very 'fun' fun fact, but it's a pretty amazing statistic, isn't it?

So how do you find the right bank for you?

1. Assess and analyse your existing banking arrangements

For many of us, our banking arrangements have evolved over a number of years as our financial needs have changed. We've added different credit cards, new loans for various projects, extra insurances, new investments.

What started out as maybe one savings account or loan has now grown into a maze of financial products. Naturally, this has been a smart marketing tactic of your bank, which has cross-sold you products knowing the more embedded it is in your financial life, the harder it will be for you to leave. And we get lazy. We know it's a complex relationship and just can't face the effort of assessing the alternatives.

Start from the top down with these simple questions: does my bank meet my financial needs? Are its services right for me? Is it responsive to problems that arise? Does it present proactive suggestions? Does it understand my particular needs?

Answering these simple questions will give you an idea of how committed you are, or whether it's time for a change.

2. Cull unwanted accounts and products

How many banking accounts and products do you actually have? I reckon you'll be stunned at what you find. All those dormant accounts just sitting there forgotten, the extra credit cards you've been offered in the past, the insurance cover that's now inappropriate, the investments that looked like a good deal at the time but not so much now.

Cash in, close or exit those accounts that don't serve a purpose or fulfil a financial need. Most of them will, more than likely, be attracting unwanted fees that far outweigh any benefits.

Simplifying your banking to what you actually need is a critical foundation from which to drive change.

3. Compare your accounts with the market

This is the real nitty-gritty of assessing whether your existing bank is either ripping you off or providing value for money.

Start with the comparison websites such as canstar.com.au or finder.com.au and individually benchmark each account with its competition. Focus on the interest rate, fees, returns and services (features) that are linked in. As you work through the different categories of accounts, loans, cards, insurance and investment products, you'll soon start to get a feeling for whether your bank's products stack up against the competition.

As you do your comparisons, you'll probably see common financial providers consistently appearing as leaders in several categories, indicating which institutions are the best rated overall. Both Canstar and Finder, for example, will give a star rating for the best product in each category – home loans, no-frills credit cards, online savings accounts, term deposits, etc.

I won't personally recommend any products in this book because they change all the time and I don't want to mislead you. I might think one is pretty good now, for example, but a better alternative could be released next month. That's where I got the idea for a weekly newsletter attached to the purchase of this book. If you sign up for it, I'll let you know whenever a good new alternative becomes available.

4. Ask for a better deal from your existing bank

After your assessment is complete, if you've realised your bank isn't doing the right thing by you with fees, returns and services, it's decision time. You're now armed with all the facts and you know exactly what your banking position is.

Is the situation bad enough that it's worth your while to shift banks? If the answer is yes, your first move should be to approach your existing bank. Knowledge is power. Calmly explain the situation, show the better offerings of competitors and ask what the bank is going to do about it.

They'll know that you know what you're talking about, and their head office would have told them it's cheaper to keep an existing customer than find a new one. If you're a good customer who has a range of products with them, they'll generally try to match a competitor's offering.

Frankly, even if you're annoyed with your existing bank for ripping you off in the past, if you can get a better deal with them and not have to move, it's usually less hassle to stay.

If they won't play ball, pull the plug. But not straight away.

5. Line up a new financial partner first before letting go of the old

You might be just itching to recreate a movie scene and tell your bank to get nicked in a dramatic way, but please don't do that. Take a deep breath instead and visit the alternatives first. The last thing you want is to be left in limbo.

While your research has found you a couple of alternatives you like, still take time to ask savvy family members, friends and colleagues for recommendations on who they use. They may have a good personal banker or financial adviser who'll take you on.

Visit the alternative banks and don't just talk about replacing the products you already have. Ask if they also have alternative solutions. Service is important, and so are the tools they have on offer. If you're a 'bricks and mortar' banking customer, are their branches and ATMs conveniently located? If you're a digital customer, are their online banking platforms and resources good? It's not enough for the new bank to have great products, you need to 'feel' good about using that bank too.

Most importantly, do they want you as a customer? Some banks have strict criteria about the type of new customers they want and who to shower with kindness – make sure that's you. For example, some banks may not want to lend to property investors or people buying home units in inner-city suburbs or those with constant outstanding credit card balances.

Ask what they can do to help close down existing accounts at your old bank/s and transfer them. Some banks have quite sophisticated services that basically handle all the paperwork in closing down accounts and setting up new ones. It makes it so much easier.

6. Take the plunge

It's a big decision. But you've done your homework, an alternative is keen to have you as a customer, your money will be invested in better products and the returns will be much higher – so make the decision. Walk. Show that you won't be pushed around and that you're doing the best thing for you, your family and the future.

KOCHIE CALCULATOR: POTENTIAL INTEREST-RATE SAVING

Let's go back to your first task in this section: making a call to the bank to ask for a discount on your mortgage interest rate. When I've challenged people in the past to do this most have secured at least a 0.25% interest rate discount – some up to 0.7%.

On an average home loan of $400,000 over 30 years at 4% compound interest, you'd be making monthly repayments of $1910 and pay a total interest bill over the 30 years of $287,479.

Say you make that simple call to the bank and they agree to a 0.25% discount on your mortgage rate to 3.75% a year. Your monthly repayments would drop to $1853 (a saving of $57 a month) and the total interest over the loan would be cut to $266,887 (a saving of $20,592).

If you can snag a 0.5% discount, the monthly repayments would drop to $1797 (a $113 saving a month) and the total interest to $246,625 (a saving of $40,854).

They are big savings from just one simple phone call asking a simple question. Once you get over the nerves, you'll be proud of yourself. Good job! You're not one of those people who just grumbles about the banks – you've taken action.

Be a constantly savvy bank customer – it's worth it

Okay, you're satisfied you're now with the right bank. Don't sit back and think, 'Phew, that job's done now. I don't need to think about it any more.' Nope. Be vigilant. Banking needs your constant attention. It's not hard and it will be worth it.

Why? Think about this. Australia's banks are some of our largest and most profitable listed companies, with the Big Four producing around $30 billion in profit each year. How do they make such big profits? From us, their customers. By not passing on full Reserve Bank rate cuts, charging sneaky or excessive fees, not bothering to tell you there are better deals available.

Don't get mad, get even! Here are five of my favourite habits for turning the tables on your bank and making sure you're getting the best possible deal all the time.

1. Negotiate on EVERYTHING

If you don't ask, you'll never know. Simple.

What can you negotiate? Everything. You've discovered you can negotiate the interest rate on your home loan (the headline rate is for mugs). Now negotiate your credit card annual fee, your regular bank fees (ideally you want to stop paying them) and even the perks you receive. You may be surprised at what the banks are willing to offer straight off the bat.

Remember to go back to the comparison websites regularly, to ensure your bank products aren't being left behind by better deals from competitors. It never hurts to go in with a bit of extra ammunition.

2. Stop paying unnecessary fees

Credit card fees, account fees, ATM fees – Australians are up to their eyeballs in unnecessary fees, and if you have any sense you won't be happy about it.

The first step is to look at all your banking accounts. Cut redundant accounts, make sure the accounts you have are the best ones for your circumstances, understand the conditions of the accounts, and always stay within the terms. Cancel unneeded credit cards, switch to a fee-free bank account, organise your finances to avoid overdraft or late fees, and put the money back into your own pocket.

3. Maximise the interest you receive

Interest goes both ways: make sure you're maximising the interest you *earn* on your own money as well as minimising the interest you *pay* to the banks (see more on that across the page). Savings sitting in transaction accounts earning piddly returns are actually going backwards thanks to inflation, so compare the higher-interest online savings accounts in the market and find the best place to store your money. As I said before, I won't recommend certain accounts here because they change constantly.

So sign up for the newsletter and I'll provide guidance on accounts that are relevant right now.

Take advantage of bonus periods and other offers to eke out every last cent of interest you can from your bank. Remember, your bank would do the same to you.

4. Minimise the interest you pay

Paying interest is a parasite on your wealth, sucking money out of your pocket and straight into the bank's. So you should always aim to pay the lowest amount of interest possible.

Focus on cutting out 'bad debt' like credit cards and car loans first. These generally charge the highest rate of interest, and in the long term they don't get you anywhere. Once you've ditched these, turn your attention to bigger debts, such as the mortgage. Yes, negotiate the rate, but also do everything you can to get ahead on your repayments (mortgage offset accounts can be a great option here – see below). The quicker you can pay off the principal, the less interest you'll have to pay to the bank.

Don't roll your eyes. I know what you're thinking: 'Come on Kochie, that's easier said than done. Don't leave me hanging. Where the hell do I start?' Never fear, my fiscal warrior, Step 3 in our 11-step process deals with cutting your debt. Read on.

WHAT IS A MORTGAGE OFFSET ACCOUNT?

An offset account is a savings or transaction account that's linked to your home loan account. The balance in that account (or part of it) is 'offset' each day against your home loan balance, and you're only charged interest on the difference between your total loan balance and the amount in the offset account. The logic is that if that savings account stood alone it would earn a small amount of interest on which you'd be taxed. By keeping it in an offset account you don't earn interest but you save the 4% loan interest.

WHAT HAVE WE LEARNT?

I bet you're surprised, after doing your household budget, how different reality can be from your perception of where you spend your money. You'll now be aware of how you can manage those costs more effectively. Keep reading for lots of good ideas on how to prune those costs.

You'll have your financial documents organised and under control now, which will make things so much easier to manage, and bring peace of mind to you and your loved ones.

And don't marry your bank. Constantly make sure they're doing the right thing by you in terms of interest rates and fees. If not, don't be afraid to shift to an alternative – once you're sure it is a better option.

HOMEWORK

KEY POINTS

- Complete a household budget

- Get organised, documents-wise

- Take a good hard look at your bank

HOMEWORK

- ☐ List all the income you earn and all your expenses

- ☐ Buy that expandable file to store all your important documents, and tell your loved ones where to find it

- ☐ Make sure you have the right bank accounts for your circumstances

NOTES

STEP 3: TAKE THE NO-DEBT/ LOW-DEBT PLEDGE

Then whip your mortgage into shape, take a scalpel to your credit card debt, and inoculate yourself against financial crisis.

> **DO THIS NOW**
>
> Take the debt pledge:
> I, _____ , swear that
> I will no longer accept high debt as a way of life.

DON'T LET DEBT GET YOU DOWN

Okay, if you've read straight on from the last chapter, stand up, have a jog on the spot to get the blood pumping, and grab a cup of coffee or tea. I want you at your best for this next section.

If you discovered when doing your household budget that your expenses exceed your income, or close to it, this chapter will be a vital part of your money management process. If you're already in debt (apart from your mortgage), it will be even more important. But even if you're not in debt, there will be lots of valuable tips for you in here, including how to tame one of the most beastly debts of all: the monthly mortgage.

In this chapter, I'll show you the tools you need to get ahead of your debts and stay that way. You'll learn to:

* find realistic and manageable ways to pay off your debts
* stay debt-free and improve your credit rating
* get your home loan under control
* weather any unforeseen financial storm.

 *Australia is reported to have some of the highest personal debt levels in the world, up there with Denmark, the Netherlands, and Norway.*

TAKE CONTROL OF YOUR DEBT

Debt can easily get out of control. According to the ABS, the average Australian household has $17,000 in consumer debt (excluding the mortgage), with $3273 on their credit card/s, $2062 of which is earning interest – really high interest.

So Step 3 of your money makeover is about getting that debt under control through the power of your credit rating, knowing how to get out of a crisis and using some nifty expert strategies that give you better solutions.

Whenever Libby and I are asked, 'How do I get on top of my debt?', our first piece of advice is always, 'Use your savings to pay off your debt', because it's no use earning a much lower amount of savings interest when you're paying a much higher rate of interest on your loans. It just doesn't make sense, as you'll see on page 48.

There's nothing worse than feeling overwhelmed by debt. It's a harrowing experience that can often seem to have no end. But there is a solution. It's never quick or easy, but you *can* get out of the debt mire. Don't accept debt as a way of life. Take control of your money and secure your financial future.

TAKE THIS QUIZ:
Do you have a debt problem?

Are you:

1. spending more than you earn each month and regularly dipping into your savings or putting day-to-day expenses on credit because you have no money? Y/N
2. only able to afford the minimum payment on the monthly credit card bill and so not prepared for unexpected expenses that could crop up, like house and car repairs? Y/N
3. receiving legal notices in the mail? Y/N
4. taking menacing phone calls chasing payment? Y/N
5. enduring relationship instability such as marriage or relationship breakdown? Y/N
6. adopting bad lifestyle habits such as increased drinking, smoking and gambling? Y/N

> If you answered yes to one of these questions, you need to start changing your habits – don't worry, I'm about to show you how. If you answered yes to more than one of these questions, I'm afraid you have a serious debt problem. And I'm here to help.
>
> Be honest. These are all telltale signs of financial distress and a warning that you must act now to resolve it. The worst thing you can do is ignore your debt problems until it's too late, hoping things will work out for the best and your creditors won't notice.

My seven-step debt diet

I'm going to start by putting you on my seven-step debt diet. Instead of cutting out carbs I want you to cut out credit. Instead of getting rid of kilos you'll get rid of unwanted debt. Your household budget is your training program – stick to it and you'll soon be on your way to a whole new you.

1. Face reality

Many people ignore their debt problems until it's too late. The sooner you act, the better off you'll be.

2. Ask for help

If you're in trouble, talk about it. It will probably be much less painful than you think. Credit card companies and financial institutions will be much more lenient if they know you're trying to tackle the problem. Talk to them about a payment program to help manage your debt. Ask if you can reduce or postpone some repayments, or pay less interest while you get back on track.

3. Make a budget

Remember the budget you did in Step 2 (page 30)? Do it right now if you haven't already. Then for the next month write down everything you spend and examine what you've done. You'll be amazed, and maybe a little horrified, at where your money has gone, but I bet you'll think twice in future.

Balancing your family budget so that your outgoings each month match your income is a great first step, because you're living within your means. But to get ahead of the game, that family budget needs to make a surplus – leftover cash – to put towards a debt-reduction plan. The fastest way to pay off what you owe is to make extra repayments. Look at your budget and work out the maximum you can afford to pay off your debts every month. Make 'extra debt repayments' a line in your budget, as a reminder that your income has to cover it. Once you've completed this chapter, make sure you read Step 4, which is full of ways to reduce your spending and achieve that monthly surplus.

Each pay period, set aside money to cover your basic expenses such as food, transport, utilities, and rent or mortgage payments. Make sure you contribute each month to an emergency account to cover any unexpected bills. Then use all the cash left over to pay down debts like your credit card bill. As you'll see over the page, there's no point saving it when you have debts to pay.

If you're not making much of dent in your overall debt you'll have to increase your income. Take a look at Step 5 for ways to generate more income.

4. Stick to the budget

You need to start living within your means so you don't slip any further into debt. From now on use cash (or a debit card) for everyday expenses like groceries, clothes and entertainment so you only spend what you have. Resist impulse buys and save up for big purchases. It might be hard at first, but it will get easier over time. Set yourself a goal to work towards once you're out of debt, and remind yourself of it when things get tough.

If you're going to struggle with the temptation of credit, get rid of it. Replace your credit card altogether with a debit card. It allows you to purchase things online or over the phone like a regular credit card but only uses the money you already have – so you can't go further into debt.

5. Don't fall in to the minimum payment trap

The monthly credit card bill looks horrific, but then you take comfort in the much smaller minimum balance owed. Big mistake. Sorry to break it to you, but it will take years to eliminate your debts if you only make minimum repayments. Your credit card provider will charge interest on the rest of your bill, adding to your overall debt.

It's important to understand that the minimum payment on an outstanding credit card balance won't cover the interest payment. That shocks most people, because there seems to be a myth that the minimum payment covers the interest but doesn't pay off any of the debt.

That's wrong, I'm afraid. Your card issuer sets the minimum monthly repayment on your credit card. This amount varies between credit card issuers but is usually calculated as 2–3 per cent (although it can sometimes be up to 10 per cent) of your closing balance, with a minimum dollar charge of around $20–30. Compare that with the actual interest rate charged on the whole amount, which can be 12–21 per cent – that's a big gap! So not only does the principal compound, but so does some of the interest. It's just so dangerous.

KOCHIE CALCULATOR: THE DANGER OF MAKING ONLY MINIMUM PAYMENTS

Tom has a $5000 outstanding balance on a credit card charging 15% interest. If he pays $250 a month to get that balance down, it will take him two years to pay off the debt for a total interest bill (on the $5000 balance) of $790.

If he just paid the minimum balance of $100 a month, it would take just over 24 years to pay it off and he would have paid a total of $7245 interest — on a $5000 balance.

This minimum payment trap is scary.

6. Pay off your most expensive debt first

It's common sense, but you need to pay off the debt with the highest interest rate first. Credit cards are charging up to 21 per cent interest, so focus on that debt to start with, then look at personal loans, which will be costing at least 10 per cent interest.

Don't even think about saving or investing until you've paid off your bad debts. There's no point playing the share market or investing in a managed fund when you're being charged 20 per cent interest on your credit card debt. Your home loan is probably your cheapest debt, at around 4 per cent. Borrowing to buy a home or invest in quality shares or property is generally considered to be good debt, and not as much of a concern.

KOCHIE CALCULATOR: SAVINGS VERSUS PAYING OFF DEBT

Let's still use Tom and his $5000 credit card balance on which 15% interest is being charged. He wants to pay the balance off over six months, which would need a monthly repayment of $870, and would result in total interest of $221 over the period.

If, at the same time, he has $5000 in a term deposit earning the current rate of 2.8% interest, he would earn $70 interest (and have to pay his marginal rate of income tax on it).

So he would have *paid* $221 interest on his credit card and *earned* just $70 on the term deposit, leaving him $151 behind.

If you have debt, you should have no savings (apart from your emergency money). It should all go into the credit cards or loans instead. Think about it logically. Why have savings earning 3 per cent (at best) when you're paying 10–18 per cent interest on loans and outstanding credit card balances? As I've said, just doesn't make sense.

7. Consider consolidation

Credit card debt can be a tough burden to carry, especially when you're finding it hard to even make the minimum monthly payment. Sky-high interest rates continue to compound and grow the interest cost each month. Throw in maybe a mortgage and another credit card, and things can quickly appear unmanageable.

If this is you, you need to minimise the interest you're paying – for example, through a 'zero rate transfer credit card' (see page 51), or by consolidating multiple expensive high-interest debts by bringing them all together onto the lowest possible rate and setting up a payment plan to wipe the slate clean.

But just as it would have been a good idea to have spent some time researching that credit card or loan before signing on the dotted line, you need to do some research to consider which type of debt consolidation is right for you. As with most financial products, there's no one-size-fits-all approach.

To help navigate the area, here are the three options to consider, and a checklist to find out which is right for you.

KOCHIE CALCULATOR: AN EXAMPLE OF CONSOLIDATION

Alice has three credit cards with outstanding balances of $15,000 each and an average interest rate of 15%. A good strategy for her could be to take out a personal loan for $45,000 at a 13% interest rate and a set term of five years, and use that money to pay off the credit cards straight away.

Over the five years, her monthly repayments on the personal loan would be $1023 a month and she would pay a total of $16,433 interest. To pay off her credit cards in the same time period, she would have to pay $1065 per month for a total of $19,397 interest. By consolidating her debt, Alice saves $2964.

Option 1. Combine your debts in a personal loan

The key benefit of a personal loan is that it has a set term. That means the repayments are calculated so that at the end of the loan period the debt is cleared.

While you might still have to pay interest of 8–14 per cent, that's still probably lower than your credit card, and the set term could mean a bigger saving because it makes you clear the balance once and for all.

There are also a lot of non-bank financiers who offer good options in the personal loan market with comparatively low interest rates. Look at some of the credit unions and regional banks as alternatives. As I mentioned in the last chapter, credit unions and regional banks are governed by the very same rules as the big banks. There's also a bunch of what are called 'peer-to-peer lenders', which offer attractive rates to borrowers with good credit ratings (I'll explain the importance of your credit rating shortly). At the time of writing, personal loans from peer-to-peer lenders like SocietyOne were charging an interest rate of 9.5 per cent.

WHAT TYPES OF LENDER ARE AVAILABLE?

It's not just the big banks that lend money. There are also numerous other lenders in the marketplace. They include:

* **Credit unions, building societies and mutual banks:** these are member-owned financial institutions and therefore are not-for-profit institutions. They're often local organisations with only a few branches, but can provide fee-free access to ATMs throughout Australia and the usual online services. Others are profession-based, such as the Teachers Mutual Bank.
* **Regional banks:** these are smaller than the Big Four banks but larger than community banks. They're often state-based, but many have a smaller presence in other states. Examples include Bendigo Bank, Adelaide Bank, the Bank of Queensland and ME Bank.
* **Community banks:** these are banks owned by local members of the community but operated by a larger institution. Many branches of Bendigo Bank in country towns are operated in this way, and were created when bank closures left the town without financial services.
* **Peer-to-peer lenders:** newcomers to the Australian market, peer-to-peer lenders raise money from investors and then lend it out to borrowers. Because their investors are looking for a reliable return on their investments, the loan conditions can be more stringent than those of other institutions, such as an excellent credit rating.
* **International banks:** these are local versions of large banking companies based overseas. Examples include HSBC and Citigroup.

Be aware that some smaller institutions are actually subsidiaries of the Big Four, including Bankwest, St George Bank and the Bank of Melbourne.

Option 2. Transfer all your credit card balances onto a zero rate transfer credit card

This is a popular option because the balance transferred often enjoys an interest-free period, which can be as long as 14 months. This could give you the space you need to bring down the debt without having to pay the usual high interest rate. The key to making it work is setting up your own repayment plan, just as a personal loan would, to ensure you clear the debt during that interest-free period. Because no interest is being charged, it's easy to work out your repayment amounts – just divide the balance by the number of interest-free months on offer and you'll have the monthly payment you need to clear the debt.

Ideally, a zero per cent balance transfer card will also offer a low interest rate on new purchases too, but your focus should be on reining in spending and paying off your existing debt, so that should be a secondary consideration.

Just be aware that once your interest-free period ends, the balance will revert to the normal interest rate, which could be as high as 21 per cent. You could then find yourself rolling the balance over again, which can incur costs and have implications for your credit history.

As I said, this works best when you make a commitment to yourself that you'll pay off the balance within the interest-free term. See it as a circuit-breaker to pay that credit card balance off once and for all, and have the discipline to stick to it. If you're worried about falling into debt again after that, close the account as soon as your debt is paid off.

Option 3. Consolidate all your debts into your mortgage

If you have a home loan and have accrued a bit of equity in the property, this approach can be a great way to save on interest. But, just as with credit card balance transfers, you need the discipline to increase your mortgage repayments to clear the extra debt as quickly as possible. Be aware that this approach turns your unsecured debt into secured debt, which means that if you don't meet your loan repayments then the bank could sell your home to recover their loan.

WHAT IS SECURED DEBT?

With secured debt, such as a house or car loan, the loan is 'secured' by an asset the lender can seize and sell if you default – the house or car. With unsecured debt, such as your credit card debt, there's no asset to secure the loan, so if you default the lender can take legal action against you. With unsecured debt the interest rates are usually higher.

The logic is that you transfer those pesky outstanding credit card balances incurring high interest (e.g. 20 per cent) to your home loan, which currently incurs an interest rate closer to 4 per cent. It's a good decision. But then you have to commit to making extra home loan repayments to pay off those balances as quickly as possible – start by contributing the interest payment differential (e.g. between 20 and 4 per cent, so 16%).

If you've already paid down the home loan principal by more than the debts you need to pay off, just transfer the debt amount out and pay off the credit cards – tell the bank that's what you're doing. Otherwise talk to the bank about lifting your mortgage by the amount of your debt to pay off the credit card balances.

KOCHIE CALCULATOR: TRANSFERRING CREDIT CARD DEBT TO A HOME LOAN

Alice transfers her $45,000 outstanding credit card balances with their average interest rate of 15% to her mortgage at 4%. Let's see what difference that makes:

- At 15% interest that balance would grow to $51,750 after one year – $6750 in interest.
- At 4% interest that balance would grow to $46,800 after one year – $1800 interest.

So Alice's interest saving from consolidating credit card debt into home loan is $4950.

BUT: Alice must use that $4950 saving to pay down the $45,000 starting balance, otherwise she won't get ahead . . . and that's the point.

How to choose a debt consolidation that's right for you

Picking the right option involves drawing up a realistic budget (factoring in debt repayments) to get an accurate picture of the time it will take to pay off your debt.

Go back to your budget and work out what you can pay. If you've budgeted for savings, put these towards your debt. There'll be time enough to save for that holiday once your nasty debt is gone for good. Be honest about your self-discipline in making repayments, because if you choose an overly optimistic repayment term, you may end up taking longer and incurring additional interest. Similarly, a loan term that's too long, even at a very low rate, can accrue significant interest charges. Use an online calculator and tweak the monthly payments and the time frame until you find a workable solution.

STEP 3: TAKE THE NO-DEBT/LOW-DEBT PLEDGE

Once you've got your repayment plan sorted, it's all about getting the best deal possible. This means comparing the interest rates, fees and charges, and checking that the loan term is right for your repayment plan and discipline.

Finally, always avoid financiers that make big promises about getting you out of debt quickly, and check that your credit provider is licensed by our financial regulator, the Australian Securities and Investments Commission (ASIC) – visit asic.gov.au or its personal finance website moneysmart.gov.au. Beware some of those debt consolidation companies that advertise aggressively in the media. They often have a sting in the fine print and are not the answer.

WHICH DEBT CONSOLIDATION OPTION IS RIGHT FOR ME?

Option	Pros	Cons
Combining debts in a personal loan	Set term means you know exactly how much to pay to clear the debt	You need to shop around to find a good rate
Transferring debts to a zero rate transfer credit card	Zero interest period allows you to pay off the debt without paying interest	You need to be disciplined and make sure you pay off the balance before it gets rolled over at the (much) higher rate. Find a card with no balance transfer fee
Consolidating debts into mortgage	You can use the equity you already have in your house to absorb the debt and pay it off at a much lower interest rate	You need to make sure you increase your payments until the extra debt is cleared, because it's now secured by your house

For even more tips on getting out of debt, see my eight-point action guide for handling a personal financial crisis, later in this chapter (page 58).

THE POWER OF YOUR CREDIT RATING

If you've ever been late in paying a bill or defaulted on a loan, then chances are it has been recorded on your personal credit rating. And while you might not think too much of it, you can be sure that every financial institution in the country takes it very seriously. But don't panic: I'm going to step you through what it means and what you can do about it.

Why is your credit rating so important?

When the day comes to apply for a new form of financial credit, like a credit card, car loan or even mobile phone plan, that blemish might see you get knocked back or charged extra interest because you're a 'higher risk'.

You see, the company lending the money will run a credit check on your application, and if you've taken out any form of credit in the past they'll receive a report on whether you pose a credit risk or not. This report outlines things like whether you've taken too long to repay a debt, whether you have any current overdue accounts, and other personal details they deem relevant.

In fact, not so long ago the federal government changed the privacy and credit regulations so that even more of your payment history is recorded on your credit report. So more than ever, if you're unsure of the details of your credit rating, it's worth taking the time to check it, especially if you're planning on borrowing any time soon.

How to check your credit rating

Credit agencies are required to provide you with a free copy of your credit report every 12 months if requested, or if you've recently been rejected for credit.

Your credit report includes information on debts like your mortgage and credit cards, all the way down to your monthly bills. It also includes any application you make for credit, any time you've defaulted on a debt and if you're guarantor for someone else's loan.

Two of the main credit agencies are Equifax and Dun & Bradstreet. They each have a specific process to follow to request a free copy of your credit report. If you're in a hurry, you can also go to Get Credit Score (getcreditscore.com.au) for a free credit score and quick summary of your credit report, but make sure you read the terms and conditions. This online service is a handy way to get an idea of what your credit report looks like and how you appear to lenders when they're reviewing your application for credit.

Improving your credit rating

Poor credit ratings can be caused by missed or late payments, defaulting on a debt, being rejected for a loan or mistakes made by a creditor or credit rating agency. Other things, like a patchy employment history, having an excessive amount of debt, or regularly changing your address can also weigh you down.

If you've mistakenly received a black mark against your name, get in touch with the ratings agency or creditor directly (if they've incorrectly listed you as defaulting or being late on debt repayments) and request to have this rectified. The credit rating agencies must correct any mistakes.

Once you've checked that your record is accurate, you can start improving your financial situation, which starts with paying every bill and loan instalment on time. While overdue or defaulted debts won't be removed from your record until five years have passed, it's good practice to turn over a new leaf and start building a positive track record now.

From there it's all about staying on track and limiting the amount of new debt you take out. Don't apply for needless credit cards, and work through your budget to understand your situation before applying for any new loan, to ensure it's worthwhile and within your means. If you have a patchy credit history, it may be worth waiting to apply for a serious debt like a home loan until you've been at your current job and residence for at least a year.

By keeping your credit record clean and limiting the amount of debt in your life, you'll be in the best position to negotiate favourable terms when the time comes to borrow again.

Use a good credit rating to your advantage

A good credit rating means you're reliable in meeting your obligations – you're low risk. With most credit products, financial institutions treat everyone the same and try to impose the same interest rate, which takes into account a certain amount of defaults from customers who aren't as good as you at making repayments. In effect, you're paying a higher interest to compensate the bank for those other customers.

If you have a good credit rating, you should used it as a powerful weapon when negotiating better deals. When you're talking to the bank about a loan, explain that you want a discounted interest rate because you're a good credit risk. Ask them to check your credit rating and explain to them that, as a lower risk, you should get a lower rate.

TAMING THAT HOME LOAN BEAST

It's the biggest financial commitment of most average Australians – making the monthly mortgage repayment. It's an expensive business servicing a mortgage, even at these historically low interest rates, and it will become a whole lot more expensive if interest rates rise in the future.

But there are ways to reduce that mortgage quickly and relatively painlessly to save interest. If you're currently facing a bulging debt burden to finance your castle, here are five hot tips to lessen its girth and get it under control before any rate rises.

1. Increase the frequency of your repayments

If you currently make repayments monthly, change them to fortnightly. If you make them fortnightly, change them to weekly.

The advantage of this slight tweak is twofold. In a calendar quirk, changing your repayments to a more frequent cycle will mean you make extra repayments each calendar year. Also, by increasing the regularity of your repayments you'll end up paying less interest on the loan as there'll be less interest compounding each period.

KOCHIE CALCULATOR: PAY LESS INTEREST WITH MORE FREQUENT REPAYMENTS

Let's keep using the $400,000 home loan (see page 37) as an example with a 4% interest rate over a 30-year term. Monthly repayments would be $1910 with a total interest bill over the loan of $287,479.

If you cut those repayments in half (to $955) and pay fortnightly, you'll save $44,880 of interest and cut the term of the loan by four years.

Pay weekly ($478) and you'll save $45,633 in interest and cut the term by more than four years.

---

2. Keep repayments constant when interest rates fall

If the Reserve Bank cuts interest rates again (unlikely but not impossible), or you followed my advice at the start of this chapter and negotiated a discount on your rate, don't go book a holiday on the savings. Instead of taking the opportunity to reduce your repayments, keep them constant at the old higher rate.

You've already budgeted to pay a certain amount off your mortgage each week so, if you can afford to, keep doing it. The long-term dollar savings and reduction in loan time can be considerable, especially in the face of successive rate cuts. This is because the more you pay each time, the faster you get to paying off your principal rather than just the interest, which means that the proportion of each payment that's interest will start to fall and the total interest you pay will fall too.

3. Budget for an extra $100 a month

If your mortgage doesn't have you pressed to the wall, see if you can rustle up an extra $100 a month out of your budget. Or put a tax refund, bonus or inheritance/windfall against the mortgage. The impact is huge.

KOCHIE CALCULATOR: THE EFFECT OF EXTRA MORTGAGE PAYMENTS

If we put an extra $100 a month into our $400,000, 30-year mortgage at an interest of 4%, the total interest will fall to $258,480 (for a saving of $29,000) and the term will fall to 27 years and three months, shortening the mortgage by a whopping two years and nine months.

If we keep paying at the original rate but add a one-off bonus or windfall of $10,000, the total interest will fall to $271,480 (saving $16,000), and the term will be cut by one year and four months.

4. Ask your financier for a better deal

Yes, I'm nagging you. If you didn't follow my suggestion earlier, do it now. It's so important.

5. Look around for a better deal

Yep, nagging again.

HOW TO COPE WITH A PERSONAL FINANCIAL CRISIS

You wouldn't wish a PFC on anyone. It can feel as though your whole life is about to come crashing down like a house of cards. The crisis can be so debilitating that people can be almost paralysed into inaction. They literally go into the bunker and hide. Unfortunately, that aggravates the problem rather than solves it.

A PFC can be triggered by a range of personal factors around money, but the most common is a debt burden that has careered out of control. The good news is that, with discipline and some hard work, there is a way out. Here's my eight-point action guide for handling a PFC, so you can turn things around as quickly as possible.

1. Don't go it alone

If you're drowning in debt or simply don't see a way out, there is help available.

Financial counselling (which is a completely different thing from financial planning) is a free, independent and confidential service provided by many non-profit organisations that's aimed at helping you get back in control of your money. Contact Financial Counselling Australia on 1800 007 007 or visit financialcounsellingaustralia.org.au to find a counsellor near you. Do this to make sure it's a legitimate counselling service and not a company aiming to get even more money from you.

2. Understand the big picture

I've said it before and I'll say it again: budget, budget, budget. Before anything else, draw up a list of all your assets and debts to get a bird's-eye view of where you're at financially. Then build a budget to work out where your money actually goes (see page 30). Run a fine-tooth comb through last month's receipts and bank statements to double-check you've listed all your expenses accurately.

3. Set yourself a realistic deadline

If you're in a sticky financial situation, your main goal is probably to get out of it as quickly as possible, which is perfectly reasonable. But it's not a good financial goal. A good financial goal has a definite deadline and can be broken down into smaller, more manageable steps.

For example, rather than say, 'I want to pay off my credit card', it's much better to say, 'I want to be rid of my credit card debt by Christmas, which means I need to repay $150 a week for the next four months'.

4. Take control of your spending . . .

With a budget and some well-defined goals to work towards, it's time to take control. Think about your spending in terms of wants and needs. Needs are non-negotiable – for example, you'll always need to make room in your budget for groceries. Wants are nice to have, such as catching the latest movie, buying new clothes or eating out – but if you're in the midst of a PFC these should be the first things to go. I know this sacrifice could be hard to accept, but remind yourself that it's only for a short time, and how good it will feel not to have all that stress any more.

5. And your debts

Go back to page 45 for a detailed look at how to tackle debt, but to save you flicking back, I'll recap the key points here.

If you're having trouble repaying a debt or bill, speak to your lender or biller immediately. They may be willing to negotiate more favourable terms and you could avoid a black mark on your credit report. Financial institutions and businesses in general hate surprises. If you have a problem paying a bill or a debt, the earlier you can warn them the better. And be honest. Explain the problem, why you need a bit of leeway, and the plan you've put in place to make sure you can get back on track. Believe me, they'll be more inclined to be flexible and work with you rather than against you.

Next, look at whether you can minimise the interest you're paying, for example by consolidating multiple debts to reduce the overall interest you pay (see page 49). Find out your credit score (see page 54) then either go to your bank and get a better deal on consolidating debts into a personal loan or use an alternative like a peer-to-peer lender.

Finally, try to channel all of your additional money into making extra repayments, which will save you interest and help you pay off the debts faster.

Remember, don't be afraid to use your savings to make extra repayments. Money in the bank only earns around 3 per cent these days, while credit cards or personal loans still charge interest rates in the double digits.

6. Sell your assets

Naturally, if you have share or property investments that can be easily sold, they can generate cash to get you out of trouble. Or maybe you have a second car or a luxury such as a boat or motorbike or Xbox.

You're in financial trouble so there's no room for luxuries. Maybe even consider downsizing from the family home or unit to a more affordable alternative and using the difference to pay down your debt.

7. Focus on income generation

Cutting costs (see Step 4) can only get you so far. Once you've slashed to the basics there's not much more you can do except focus on the other side of the family budget – earning more income.

Step 5 of this book is all about increasing your income, so make sure you flip over to get more detail. Turning a passion or hobby into a money maker is a good start – everything from selling craft online through to being a handyman or cooking for local cafes. In this era of so-called 'collaborative consumption', part-time jobs like turning the car into an Uber or delivering food from restaurants are booming, and make great flexible money earners. Not only will it increase the family's income, and take financial pressure off, but it will also give you a sense of your own financial independence and can be hugely beneficial to mental wellbeing. Of course it's all about balance: you don't want to work yourself into the ground or have no time left for your family. My main point, always, is to remember you have options, to find what works for you, to push yourself and to *be creative* with your finances.

8. Plan for the next PFC

If all goes well, the steps I've outlined will help you take control and get through your PFC (and improve your daily financial habits too). But a PFC could happen again, so make sure you're prepared.

Once you've combated your short-term financial crisis, it's just as important to look further ahead to ensure you're in a better position should you get into strife again. This starts with setting two- to three-year financial goals, and building an emergency fund equal to 10 per cent of your income. Start setting aside money in a savings account for the purpose of covering unexpected expenses. This is what's known as a rainy-day or emergency fund (more on this on page 99).

Just as important is reviewing your will, superannuation and estate planning, as well as embarking on a financial education program. This process can be made easier with the help of a financial planner, and also Step 6, which is all about future-proofing your finances.

And make sure to do a full review of your insurance, both for your belongings (think home, contents and car for starters) and for you and your family (life, income protection, health, and total and permanent disability insurance).

This will ensure you can weather the next PFC if it comes along.

STEP 3: TAKE THE NO-DEBT/LOW-DEBT PLEDGE

WHAT HAVE WE LEARNT?

Have I taken the panic out of your views on debt? I hope so. We've worked through some great strategies for paying off a troublesome debt, managing your mortgage, improving your credit rating and conquering a personal financial crisis. It all requires patience and discipline, but keep your eye on the prize and you'll get through it. I have confidence in you!

HOMEWORK

KEY POINTS

Minimum credit card payments have a bad long-term impact

Consolidating your debts might be the answer

Your credit rating is important

Don't be scared of a personal financial crisis – be prepared!

HOMEWORK

☐ **Commit to paying off more than the minimum each month, check the details of your credit card and make sure you have the cards that are best for you**

☐ **Look at how you can consolidate high-interest debt into a single card with an introductory zero per cent rate, or into less expensive loans, such as a personal loan or your home loan**

☐ **Once you know where you stand, you can either work towards improving your credit rating or use it to negotiate better deals on your financial products**

☐ **If you are in the midst of a PFC, understand the best options and choose what's right for you**

4

STEP 4: CUT COSTS TO GROW HAPPINESS

And while you're there, plug the spending leaks so that you can afford the fun stuff and luxuries that really matter to you and your family.

> **DO THIS NOW**
>
> Write a list of all the things you'd love to do but can never seem to find the money for. It might look like this:
>
> 1. Buy a new guitar.
> 2. Be in Paris for the spring.
> 3. Travel to the MCG for an AFL Grand Final.
> 4. Trade in the family rust bucket for a new car.
> 5. Be able to afford braces for the kids' teeth.
> 6. Build a new back deck.
>
> As you work through this chapter and figure out how to cut expenses, keep your list to hand. It will motivate you to start slashing!

PAY ATTENTION TO WHAT YOU SPEND

You work so hard to earn every single dollar and you constantly stress to make ends meet. It's the mounting pile of bills, while you're still trying to fund a decent lifestyle, that's the cause of most of your financial heartache.

I know you have a household budget, *but* just how well do you manage all those day-to-day expenses? Just how good are you at plugging all the little financial leaks, and how creative are you at slashing costs? You need to consider everything from the supermarket shop and asking for the best deal on everything, right through to things like energy and car costs. You'll be amazed what a little creativity, knowledge and discipline can save.

The bottom line is making sure that the household budget you completed back in Step 2 is in surplus – that you spend less than you earn – so that you can use any extra cash to pay for that list you've just completed.

In this chapter, together, we'll take a forensic look at:

✱ your key living expenses and how you can cut them
✱ how to negotiate a better deal on just about everything
✱ a few strategies on how to afford those little, and big, luxuries of life that up until now have seemed unreachable.

By the end of this chapter I reckon you'll be surprised at just how within reach those luxuries really are.

What I'm trying to say is that I'm not going to be the fun police here and force you to live like a monk. I want you to keep spending, within reason, on the things you are now, but at a lower cost so that you can afford more.

Let's get a little mantra in our heads: 'Don't buy things I can't afford, with money I don't have, to impress people I don't necessarily like.' Got it? It's all about getting our priorities right.

STEP 4: CUT COSTS TO GROW HAPPINESS

SPEND LESS ON THE NECCESSITIES

Day-to-day living is expensive, and some big, unavoidable items eat up a large chunk of our personal finances. Here are some solid tips on how to save money and get the best deals on some of life's bigger expenses, like:

- groceries
- home energy and major appliances
- travel
- clothes.

And I've added a few tips at the end about common ways people waste money unnecessarily.

Groceries

You don't need me to tell you that groceries can be a big hit to the family finances. But it's certainly a blow that can be softened. What if I said you could cut your fruit and vegetable shopping bill in half?

Fruit and veg: cooperative shopping

Forming your own cooperative with a group of neighbours, family or friends to buy fruit and vegies can cut hundreds of dollars from the yearly shopping bill. All you need is a bit of nous, a sense of purpose, and some grit and determination to get started. Actually, getting started is probably the hardest part. Once you develop a pattern, cooperative shopping is as easy as peeling a mandarin.

First, you need a commitment from a good number of people. Groups I've spoken to tell me 10 families is a manageable number. You'll find that after talking to one person and getting an enthusiastic response, they'll talk to someone else, and that someone will talk to someone else, and so on. Before you know it, you'll have the number you need.

Get everyone together for a cuppa and discuss the rules (see the examples on the next page). The group should understand exactly what their rights and obligations are, so there's no confusion in the future. Write down the rules and give a copy to everyone. The most important rule everyone should agree upon is that no one person has the right to make the rules on behalf of the group. If rules are going to be changed, everyone should be given the chance to vote.

It's important to work out a basic shopping list that will form the basis of every shop – the fruit and vegetables that are staples for all families. But always have the flexibility to take advantage of seasonal items when they're at their cheapest. Nominate an amount to be spent each week, say $300

(10 families at $30 a time), then nominate a day and time for shopping. Believe it or not, it can be fun when your turn comes around. Some of the groups I've dealt with use the visit to the local markets as a family outing.

As you're a big buyer, use that muscle to pin down the best deals. Don't be afraid to haggle with the stall owners, because you have nothing to lose – but be good-natured about it and have some fun. Also bear in mind that a drop in price isn't your only bargaining chip. Ask for extra quantity or a sample of other more exotic alternatives for the group to buy.

The shopkeepers I've spoken to love dealing with co-ops because it ensures them regular big orders and it cuts down on handling costs. Do a survey of several suppliers, explain that you'd like to buy in bulk and pay less, and keep notes on what they say.

WHAT MIGHT A COOPERATIVE SHOPPING GROUP LOOK LIKE?

Each co-op will be different, but here are some sample ideas for a co-op of 10 families (I recommend not having any more than 10):

* Roster the shopping in pairs. Each person then only does a stint every five turns.
* Shop weekly or fortnightly.
* Each family contributes $100 per week, to be paid into the relevant account in advance.
* Keep a pattern to the roster, so that everyone knows who's doing what and when, and where to pick up their goodies.
* If shopping in-store, deal only with store managers, so you develop a personal relationship. Discuss what's cheap and the quality of what's available at the time of each shopping trip.
* While one person is packing the fruit and vegies, the second person is writing down the prices. Remember, the supplies have to be easily divisible into 10 – half a watermelon, an ice-cream container of grapes or a certain number of oranges for each family.
* Make sure you've packed 10 boxes for the families to take away.
* Shop in the morning of a particular day, and agree that families should pick up their boxes in the afternoon or early evening of the same day.
* Purchases to be listed with prices achieved.
* Have a meeting of all co-op members at least every two months.

 *A little secret from a couple of groups is to keep part of the cash each week shop for a surprise 'treat' for each family – a special cheese, fish, fruit etc. The choice is up to that week's buyer and adds a bit of anticipation to the group.*

Tactics for beating the supermarket

Every weekly shop is like a battle against the supermarket to get the best value. You know they want you to spend more. The challenge is finding out where and how.

Here's my list of traps to avoid in the supermarket minefield:

* **Eye level is buy level.** The products that stare out directly at your face will be more expensive than the alternatives at your feet. Food companies pay big money to be displayed at eye level.
* **Honey, we shrunk the product.** Look out for manufacturers sneakily reducing the size of the pack by 10–30 grams but keeping the price the same. It's hardly noticeable, but you're not getting the same value for your money.
* **Economy-sized products.** I've found instances where the larger size wasn't actually any cheaper. Check unit price labels (per 100 grams/ml) beneath the price on each shelf label.
* **Individually packaged foods.** Those little bags of baby tomatoes or crackers and cheese (for lunchboxes) might look cute, but you'd probably get more for your money if you bought a full-size bag and divvied it up yourself. Again, check the unit price.
* **Bagged salads.** It doesn't come with any of the fun stuff like avocado, chickpeas, egg or celery (I could go on), so you're really just buying a few types of pre-cut lettuce, baby spinach or rocket. Buying the leaves and the tasty stuff separately will definitely stretch your dollars further.
* **Pre-chopped anything.** Are you really getting more celery when it comes in little diced pieces rather than stalks? (Unlikely.) And pre-cut produce has to be less eco-friendly than its whole counterparts because of the extra packaging.
* **Added flavours.** These mean added costs when you can do it all yourself. Why pay a 30 per cent premium for garlic prawns when you can buy the fresh prawns, spend 20 cents on garlic butter (make your own from garlic and butter) and get the same meal?
* **Anything with a celebrity's or cartoon character's face on it.** An alternative product has to be cheaper because there's no royalty going to the celebrity you love from that TV cooking show.

- **Shiny fruit and vegetables.** Looks can kill . . . your budget. Some supermarkets now sell imperfect fruit cheaper. A few blemishes might make it uglier (a matter of opinion) but it still tastes delicious.
- **Products with 'new' features.** Companies are hoping you'll pay extra for the newest thing. Maybe a tomato sauce bottle with a new spout, or a nappy with new, innovative tabs – anything where you see new convenience features will probably cost more.
- **'Healthy' food products.** Making existing foods 'healthier' is a popular tactic for food and beverage companies. Be suspicious of anything with a new ingredient that's 'good for your health'.
- **Meal plans.** Pre-packaged multi-day meal plans will always be more expensive than buying the ingredients for a few days' worth of meals and cooking them yourself.
- **Anything in the checkout aisle.** The checkout is a minefield for the weak-hearted. But stay strong. Don't give in to an impulse buy. Items that people add while waiting in the checkout queue can be marked up 100 per cent.

There's a reason overpriced foods packaged for convenience still line the shelves. We're willing to pay for the convenience! Saving on salads or produce requires enough planning ahead to buy the perishables, prepare some meals, and consume them before they go bad.

Every little bit counts

Whether you shop at a big supermarket, local farmer's market or boutique grocer, there are heaps of things you can do to keep that grocery bill under control:

- Buy produce in season and on sale.
- Buy generic items where possible and stock up on staples if they're on special or available in bulk.
- Grow some vegetables or herbs of your own or start your own co-op with friends (see page 65).
- Take a list and stick to it.
- Buy ingredients rather than pre-made meals.
- Importantly, don't shop on an empty stomach.

This is all made easier if you look at what you already have at home and plan weekly meals ahead of time. Being vigilant can save a lot of money in the long run. Identifying and avoiding the rip-offs and having the discipline to stick to your guns is going to be worth effort.

KOCHIE CALCULATOR: SAVINGS ON GROCERIES

I know it seems like a lot of work but remember, according to the ABS, the average Australian family spends $236 a week on groceries, which totals $12,301 a year. It is the second-largest expense of every household behind rent or the home loan. Even if by avoiding the rip-offs you only save 10% on your weekly supermarket bill, that's:

* $23.60 a week
* $102.26 a month
* $1227.20 a year.

This equals an airline ticket to Europe or nicer birthday presents.

Home energy and appliances

You don't need me to tell you that energy costs are a massive drain on the average household budget. But whether you live in a big house or small, old or new, there are steps you can take to cut hundreds of dollars from your energy bill. Lack of energy efficiency means that the average household wastes up to $1000 a year in heating and cooling costs. And together we all waste enough energy each year to run the MCG lights for 500 years.

Changing both your behaviour and your technology can save money. The average home's energy bill is just under $1600 a year. Depending on how lax your energy efficiency measures are, or how vigilant your family is, the quarterly bill may range from $200 up to $1300.

KOCHIE CALCULATOR: ENERGY SAVINGS

According to the ABS, the average Australian household spends $49.11 a week on electricity and gas, or $2554 a year. Following the tips below could cut up 20% off that cost, which is nearly $10 a week or close to $520 a year.

Heating and insulation

Insulation has got to be the number-one single area for savings. The ceilings are the key area for heat loss, but also the walls and the floors, depending on what the house is made of. Sealing out draughts is also important. The gaps under doors, around windows, between floorboards and through a chimney can be a big source of heat loss. Any gaps between the walls and floors or ceilings should also be attended to. In older houses, fixed vents in the walls are usually not essential and can be closed off.

Room temperatures should be 18–21 degrees Celsius. For every one degree of temperature more than 21 degrees Celsius inside your home, heating costs increase by a whopping 10 per cent. Wearing warm clothing rather than wandering around the house in a T-shirt in winter will mean comfortably coping with a couple of degrees less in room temperature. Leaving the heater on all day, even on a low setting, is the best way to see your winter bill blow out. Let it run all winter and be prepared to allow another $180 for the quarterly bill.

Keeping the living room closed off from unheated rooms, putting the heater on a lower thermostat setting and using an energy-efficient gas heater or a ceiling fan to distribute heat could save another $30 per quarter for an average Australian home, according to energy authorities.

Windows

Much of a home's heat is lost through bare glass. Heavy, close-fitting curtains with pelmets are needed to cut down heat loss. Leaving windows open and the heater on could mean an extra $45 for the season, while not bothering to close the curtains or having thin or loose-fitting curtains could add around $23.

Insulation, weather stripping and good curtains in the living room alone can cut the average energy bill by $46 in the winter quarter.

Hot water

The hot-water service is the second-biggest energy sapper at home. If you haven't already got one, installing an off-peak hot-water service is an obvious starting point to cut costs. Washing clothes in cold water would save $3.50 a quarter, taking three-minute showers instead of baths can save $3.80 per person per year, and using a low-flow showerhead an extra $4.40 per person. Using a lower temperature setting on the dishwasher can also save big money.

Allowing the hot water to drip at a constant rate of a drop every two seconds will add $14 per dripping tap to your winter bill. Using an energy-inefficient washing machine, and leaving the hot-water tap running while washing your hands or rinsing plates will also run up the bill. While the clothes line or drying racks cost nothing to run, drying clothes with a tumble dryer will chew up around $24 of power a quarter.

An electric blanket bumps up the electricity bill by a whopping $25 per quarter during winter – why not try a hot water bottle? A spa and/or sauna will also chew through the power.

Refrigerator

The refrigerator is your third-largest user of energy, and many people don't operate their fridge at the right temperature. Energy experts advise that fridges need to run at only 4–5 degrees Celsius – any lower is a waste of power.

If your fridge doesn't have a temperature read-out, leave a thermometer in it for an hour or two to check.

Careless use, placement and maintenance of the refrigerator could cost an extra $8 a quarter. Keeping the coils behind the fridge clean and at least 10 cm clear of the wall will allow air to circulate around them and aid the cooling process. And the difference between a fridge with a five-star energy rating and one with just one star is around $13 a quarter.

Lighting

Even though lighting accounts for just 2 per cent of the average home's energy use (surprisingly low, isn't it?), there's plenty you can do. Using compact fluorescent and LED globes in frequent-use areas can still save you money. You'll save around $45 over the lifetime of a fluorescent globe compared to the old incandescent globes which have now been phased out, as will Halogen globes by September 2020.

Downlights and spotlights are the current fashion in home decor, with up to four per room. But it's estimated that using these lights throughout the average house will use around $38 more in electricity per bulb than a single LED or fluorescent light in each room.

Buying whitegoods

From washing machines to microwaves, whitegoods are a big one-off expense that (hopefully) last a decade or so. Of course, that depends on the quality of the item and how you look after it.

To get the best deal, don't be afraid to negotiate, offer cash and quote competitors' prices (more on how to negotiate this is coming up). Again, it's about being well informed, so use online resources to research models and read customer reviews. It also pays to sign up for email alerts from retailers to be on top of the latest sales. Sometimes the hardest part can be finding an item that will fit into the old space without remodelling your whole kitchen. In this situation, shopping around becomes even more important.

Lots of people wait until a big-ticket item dies before looking for a replacement. This means you might not get the best value and end up paying more out of urgency. So if your whitegoods are getting old or playing up, keep an eye on sales and deals before you get desperate.

Building

If you're building a home, you have the chance to do it right from the start. A little forward planning for energy efficiency will deliver savings from the day you move in. Choice of building materials, insulation, the size and direction of windows, proximity to nearby buildings and strategic use of deciduous trees can all make for an energy-efficient home.

A home built to a five-star energy rating will use about 30 per cent less energy than the average new home.

WHAT ARE THE TOP FIVE POWER SAVERS?

1. **Insulation.** Especially ceilings, but also floors and walls depending on their construction.
2. **Sealing out draughts.** Weather-stripping around doors, windows, floorboards and chimneys. Also seal any gaps where floors, walls and ceilings join.
3. **Windows.** Install curtains with pelmets. The heavier the material the better. Overlap or make as close-fitting as possible.
4. **Hot-water service.** An off-peak service will save you money, as will low-flow showerheads, cold-water washing, and using the lowest dishwasher temperature settings.
5. **Fridge.** Run it at no lower than 4–5 degrees Celsius. Keep the rear coils clean and clear of wall. Check the rubber door seal on older fridges.

Car

Property aside, cars are probably the biggest single purchase most people make. The average Australian family can spend $22,000 a year on transport, and the biggest commitment is family cars. Left unchecked, the costs of running a car can be a financial nightmare. But a little thought can save you thousands of dollars a year. With cars, it's not just the purchase cost but the ongoing maintenance you have to consider.

The decision

There are two big questions to ask yourself.

1. Do I even need a car?

The running costs can be staggering, so do the maths – petrol, maintenance, insurance, parking and rego. If you live somewhere with options (e.g. a large city with good public transport), ask yourself how often you use the car and what for, then look at the alternatives. Check out the cost of getting public transport to work, and then work out how often you need a car for other things. I have friends who find it cheaper to use the bus or train to work and then call taxis on the weekend for social occasions. They're still way in front and don't have to worry about drink driving (or parking).

Maybe look at ditching a car altogether and using a combination of public transport and car-sharing with the likes of GoGet, Hertz 24/7 or DriveMyCar.

KOCHIE CALCULATOR: OWN OR CAR-SHARE?

Lynne and David both work and have one child, Sarah. They have a Kia Rio and are tossing up whether to get rid of it. Lynne catches the bus to work each day and David the train. They use their car three times during the week, to take Sarah to soccer practice, flute lessons and karate, for a total of 20 km per week. On weekends they drive to the shops 2 km away and once a month they take it in turns to visit their parents 14 km away.

According to Queensland motoring group RACQ, a Kia Rio costs $0.48 a km to run based on an average 15,000km a year. Each week, David and Sarah drive 20 km + 4 km (to the shops and back) + 7 km (to their parents and back adjusted for one week) = only 31 km per week, or 1550km a year. However, this would realistically cost them about $145 a week when you account for not only running costs but amortising the purchase price, rego and insurance, all for a car not being used much.

If they sign up with car-sharing service GoGet, it will cost them a joining fee of $25 per driver, plus a monthly fee of $30 plus, for a small car, either $6.35 per hour + 40 cents per km or $74 per day for up to 150 km. If we spread the flat costs out over a year and assume an hour or two per weekly trip, this would be per week: $0.96 (joining fee) + $6.92 (monthly fee) + $38.10 ($6.35 × 6 hours per week on average) + $12.40 (31 × $0.40 per km) = $58.38 per week, versus $145.39 per week with the car ownership.

2. Do I need a new car?

New cars lose value as soon as they leave the dealership, dropping up to 50 per cent in the first five years. Check out used car trading websites like carsales.com.au and drive.com.au for deals.

The purchase

If you decide you do need to buy a car, unfortunately it's a bit of a minefield. The trick is to be an informed buyer and aware of the timing. If buying from a dealership, you need to know exactly what your budget is and what it is you want before walking in. Above all else, be prepared to walk away and look at the auction houses for second-hand cars with low mileage.

Understand your needs

The first step is to work out what you need from a car and figure out a firm budget, including on-road costs. Research different makes and models until you have a good feel for how much the vehicles you're interested in cost, which features to look for and good models or years to buy.

Go to your local motoring organisation website, which will have a full cost comparison for every car make and model, including those pesky hidden costs.

 *If you're buying second hand, aim for the newest car with the lowest kilometres possible within your budget, which should save on servicing down the track.*

Be prepared

Before inspecting a vehicle, put together a list of questions to ask the seller.

* **Buying new?** Make sure you ask about fuel economy, fixed-price servicing and dealer warranties.
* **Buying second hand?** Always check the car's service log, ownership history and whether it's been in a crash.

 *Don't just take the seller's word for it; check the car's registration details with your state transport authority. Cross-check the engine number against the car's paperwork, and ask for a recent roadworthy certificate.*

Time it right

Lots of car makers have mid-year sales, and there are usually end-of-calendar-year 'run-outs' to clear that year's models before new ones come in. Remember, car dealers are paid bonuses on reaching monthly targets, so that last week when they're racing to fill their quota can be a good time to negotiate a deal.

Be a smart buyer

Shop around (don't forget to look online), get different estimates and take competitive quotes to your preferred dealer. Never be afraid to negotiate; the headline price is for mugs. Make a reasonable offer, keep emotion out of it and walk away if you're not getting what you want.

STEP 4: CUT COSTS TO GROW HAPPINESS

Watch out for extras such as leather trimmings, paint guard, rust-proofing, tinting or increased security, and decide which of these you really want or need. A few hundred bucks may not seem like much in the context of a car, but it quickly adds up.

Get the best loan

If you're relying on finance to buy your car, it can be tempting to simply go with whatever the dealer is offering. Agreeing to their in-house finance deal means more profit for them, so use it as leverage for a lower price. Make sure you understand what else is out there – other lenders may be offering a better deal. Likewise, avoid locking yourself in to an expensive service plan unless the trade-off is more off the purchase price.

Look for loans with low interest rates and shorter terms. Even if the monthly repayment seems higher, you'll ultimately save on interest.

Insurance

At a bare minimum you'll need compulsory third party (CTP) insurance, and if your car is new or valuable, you'll likely also need comprehensive cover to protect you against damage to your vehicle. Compare quotes online, buy an average model, be realistic about mileage and add a second, low-risk driver if possible.

Remember, insurance premiums reflect the type of car you drive, your driving record, where the car is kept, and the age and capability of any additional people you allow to drive the car. As a general rule of thumb, if any of these elements is out of the ordinary, you'll be judged a higher risk and that will be reflected in a higher premium.

To keep your premiums down, it's best to have good security features on the car and park it securely at night. Maintaining a good driving record won't go astray either.

Running costs

You've bought the car, now what? Fill up at cheaper service stations, try to do basic maintenance yourself, and check your tyre pressure regularly. It all adds up.

Buying petrol

There's no hard and fast rule when it comes to petrol cycles. The level of the Aussie dollar and global oil price fluctuations affect the price we pay, so it can fluctuate a fair bit over the week. Rather than trying to guess when prices are going to be in your favour, look for a reliable website (e.g. NRMA in New South Wales) or app (e.g. Motormouth) to find the latest fuel prices in your area.

The big supermarket chains offer discount petrol vouchers for purchases over a certain amount. While it may only be 4–10 cents a litre, every bit helps. It also pays to check, though, that their petrol price before discount isn't 4–10 cents higher than the local competition.

The average fill on a standard car is 40 litres a week. A 5 cent saving per litre adds up to $2 a week or $104 a year.

Cut petrol consumption

Minor tweaks to your vehicle (and driving) can help make it more fuel-efficient. Get cars serviced regularly, keep tyres inflated to the recommended level, drive in the right gear and don't over-rev.

Get rid of excess weight from the car (no more sports equipment or half your wardrobe in the boot!), open your windows instead of using air conditioning (which uses up to 10 per cent more fuel), and drive smoothly – less revving is kinder on the engine and, ultimately, your wallet.

Share the driving

Find out whether any of your colleagues or your kids' classmates live in your area and offer to share journeys to work or school pick-ups and drop-offs.

Clothes

Everyone wants to look their best, and some think you need to spend a huge amount on expensive brand-name clothing and beauty products to achieve this. Stretching your budget for clothing may mean changing your expectations and using ingenuity, but you can look attractive and spend less.

Plan

Never buy clothes on impulse. Before shopping for the new season's wardrobe, have a good look at what's in your wardrobe and figure out what to buy to complement what you already have.

Budget

Work out the amount you can afford to spend on new clothes, then make a list of priorities. Spread the money around. Don't spend too much gearing up one member of the family, only to realise someone else needs new shoes and you can't wait until next month's pay comes through.

Buying at the end-of-season sales has saved me a lot of money. The children's clothes are really economical and their fashions don't change as quickly as those for adults.

Pre-loved options

There are good-value alternatives to buying new clothes, especially with children's wear, which they often grow out of before wearing them out. Garage sales and recycled clothing shops often have clothes that have hardly been worn.

An idea from the US is 'clothes-swapping parties', where friends get together with their clothes that don't fit or that they just want to change, and swap with each other. This of course works best if your friends are about the same size as you!

Be smart

If you buy new clothes, shop around for bargains. You often see replicas of the new trends in discount stores and online that are just as good, and some are even made by the well-known brands under a different label.

The other useful way of buying fashionable brands is through their factory outlet. It may be a bit of a drive, but often a couple of them are near each other, so going with a friend can make for a fun outing that's financially worthwhile.

Try a smaller wardrobe

You know those two or three pieces of clothing that just make you feel amazing? Use that theory for your entire wardrobe – two pieces of everything. Save money by buying less, and spend more on the pieces that matter.

Treat your clothes well

Looking after clothes saves money. Try, for example, not putting everything in the dryer. If it really has to go in, don't over-dry, as extra lint will come away, making the clothes thinner and causing any elastic to deteriorate faster.

The great money wasters – to be avoided at all costs

We're all different, but some things are simply never worth the money, no matter the spin you put on it.

Here are some of *my* top 'money wasters'. Feel free to add to the list.

* **Cheque accounts and bank branches.** Don't enter a bank branch again and never write a cheque or receive a paper statement again – you pay extra in fees for the privilege. Instead, go to websites like canstar.com.au, ratecity.com.au and finder.com.au to find and compare the online transaction accounts your financial institution offers. Pay your bills either

by transferring online or through BPAY. You'll slash bank fees and earn interest. Don't be scared if you haven't done it before – it's not hard. My 84-year-old mum has taken to online banking like a professional.

* **Bottled water.** Come on . . . really? We whinge about paying $1.50 a litre for petrol but are happy to pay $2.50 (or more) for 350 ml of water we can drink for free from the tap. At $2.50 a day, that's $17.50 a week, $910 a year. We have some of the best tap water in the world. Buy a re-usable drink bottle and turn on the tap.
* **Delivered food services.** It's so fashionable to have lunch or dinner delivered to your home or office. At $5 a drop-off, surely it's easier and cheaper to go for a healthy walk and pick it up yourself.
* **Credit card interest.** I know I've covered this in the debt section, but credit cards really are a scourge on the family budget. You might think a credit card is essential for phone or online purchases and transactions, but a debit card offers the same convenience, using your own money and incurring no interest. If you must have a credit card, see Step 3 for more tips.
* **Extended warranties.** The chances of you using an extended warranty are so small that it's not worth it in the vast majority of cases. And many of the 'in-store' warranties that are offered don't even cover the most common causes of failure in the product. Why are they offered? A retailer may make a 20–30 per cent profit on selling a product, but makes almost 100 per cent profit on selling you an extended warranty.
* **Long-distance telephone calls.** Most wireless broadband services allow free or low-cost access to local, interstate and overseas calls. Using services like Skype, FaceTime and WhatsApp can slash costly phone bills. The power of smartphones means you can make these calls from anywhere. We have children and grandchildren living in London and Hong Kong, but never pay to call them. Libby and I were hiking in a remote part of the Flinders Ranges in South Australia when our daughter rang on FaceTime. We chatted, showed her the scenery and then continued walking. It's that easy and costs very little . . . even after taking into account data prices, which are dropping dramatically.
* **Brand names.** From prescription drugs to fashion and food staples, there are cheaper generic alternatives of the same quality as the bigger, more expensive brand-name products. Often the goods are produced at the same factory using the same ingredients. Granted, some brand-name items are superior (I'm very fussy about toilet paper) and are market leaders for a reason. But there are just as many where it seems you pay a higher price just to subsidise their marketing campaigns. Surely rice is rice and paracetamol is paracetamol, no matter what the brand.
* **Forgotten direct debits.** Go through your credit card and bank statements line by line and highlight those regular direct debits to make sure they're what you think they are and that you still need them.

STEP 4: CUT COSTS TO GROW HAPPINESS

We'd always thought a yearly $49.95 charge on our credit card was a magazine subscription and just kept paying it. It turned out to be a portable wireless connection we'd bought years ago and no longer used! Assess direct debits for subscriptions, club fees, gym memberships and donations to see if you actually want or use them.

* **An expensive coffin.** I've gone through a stage recently of attending a few funerals, and it amazes me how elaborate and expensive the caskets can be when they're about to be burned or buried for a long time. It sounds a bit morbid, but wouldn't you rather leave that money to family or donate it to charity, where it will be put to much better use?
* **Being disorganised.** Have a good look at yourself and the way you manage your money. Extra bank fees from dipping into your overdraft or not paying the credit card on time because you forgot, rather than didn't have the money, are just wasteful. Things like automatically paying an insurance premium rather than checking whether there are better deals, leaving lights on in unoccupied rooms and not using discount coupons are all money-wasters but also easy to avoid.
* **Buying steak at a restaurant.** Maybe it's just me, but I'm constantly disappointed paying $30–40 for a steak at a restaurant that appears to be no better than what I cook at home from the butcher for $5.

TAKE THIS QUIZ: Are you wasting money?

Ask yourself:

1. Am I automatically renewing an insurance premium without comparing?   Y/N
2. Am I unnecessarily buying premium petrol?   Y/N
3. Am I paying for internet services I don't use?   Y/N
4. Am I paying for unnecessary extended warranties?   Y/N
5. Am I prone to impulse buying because I don't make, and stick to, a shopping list?   Y/N
6. Am I too lazy to compare alternatives when I shop online?   Y/N

If you answered yes to any of these, have a good look at your shopping habits and think about what you can change plug your spending leaks.

HOW TO BE A GREAT NEGOTIATOR

You've done your online comparisons, you know what you can spend, and the time has come to clinch a deal. But deal time can come with anxiety, embarrassment and a good old fear of failure. It doesn't matter whether it's negotiating the purchase of the house of your dreams, a new car or a piece of clothing, some people are simply uncomfortable with closing a deal for a great outcome.

My brother is the world's best negotiator. He asks for a better deal on everything he buys and invariably succeeds. He always mentions any anniversaries or birthdays when he books a restaurant or hotel, which usually gets him a free dessert or wine or an upgrade to a better room.

Follow these eight simple steps to become a great negotiator, and I guarantee you'll get a better deal on virtually everything.

1. Be private

A salesperson will be less likely to negotiate with you if they know they're going to have to give that same deal to 10 other shoppers nearby. So take them aside and keep the conversation between the two of you. That way you have their undivided attention, and they can focus on your deal and not be distracted by others wanting to ride on your coat-tails.

2. Be friendly

Nothing annoys a salesperson more than an aggressive confrontational customer trying to bully them into a better deal. It becomes a battle of egos, which the customer rarely wins. So be nice. Come in with honey, not vinegar. A low-key, friendly customer with lots of charm sets a great mood and shows they're willing to work with the salesperson for a deal that will work for them both.

3. Give them an incentive to bargain with you

Businesses want to build a connection with customers that will lead to future sales. That's why everyone wants your email and mobile details, and for you to 'like' their Facebook page and follow them on Instagram. So let them know it's worth bargaining with you because you'll be a great long-term customer. If you're buying a car at a dealership, tell them you're planning on bringing it back to them for repairs. If you're at a local homewares store, tell them you always try to support local businesses when you can. Agree to sign up for their newsletter and mention how you follow their social media.

4. Don't be so blunt with your questions

Don't bluntly ask, 'Can I get this for 20 per cent off?' It's not so easy for them to say no if you make your questions open-ended and say, 'I really love this couch, and it would fit perfectly in my lounge room, but it's a little out of my budget. Is there any way you could help me?' You want to engage them, appeal to their sense of fairness and compassion. Give them a chance to work with you rather than cut you off with a definitive answer.

5. Show you're smart

You want to come across as an educated, qualified buyer, because in a salesperson's mind that will make you a customer who's ready to buy now, rather than a tyre-kicker on a fishing expedition. Salespeople have sales targets and are focused on those who'll provide a quick sale so they can move on to the next customer. It's a process for them. So mention you're a collector to the antique dealer or share some specific knowledge about the technology in that bed you're considering. It shows you're ready to make a decision.

6. Do your research

It's so easy to research just about anything on the internet. And when it comes to negotiating, knowledge is power. If you do a little research beforehand, you and the salesperson will both know what a fair price is, and you'll avoid asking for an unrealistically low price they'll reject instantly.

7. Silence is golden

A negotiation should have an easy rhythm to it, and silence is a key feature. Silence is also a great tool because it builds anticipation and pressure in a non-threatening way. It will often lead the seller to say yes to your offer just to break the silence. Try those silent pauses out. You'll be amazed by their impact.

8. Understand the product cycle

Most stores look to clear their shelves right before the end of the calendar or financial year, which means that sellers will be more likely to bargain with you at those times.

Car sellers have monthly targets, so buy at the end rather than the beginning, when they'll be under pressure to move stock. There are also likely to be better bargaining outcomes in highly competitive industries.

Learn the art of regifting. It can seem a bit callous, but it's all about maximising someone else's generosity. Returning gifts to the store is always easier with a receipt, so if you can, tactfully get it from the person who gave you the gift. Even without the receipt, the store might give you credit or exchange, particularly if they can scan the barcode and determine the item did come from them. If you can't take it back, wait for an opportunity to regift it. Make sure it's in its original packaging and doesn't look opened or used, don't give it back to the person who gave it to you, and only give it to someone if it suits them and you think they'll appreciate it.

AFFORDING THE LITTLE LUXURIES

Sticking to a budget doesn't mean you have to deprive yourself of life's little luxuries, you just have to plan for them, keep impulse buying under control and have a savvy strategy. When drawing up your family budget, work out how much you can afford to spend on luxuries like dining out, non-essential shopping or holidays, and treat these items as an expense.

A colleague at *Sunrise* received a very pleasant surprise from his wife for his 50th birthday – an all-expenses-paid holiday for them both to attend the Italian F1 Grand Prix. She had secretly put away $50 a week for two years and hunted down great travel deals. It can be done.

Use simple tactics to afford luxuries

Surfing the internet makes it so much easier to hunt down the best deals. Here are a few tactics I swear by:

* **Buy second hand.** Use online marketplaces. Gumtree and eBay have bargains on everything from strollers to TVs that are still in mint condition.
* **Use paper coupons.** Don't be embarrassed to save coupons. They'll save you money on luxuries as diverse as dinners out and dry-cleaning. Keep them in your wallet or by the door so you don't forget to redeem them.
* **Look for online coupons.** Before making an internet purchase, do a quick search for a relevant coupon code to get a discount. Type in the product name and the word 'coupons' to find out what deals are out there.
* **Buy fancy ice cream at the supermarket.** Instead of spending $6 on a scoop at a specialty ice-cream shop, splurge on the most expensive litre at the supermarket. It'll cost you about the same and last the whole week.
* **Buy in bulk from markets.** Get luxury groceries or organic fruit and vegetables with great quality, great value and a great experience. Make it a weekend tradition.
* **Grow your own herbs.** Grow basil, mint or parsley on your windowsill or balcony. Fresh herbs take your home-cooked meals to a whole new level.

Travel without going broke

Family trips needn't cost the earth to be fun. But you need to plan well ahead and understand where the savings are, particularly if you have a tribe of children and don't want to constantly hear the traditional family holiday chant, 'I'm bored.'

Libby and I went into shock when our eldest turned 12 and most airlines said she had to go onto an adult's fare. It got even worse as the other three children passed this same milestone. We very quickly realised we had to get smarter when it came to planning our family getaways.

Travel slower

It's more cost effective to take fewer, longer holidays. Once you've sunk the money into getting there, the cost per day goes down the longer you're away. Longer holidays also motivate you to use budget-conscious strategies like buying groceries and lounging by the pool, because there's no pressure to fit every restaurant and activity into a few days.

Time it right

Shoulder seasons mean the weather is still nice and the value is there. By choosing to travel six to eight weeks before or after high season, you save money on everything from flights and accommodation to car rentals and sightseeing.

Choose your destination wisely

If you want a luxury holiday, find a country where your dollar can stretch further. Pay close attention to foreign exchange rates, which can drastically alter the final price of the trip. Asian or Pacific destinations such as Vietnam, Cambodia or Tonga often have great deals on luxury travel because of the conversion. Travelling in a country with a weaker currency than the Aussie dollar will make it seem like everything in the country is on sale.

Make use of travel cards (available from most banks or financiers), and load up the currencies you'll need over the year leading up to a big trip. Watch the currency movements and buy when the exchange rates are good.

Use rewards

Yes, I'd rather you didn't have a credit card at all, but one way to travel in luxury is to use credit card rewards. If you've always wanted to experience a premium economy or business class flight, use your credit card points to travel in style – for free (but you'll still have to pay those pesky taxes). When it comes to frequent flyer points, all the experts I've interviewed over the years say you get the biggest bang for your buck by paying cash for a cheap fare then using points to upgrade.

Rent an apartment instead of a hotel room

Opting for an apartment, cabin or beach shack rental instead of a hotel room not only saves money but, typically, offers more space and flexibility. This is especially true for families. We've often found that we can rent an apartment for, say, $150 per night, whereas two hotel rooms would be $300 per night.

We're cutting the cost in half, we can save more by cooking our own meals, and we also get a nice living room with space for the kids to play and eat.

Start your search on home-sharing platforms like Airbnb and Stayz where it's easy to filter for certain preferences, including number of bedrooms and proximity to public transport. TripAdvisor has a similar home/apartment rental search engine. If you live in a city, think about swapping with someone who lives in the country or has a place on the coast, or vice versa, using websites like homeexchange.com and aussiehouseswap.com.au.

If you do book a hotel . . .

Book the cheapest, worst room in a good hotel. No matter whether you're sleeping in the royal suite or the broom closet, the pool, day spa, restaurant, gardens and city sights are exactly the same for everyone. Very few book a hotel to spend all day in their room.

Remember, always ask for an upgrade – on everything. There's no harm in asking!

Mystery hotel rooms are another option – luxury hotel rooms advertised at a discounted rate by keeping the name of the hotel a secret. Most of the popular accommodation websites – Wotif, Expedia, Lastminute, Groupon and Scoopon – will offer these types of specials.

Buy groceries

If you do stay at a hotel, avoid the buffet breakfast unless it's included free as part of a package. Breakfast is a hotel's most profitable meal – and your biggest waste of money. While $25 per person might not seem outrageous, it quickly adds up. Pick up staples like yoghurt, cereal and fruit from a supermarket instead. The kids won't care and your wallet will thank you.

Having an apartment with a kitchen lets you cook meals instead of always going out for restaurant meals. Or make your own breakfast and lunch and use the money left over to go out for dinner.

Some restaurants offer bargain rates during the slow times of the day. So, by eating your main meal at lunch or an early dinner before 6 pm, you can cut your restaurant bills considerably.

Choose activities carefully

Don't overcommit to a hectic (and expensive) schedule. A bit of planning goes a long way. A Koch tradition is always a hop-on hop-off bus tour as soon as we arrive in a new city. It provides a good quick whiz around the most famous sites and an opportunity to see which ones are worth coming back to for a more comprehensive look.

The bus guide, and local tourist bureau brochures, will provide a good idea of the popular free attractions and tips on where to buy cheap tickets to shows. Remember that if you have little kids, they often lose their stamina after a couple of hours, so big, expensive all-day tours will be a waste of time and money.

Mix paid activities, like visiting museums, with simple, relaxing free ones, such as a day by the hotel pool or exploring a local park. Even with museums, check on TripAdvisor if they have free entry after, say, 4 pm, which may leave two hours to have a look. We used to do this a lot to see whether a museum was worth coming back to and paying for a longer look.

It's the little things

You don't *need* to spend thousands on fancy hotel rooms or Michelin-starred restaurants. Just stroll the streets or sip a cappuccino at a local cafe. Window-shop. People-watch.

Nice luggage

Designer brands don't always equal quality. Check out discount luggage stores for better known brands at cheaper prices, or peruse second-hand stores and online outlets.

Celebrate Christmas without breaking the bank

Approaching the biggest spending speed-bump of the year, Christmas, can be hard. Summer holidays are a cornerstone of a family's year, but there are plenty of ways to keep holiday costs under control while also maximising the fun.

Keep a price limit on gifts

Whatever the size of your family or group of friends, it's very easy to go overboard with gifts. Even when strictly setting out to buy a few little things, invariably it ends up costing way more than you thought.

The key here is to make a budget and stick to it. Take a minute to write down who's getting a gift this year, spread out your budget accordingly, then only spend that amount on each gift. End of story. If there's something special that absolutely must be bought, chip in with others to keep it affordable for everyone.

A popular alternative to spreading the budget is Secret Santa, where you draw a name out of a hat and buy a gift for that one person. It means everyone gives and receives something, but it keeps costs down.

And don't waste money on wrapping paper – it usually gets thrown out anyway. A lot of places offer free wrapping; otherwise, newspaper or brown paper with a ribbon does the trick.

Plan your meals

If you haven't got your kitchen budget sorted, get onto planning it early. The biggest hit to the savings is usually unplanned meals, so plan ahead and buy the essentials in bulk. If you hit the shops with clear meals in mind, the savings can be huge.

If you're hosting a Christmas lunch or dinner, don't hesitate to ask for a hand. Again, plan out what you'll need so that when people ask what they can bring, you have a good answer on hand. An extra bottle of wine or dish to share makes a big difference. Most people want to contribute something if they're coming over, so it's a nice way to involve everyone too.

Holiday around home

Holiday entertainment and trips don't have to stretch the family budget. In fact, summer's the best time of year for cheap entertainment, steering you clear of shopping centres and online shops that weasel their way into your wallet.

If there are essential items you need, by all means hit the post-Christmas sales for a bargain, but prioritise getting to the beach or the park for a picnic or visiting an outdoor film festival. It'll leave your bank balance better off and also help you relax, which is what holidays are for.

Make use of reward programs

A lot of credit cards, health insurance funds and motor vehicle memberships have perks and benefits that members don't use. Cheap movie tickets, free travel insurance and affordable foreign exchange options are just a few of the benefits I've come across but wouldn't have known about without looking. So get all your cards out and take an hour to flick through the membership benefits online to see where you can save this season. There's a good chance you're missing out on some great year-round deals.

On the flip side, don't let fees add up over the holidays. Pay with debit cards and cash where you can, and always plan ahead to withdraw from your own bank's ATMs. It's simple stuff that can make a bit difference.

Now this all sounds pretty straightforward, and it is. Yet, come the silly season, people still lose track of their financial fitness and wake up with a New Year debt hangover they could have easily avoided. So plan ahead now and show some discipline – it'll help lay the platform for a financially fruitful year ahead.

Home

Zhoosh up your home with these simple, affordable strategies:

* **Paint your front door.** Not only will this add charm, but it will also raise the value of your house. Not bad for a $15 can of paint.
* **Have amazing showers.** Replicate that luxury-hotel shower experience by upgrading your showerhead (while making sure it doesn't waste water).
* **Create a home bar.** Nothing says luxury like a home bar. Some glass decanters will class up even the most bottom-shelf liqueurs.
* **Spruce up an old mattress with a topper.** I can't understand people who put up with a bad mattress. If you need a new mattress but aren't ready to spend, get a luxury mattress topper and sleep soundly.
* **Splurge on bathroom accessories.** Save money by buying basic soap but get a fancy soap dispenser or soap dish to add elegance.
* **Get mood lighting.** Because nothing feels as romantic as sitting in a room full of candles or dim lighting – no matter the state of the furniture.

Entertainment and dating

You might feel guilty about treating yourself to a bit of romance when there are bills to pay, but I'm a firm believer in making time, and money, available for your relationship. Try these guilt-free tips for keeping the romance alive:

* **Indulge in free luxury experiences.** Look for free and discounted nights in your city by checking your council events, local library and suburban newspaper. There are so many jazz, opera, symphony 'in the park' festivals around Australia.
* **BYO to restaurants.** You might be slugged corkage, but a bottle that costs $20 at the shop can cost $70 or more at a restaurant, so this is a great way to enjoy top-notch wine without paying top dollar. Some licensed restaurants have specific BYO weeknights and drop corkage fees.
* **Plan a high-class picnic.** Buy some fancy cheeses, baguettes and a bottle of bubbly. Wait for a sunny day, put it all in a basket, and you've got yourself an unforgettable date.
* **Hang out in hotel lobbies.** Hotels always make me feel like I'm on an adventure, and the fancier the better. Just grab a book and lounge in a nearby hotel lobby, or order a glass of wine from the bar and linger (but don't be creepy!).
* **Go to art exhibition openings.** Hit up an art gallery on opening night and indulge in some free wine and cheese.
* **Watch a sunset at the beach.** I love the beach. It instantly relaxes me.

Sunrises and sunsets make me slow down and gaze in awe at nature's beauty. A bottle of wine cooling in a rockpool . . . aaaaahhhh.
* **Check out the fanciest happy hours.** Instead of going to your neighbourhood burger joint during busy hours, head to the happy hour of your favourite fancy restaurant, bar or pub. Bonus points if it's on a rooftop!

Fashion

I admit I'm no style icon, but I do understand people who are and who love buying, wearing, shopping for and enjoying new clothes. It reflects their character and style, and makes them feel good. Here are a couple of tips to find the right balance:

* **Buy second hand.** Second-hand shops are a great place to get designer and high-end clothing for reasonable prices. Look for specific brands you love.
* **Rent a good outfit.** Blokes have been renting tuxedos for years, and now ladies can rent designer outfits from internet platforms like GlamCorner and The Volte. Rather than spend $500–1000 on a gown, look amazing for $100.
* **Tailor your clothes.** Splurge on tailoring for a couple of basic pieces. Libby does this all the time. You'll keep them longer and wear them more. And they'll look more expensive because of how well they fit you.
* **Costume jewellery rocks.** Diamonds may be a girl's best friend but cubic zirconia looks the same and is a better financial deal. No one ever comes up with a jeweller's glass to check on the quality of the stones and metal. There's an enormous range of good-quality costume jewellery available.

Beauty

Want to pamper yourself but worried about the cost? Libby and my daughters have it sorted:

* **Start your own day spa.** Buy some good nail polish and take the time to do a home mani-pedi. A foot soak and some fresh polish go a long way towards relaxation.
* **Coconut oil.** From eye make-up remover to face mask, conditioning treatment, cuticle cream *and* cooking oil, coconut oil is a bit of a wonder. It smells delicious, feels amazing and will make you feel a million bucks for under ten bucks.
* **Buy chemist-brand make-up.** You don't have to spend hundreds to get quality cosmetics. The home-brand products can be just as good.

- **Get student massages.** Most massage and beauty schools consistently need people for their students to practise on.
- **Be a hair model.** If you're lucky enough to get an experienced student, you can get a $75 haircut for under $20.
- **Pamper your make-up brushes.** Using baby shampoo to wash them regularly will not only help you avoid skin breakouts, but also keep brushes soft and clean-smelling.
- **Drink lots of water.** Hydration is terrific for your general health and amazing for your skin.

NOTES

WHAT HAVE WE LEARNT?

Now that wasn't so bad, was it? My aim was to make sure you get value for money, and now you know how to save on all of the basics, from groceries, to energy, appliances, cars and clothes, and how to live the high life on a budget. Ease yourself in by making a commitment to look into at least one of my suggestions for saving each week over the next month or so.

HOMEWORK

KEY POINTS

- **Focus on groceries, your second-biggest expense**
- **Ask yourself if you really need that car**
- **Negotiate on everything**
- **Plug the financial leaks**
- **Spoil yourself**

HOMEWORK

- ☐ **Adopt a supermarket strategy and start a neighbourhood buying co-op**
- ☐ **Do the numbers, look at car-sharing alternatives**
- ☐ **Do your homework, compare, ask for a better deal**
- ☐ **Cut silly stuff like bottled water and save big bucks**
- ☐ **Don't give up your luxuries: find cheaper ways to enjoy them**

NOTES

STEP 5: GROW YOUR INCOME

Ask your boss for a pay rise. But if that goes south, investigate working for yourself or getting a side hustle.

DO THIS NOW

1. Write down your annual salary here:
   _____

2. Calculate 10% of your annual salary (i.e. your salary × 0.1):
   _____

3. Multiply that 10% figure (i.e. the figure in the line above) by 5:
   _____

Quite a big sum, right? If you're on a salary around the Australian average ($80,000), you probably got somewhere around $40,000. That's right, if you manage to secure just one pay rise of 10%, that's an extra $40,000 in your pocket over five years. And imagine if you received a pay rise *every year*? Want to learn how? Read on.

HOW CAN YOU GET MORE MONEY COMING IN?

Whenever anyone talks about building wealth and getting their money under control, they always focus on the household budget and cutting costs. They seem to forget about the other side – the income bit. Focusing only on cutting costs can be horrible. Earning more income could be a better option, and might not be as hard as you think.

This step is all about earning more cash, by:

* grabbing hold of career opportunities that come your way
* negotiating better pay
* striking out on your own and being your own boss
* developing a side hustle or turning assets into cash.

DO THIS NOW

* List two or three career opportunities you *haven't* made the most of. Are you kicking yourself about them?
* List two or three opportunities you *have* made the most of, and reflect on how that felt and where it got you. Feels good, right?
* Think for a moment about opportunities that might present themselves in your career and how you might take advantage of them. Is there a big project coming up that you could put your hand up for? Can you take on the responsibilities of a manager going on leave?

STEP 5: GROW YOUR INCOME

GET THE MOST OUT OF YOUR CAREER

Everyone dreams about winning Lotto or receiving a big inheritance, and for most people these two options remain a dream. But you know what? You do have the opportunity to fulfil that dream by creating your own Lotto: your career.

Make the most of your job and your career, and if you're in the right field there's the potential to win Lotto-type returns. We often forget about it because it just comes into our bank account regularly, but boost that pay cheque and it can do wonders for your future. Increase your salary from $40,000 to, say, $80,000, and over 12 years you're earning almost $1 million.

Now I know doubling your salary won't happen overnight, but rather than dreaming of a windfall, why not take control of your earning power? We all have a dream job. A job that will take us out of the current grind and transform our life. It may be a job that allows us to travel the world, be our own boss or get out of the rat race altogether to tranquil rural surroundings. Whatever shape the dream takes, for most it remains a dream but for others it's a reality. Often the reality doesn't quite match the dream, but some people have shown it can be done.

A dream helps, but you also need the skills and the opportunities – and it takes plenty of hard work to create them. This also involves being realistic enough to assess whether the goal is achievable and whether it's actually what you want.

Think realistically about the change in lifestyle. For instance, many people want to be self-employed so they can be their own boss and take holidays whenever they like. But many self-employed people can end up slaves to their business and rarely get to take holidays.

Grab your opportunities

Some people's success seems so crazy and out of reach. I wish I had a dollar for every time I've been asked this question: 'How on earth did a finance journalist end up hosting *Sunrise*?' The answer is always the same: 'Sheer arse.' That's what life's all about. Taking advantage of opportunities and seeing where they'll take you. Of course *Sunrise* was one of the biggest opportunities of my life.

For 11 years I'd been the finance editor for the Seven Network, which included daily segments on the *Sunrise* breakfast program hosted by Chris Reason and Mel Doyle. Unfortunately, Chris was diagnosed with cancer and needed treatment for three months, so I was asked to fill in for that period. Thankfully, Chris's treatment was successful, but he was advised, for health reasons, not to return to the physically demanding role of daily breakfast television.

At that time, a young punk called Adam Boland was put in charge of the show and asked me stay on full time. Originally I said no because I had no ambition to be a newsreader, but I said I'd consider it if I could inject some of my own personality into the show and basically be myself – be normal.

Adam had the same idea, and said he'd protect me from any fallout from management. The executives at Seven were more than a little nervous, but as *Sunrise* was coming a poor second to its major competitor and the network had big headaches at the other end of the day in prime time, they didn't really care what we did and we sort of slipped under the radar.

That's how I got onto *Sunrise* – sheer arse . . . and the rest is history.

After we'd become the top-rating breakfast show on television I asked Seven's big boss, David Leckie, whether he'd ever have approved *Sunrise*'s format had he known what we had planned. His answer: 'No way.' *Sunrise*'s success is all about setting goals, being different, loving the viewers and sticking to the plan. Life's full of opportunities. It's exciting: you never know where it will lead, but it's all about grabbing those opportunities and hanging on for the ride.

Your current job is a building block of your career, which is a critical part of your being because it affects your whole life. From self-esteem to social interaction and financial reward, *your career is at the centre*.

TAKE THIS QUIZ: Career self-assessment

Self-assessment is important when planning a career strategy. Write down your answers to the questions below.

1. **What skills do I have?**

2. **What are my strengths and interests?**

3. **What do I like doing at work?**

4. **What don't I like doing at work?**

5. **Am I in the right job for my interests, strengths, likes and dislikes?**

Review your answers and see if they point towards your dream career or at least a career change.

Work on your self-confidence

'Always have enough confidence in yourself to give anything a go. But also have enough confidence, if it doesn't work out, to go and do something else.'

It's the single best bit of advice I've ever received, and I've tried to follow it to the letter. It came from my father, and I'm trying to pass it down to my children. In essence it means 'never be scared by an opportunity'. Grab it, give it your best shot, and if it doesn't work out, then move on to something else. But never be left wondering, 'What if . . . ?'

I just don't understand people who stick with a job they don't like. I can hear some people saying, 'It's easy for you to say in your fancy, well-paid media job.' Fair enough, but it's a tragedy to be stuck doing something that you hate, so if you can, I encourage you to strive for a job you enjoy.

I can understand there are people who don't want much from their job because they have other exciting priorities in their life and a job is simply a means to another end. Their life revolves around family, friends, community groups or hobbies.

What I can't understand is people who simply grumble about their job and do nothing about it. I don't want to be too blunt, but get off your butt and do something about it – life's simply too short.

I firmly believe *it's a confidence issue.*

Look for a speciality, be unique

When I was a young, ambitious 25-year-old journalist, I looked around at all the finance media icons to see what I could learn and how I could be as good. They were all highly skilled with great contacts and much older than I was. In finance journalism back then, age brought credibility. I could work on developing my skills and building contacts, but competing with nature was going to be a little tougher – and I even had hair then.

So I looked around for what could be the next big thing in finance journalism, something so new and different that the usual rules wouldn't apply and age wouldn't matter. As luck would have it, in the early 1980s, Paul Keating as federal treasurer was revolutionising the financial system: deregulating the banks, floating the Australian dollar and means testing age pensions.

I'd seen the boom in personal finance media in the US while visiting my parents, who were living in San Francisco at the time. So I decided to do the same thing in Australia. Instead of writing stories for Australia's chief executives, I decided to inform their families and friends about making the most of their money. At this time there were no personal finance sections in any newspaper.

It was arguably the best career decision I've ever made. At *BRW* magazine we started to see spikes in circulation when I wrote personal finance stories.

That was followed by the success of *Personal Investment* magazine, which rode the share boom of the 1980s. I happened to be in the right place at the right time in a speciality that was becoming increasingly sexy.

I think the key in any career is to look around and *find an in-demand speciality* where you can develop a unique set of skills that set you apart from the rest.

Assess the future of your job category

The economy and technology have dramatically changed the working landscape. Tens of thousands of positions have been made redundant and some jobs have disappeared altogether – including many jobs in print media, where I started out.

It's worthwhile assessing the future potential of your job and, if it's under threat, looking for a change. It might be wise to talk to your boss about transferring to a different type of work where you'd gain new skills. For example, an engineer might switch to a management role to broaden their skills and experience.

If you're in a large company, the first step is to look for the right department and job. Ignore the gossip on the grapevine and check with the personnel department to see which divisions are hiring. Internal transfers usually receive preference. Ask department heads about their long-range plans, and scan trade magazines or websites to learn which parts of your industry are expanding.

Set yourself goals

Every New Year I ask Libby and the kids what goals they've set for themselves for the next 12 months. For years they'd laugh at me: 'Don't be stupid!' As they got older, there were fewer laughs and even a couple of answers. It started to sink in.

Life's so busy these days that we don't seem to take a deep breath, stop and think about what we want to do as individuals. But if you don't have some sort of map, how do you know where you want to get to?

My brother Matt is the brains of the family and I reckon his great success comes from the fact he's very clear about his goals. He never talks about it, but years ago I came across his open diary and in the inside front cover was his list of personal goals, both short and long term. They were both career and personal goals, written down as a constant reminder. He's probably the most balanced guy I know.

STEP 5: GROW YOUR INCOME

WHAT MIGHT CAREER GOALS LOOK LIKE?

Everyone's goals will be different.

Let's take Angela, a property lawyer, as an example. Her list of career goals may look like this:

- Become a partner by 2020.
- Increase my personal brand: publish at least one article a year, speak at one conference per year.
- Give back: take on at least one pro bono case per year.

You must have a *clear sense of purpose*, define your goals, work towards them, and apply common sense, research and effort.

DO THIS NOW

Amend your budget to include a monthly contribution towards your own . . . let's call it 'Emergency Fund'.

Have a fallback position

I've always vowed I'd never depend on radio or television for a living. While they're great jobs, in some ways they're horrible industries to be in because they're so cutthroat and volatile. When you have a single income, a couple of kids and a mortgage, that volatility is unacceptable. So I've always worked other jobs on the side because I don't want to put the family at risk.

As a journalist, I'm lucky I can freelance with other groups after hours. Even when I was a young journo on the business pages of the *Australian* newspaper, I was also a contributor for the London-based *Economist* magazine. From 1988 until 2002, I ran my own publishing business, while my media work was a hobby that regularly got out of control.

In fact, one of the best pieces of advice I've received about life in the media was from the former editorial director of the Fairfax newspaper group Max Suich. I'd just started *Personal Investment* magazine, when he explained that he always kept the equivalent of six months' salary in a separate savings account he called his 'F**k off money' – a pot of cash he could fall back on if he was asked to do something at work he didn't agree with philosophically.

How often do people go against their own principles because they can't afford not to? The mortgage, credit card bills, the huge cost of bringing up kids – it's a horrible position to be in when you simply can't afford to leave.

That little stash of cash gives you the flexibility to stick to your guns.

Consider working overseas

The younger you are, the easier this will be.

I was fortunate to spend 1987 working in London, buying a small UK financial publishing business for the Fairfax media group. We had three young kids at the time, and I found it so incredibly rewarding both professionally and personally. It opened my eyes and exposed me to world's best practice, new ways of doing things and new industries. It put me outside my comfort zone. Couple this with the personal growth for us as a family, and it was a wonderful year.

I came home and started my family publishing business the following year from an idea inspired by the UK publishing group. The UK was about five years ahead in this boom and had developed specialised industry magazines for professionals in the industry. Fairfax and I started a joint-venture specialist publishing company that followed the UK trend.

Libby and I have encouraged all our children to work overseas while they can, as it's easier for younger Australians to obtain a working visa from an amazingly wide range of countries.

Slightly undervalue yourself

There's no doubt money is important. Being paid what you're worth is important. But it isn't the be all and end all.

My top priority has always been to be in a job I love and then be paid appropriately for doing it. I've always thought it's better to be happy to be paid a little below what you're worth and keep your job than push for every last dollar and run the risk of being let go at the next downturn.

Like most industries, the media runs in cycles. It will have boom years when everyone's making big money and then an inevitable bust with staff purges and redundancies. I've always figured that when those purges come and the bosses get to my name on the list they'll think, 'Hey, he does a good job and he's value for money, so let's keep him.'

So many people stress about how much they're being paid down to the last dollar. I tend to look at the other rewards first and balance them up – enjoyment, colleagues, potential, conditions.

Sure, I'm seen to have a fancy, well-paid job, but my television prominence only started in 2003. For the 23 years before that I was just one of the journalistic troops, with no real power but still the single income, four kids and a mortgage.

A little while ago I was approached by another television network to switch camps. They were offering a better deal and the executive was very flattering, outlining some exciting future projects. It was tempting. Then he brought a colleague into the meeting who played the 'bad cop': 'I don't know whether you'd be right. I don't like you having other interests because we like to own our people.' I just sat there thinking, 'This is all too hard when I really enjoy working with the team at Seven.' So I said, 'You're right. I don't think I'd be right for you either.'

I've always said to my bosses that I don't haggle about salary: 'You pay me what you think I'm worth.' But then I add that if I discover I'm way underpaid they shouldn't be upset if I leave.

It seems to have worked and, touch wood, I've never been out of work.

Let me be really clear about this though: I'm *not* saying you should leave the decision about how much you're paid entirely in the hands of your employer, or that you shouldn't ask for a pay rise every year (you should, and I'll tell you how in a minute!). Only that, in the course of those discussions, it's important to remember where you and your salary sit in the scheme of things.

Build your brand

One of the biggest assets of a company is its brand, and you should be thinking the same way about you and your career.

As life becomes more complicated and people are swamped with more and more options, consumers are gravitating towards brands they love and trust to make decisions easier. If a consumer loves a particular company they'll choose that brand no matter the competition. Look at Virgin. It started in music then went into clothes, airlines, financial services and mobile phones. The brand is so strong that consumers follow it across industries. There's no reason why you shouldn't be doing the same. That's what I did early in my career.

I wanted the 'David Koch' brand to stand for someone who provided good personal financial information to ordinary Australians in an easy-to-understand, relevant and entertaining way. Someone who took the mystique out of the complex finance world and understood the plight of average Australians.

My personal brand was moulded by the stories I wrote and products I created, such as *Personal Investment* magazine and *Money Management* newspaper. I reinforced it by talking about personal finance issues in radio interviews and being involved in the financial services industry itself.

I know I'm lucky working in the high-profile media industry, because it's one of the few industries where you're paid by someone else while they build your brand for you. But you can build your brand as well:

- Do the best you can at work and build a great reputation in your company.
- Volunteer for company projects and activities outside your speciality – it might be the social club, becoming a first-aid officer, helping on a committee.
- Get actively involved in your industry association as a member or on a committee – you'll learn a lot and make good contacts with competitors and suppliers.

Building your personal brand is all about being seen as good at your job by your boss – and the bosses of your competitors.

Just never think your brand is bigger than your employer's brand. It happens a lot in media, where 'stars' think they're the reason for the success of a show, that the only reason people watch or listen is because of them rather than the station or the show itself. A particular company and its culture may be just right for you, and going somewhere else may not be as good a fit or as enjoyable.

Find a mentor

One of my favourite movies is *Mr Holland's Opus* starring Richard Dreyfuss. It's the inspiring story of a music teacher who worked through his own personal feelings of inadequacy to become a mentor and inspiration to a whole school of kids. I've always hoped my kids would have a 'Mr Holland' in their school life and, thankfully, they all have.

For me it was my maths teacher and rugby coach, Col 'Doc' Holliday, who cared for, inspired and counselled a group of teenage boys coping with growing up. He taught me to set goals, to be courageous in what I wanted to be and to always be a team player. It was great advice.

You might not have had a mentor at school, but learning from others with more experience and wisdom is just as important after you graduate, when you're developing a career and even once you've established your career. If you don't have a mentor, look around and find one. You'll be amazed at how many people are happy to help, take an interest and give advice – they only need to be asked.

I've been lucky that, apart from Col, I've had terrific mentors at different stages of my life and career. I feel privileged that one of the people I most admire in my life is my father. As a kid, and as an adult, he was always there with encouragement for what I was doing and advice when it was needed. I knew he was always there for me. He was a wonderful resource and mate. I was devastated when he died a few years ago. There've been many others – Bob Gottliebsen, Mike Carlton and Geoff Morgan, in particular – who I consider my mentors. You need to find yours.

My lifelong philosophy is that there's always something to learn from everyone, no matter who they are or what their age.

Back your own instincts

One of my biggest weaknesses is not listening to my own instincts enough. Weird, isn't it? I don't automatically follow my own gut feeling. Everyone's under the false impression that I should be in control and know everything. Despite the outward confidence I doubt myself regularly – just like most other people. For me it's all a matter of balancing up the advice and then taking responsibility for the final decision.

I often wonder if it's because my job means I get to meet a lot of successful and important people I'm in awe of. I assume they must be better than me, that they must be good to get to that position – but I'm often disappointed after meeting someone famous. I get excited because they're so successful and after the interview I often wonder how on earth they got there. They're neither bright nor nice.

I've made some of my biggest career and business mistakes when I've gone against my gut instinct and followed the advice of someone else I thought knew better. I can't blame that person for the outcome because I made the ultimate decision, but I've learnt (probably later than I should have) that *you* know what's best for yourself. That's not to say you should never take advice from anyone. Take advice, weigh it up with your own view, and then make a decision.

Respect others

I love my job because I love finding out what makes people tick. I don't care who they are, I reckon you can learn something from just about anyone. It's one of the most powerful lessons I've picked up from my father. He was the ultimate people person. Everyone loved him. His circle of close friends had always been based on personality rather than position or wealth, and they came from all walks of life.

While we came from a working-class background, Dad became a very successful businessperson and rose to be chief executive of a major stock exchange listed company. As teenagers, my brother Matt and I would act as waiters for work functions Dad had at home, which attracted business leaders and politicians.

One uni holidays I worked for the liquor distributor of Dad's company as an offsider on a truck delivering kegs of cider to pubs and wine bars. On Christmas Eve we got back to the depot a bit late for the Christmas party and quietly walked in the back in the middle of the speeches. Well, there was my old man, the big boss from head office (who just the weekend before had been entertaining the rich and famous at home), giving the funniest, most down-to-earth speech I'd ever heard to this bunch of hardworking blokes – and they loved him. Some of his jokes were a bit crude, so you can imagine how shocked I was!

When I commented about it afterwards he said, 'Everyone's a human being and everyone deserves respect.' I've never forgotten that piece of advice.

It's one reason *Sunrise* has such a strong culture – we respect everyone who works on the show; we celebrate successes, set direction and analyse mistakes as a group. From the on-air anchors to studio floor crew and producers, everyone's treated the same.

I hope I've inherited Dad's respect for others, and it's the one thing I hope I can pass on to my kids. It's probably one reason Libby and I have a big circle of friends with only a few who work in media. We find a lot of media people live in an unrealistic privileged bubble.

Be yourself

'How can you be a finance nerd and be funny?' It's one of the most common questions I've been asked since I started hosting *Sunrise*. It always amuses me, as what you see is what you get. I've always been the same, but people have this peculiar idea that anyone who works in finance must be boring. Hopefully I've become a champion of the supposed geeks.

When it comes to your career, I've always felt you can't pretend to be something you're not. People are too smart and will eventually see straight through you. And I can't see how you could live with yourself pretending to be something different anyway – your life would be a sham. I can't stress how important it is to be true to yourself. Take comfort from the fact that the charlatans are always uncovered in the end.

NEGOTIATING A PAY RISE

Clinching that annual pay rise has never been harder. Average wage rises are barely keeping pace with low inflation. In fact, many industries have frozen salaries, cut bonuses, cancelled performance reviews and abandoned automatic rises.

So now, more than ever, you need a well-thought-out strategy to convince the boss you're worth more. I think it's important to talk to your boss regularly about your performance and how you're a key member of the team.

How to ask for a pay rise

1. Time it right

If your company is doing it tough or on the brink of collapse, now is not the right time to ask for a pay rise. But if you know your employer is doing okay, give it a go.

Approach your boss and ask for some time to talk about your performance and discuss your future. Try to do it after you've had some success, such as winning a new client, increased productivity or being praised by the boss for good work.

2. Formalise the process

The single biggest mistake people make in salary negotiations is treating them too casually. This is your livelihood we're talking about, so you and your manager need to take it seriously. This means providing warning by booking in a formal meeting, preparing yourself with a clear case for a pay rise, and following up.

The last piece of the puzzle is where a lot of people fall down: make sure you set out the next steps at the end of the meeting. Get a clear agreement on when you'll follow up, anything you need to do to secure the raise and – ideally – when it will take effect.

3. Know your value

Research how much you're worth. Scan career websites (like seek.com.au), look through online job advertisements, or speak to a recruiter in your industry to find out what similar positions are paying.

Delicately present that information to your boss if you find you're being underpaid.

4. Prove your worth

Make a list of your achievements since your last performance review and refer to them in your meeting. You may have exceeded your sales targets, taken on extra work or outperformed your colleagues in some way.

Also remind your employer of any unique skills, experience or contacts you bring to the position.

5. Seek extra responsibility
Discuss your future with the company and quiz your boss on what you need to do to succeed or reach a certain position. Ask for more responsibility. This shows you're ambitious, a hard worker and keen to progress in the company.

6. Boost your knowledge
Learning new skills can help you move up the pay scale and off that career plateau that's been holding you back. Show initiative and ask your boss what training or further education you need to move to the next level. Find out if your company will subsidise your tuition fees. If not, bear in mind that they're tax deductible.

Wage negotiation mistakes

To help you get through this tricky chat with both money in your pocket and the goodwill of your boss, here's how to avoid the five biggest mistakes people make when negotiating a pay rise.

1. They don't consider the direction of the business
As an employee you're part of a team working towards a common set of goals, so it's important to appreciate your role in achieving those goals. Too many people see themselves as independent of the business, and frame their case for a pay rise in terms of their work, not how they're contributing to the business's future.

So before you march in asking for more money, talk to your manager and the people around you to find out what they need. What are they working towards and how can you help them deliver their targets?

2. They don't do a proper self-appraisal
The worst time to ask for a pay rise is when you've been underperforming, and yet so many employees wait until they're upset about their pay rate to pose the question, without considering whether they've been exceeding expectations or not.

Regardless of how underpaid you feel right now, cool your heels and do a self-appraisal to see if you've been doing everything that's asked of you, and a bit more. If you haven't been hitting targets, hold off while you work harder over the next four weeks to get yourself into a stronger negotiating position. This will also help you get a clearer picture of your strengths and contribution.

3. They undermine themselves

Pay negotiations can be uncomfortable, especially if there's no formal structure in place to guide the timing and process of performance reviews.

In this unfamiliar environment, a lot of people go into their shells and aren't as confident in their pitch as they were when practising in front of the mirror. So much so that they end up referring to negative aspects of their performance and using self-defeating language when making their case.

Try to overcome this tendency by reminding yourself that you *do* deserve a pay rise and your contribution is important, and always refer to your projects and achievements in positive terms.

4. They don't leave themselves room to move

Negotiations involve each party giving some ground on their initial position to try to come to an agreement. Despite this fundamental principle, so many employees start with what they actually want, leaving themselves no room to move when negotiations begin. By starting with a higher target than you'd be happy with, you're likely to end up with a better outcome. It's also important to look at alternatives to money, in case that's not on the table. So spend some time working out what's valuable to you in terms of conditions or benefits (perks) – see below.

5. They don't ask at all!

If you don't ask you don't get. A good employee, happy in their work, can often be taken for granted by bosses who get distracted by high-maintenance staff.

Don't be a shrinking violet and overshadowed by others. Don't be afraid to put yourself in the spotlight and ask for a better deal.

If the boss says no

Don't threaten to quit if your boss says no to a pay rise this year. Get some feedback and ask what you can do to get a raise in the next few months. Also consider alternatives to a straight pay rise that can still make a big difference to your lifestyle.

Salary packaging

Some of the most common and popular packaging arrangements include funding a car lease, buying a laptop or salary sacrificing into superannuation to boost retirement savings. Check with your employer to see whether they offer salary packaging as a benefit, and what items they've selected for their employees to package.

Personal development

Ask if they'll invest in your development. They may be more willing to fund this if they believe the skills you gain will make you a more effective employee and help build their business and profits. It's a business expense for the company as staff training, and comes with tax advantages.

Intangible benefits

Flexible working hours or the ability to work from home one day a week could do wonders for your lifestyle and family life, and help save on child care or after-school costs.

KOCHIE CALCULATOR: THE FINANCIAL VALUE OF WORK BENEFITS

Instead of a pay rise, other benefits could include:

* Flexible working hours to finish early and save on after-school care fees: $100/week.
* Four-day working week, which saves on childcare costs: $120/week.
* Professional development courses: $1000.
* Purchase of a laptop: $900.

If you don't ensure that each year you're receiving at least the minimum pay rise (or equivalent in other benefits) to keep up with CPI, you're effectively taking a pay cut!

BE YOUR OWN BOSS

Do you secretly dream of setting your own hours, choosing your customers, or becoming the next great Aussie entrepreneur? It's easier than ever to start a business today, and a few high-profile success stories have shown us that anything is possible. Being a successful entrepreneur has always been a solid pathway to building serious wealth. But in the past, entrepreneurs have needed significant financial resources to build their business dream in retail or financial services. The digital age is changing those parameters as the internet reduces the cost of entry for entrepreneurs to test an idea, build customers and gain traction.

But while the thought of being your own boss and changing the world from your lounge room is pretty exciting, for most budding entrepreneurs the reality is very different. The solo path is a long, hard slog that requires commitment and determination, and there are no guarantees of flash cars and waterfront properties at the end of it all. You need to be passionate about what you're doing and not be in it for the wealth.

If you're thinking about starting out on your own, here's what a successful entrepreneur looks like. Do you have what it takes?

1. They (genuinely) love a challenge

Whether it's coming up with an innovative way of doing something or carving out a niche in a crowded market, great entrepreneurs aren't afraid to meet a challenge head-on. It's this competitive edge that keeps them one step ahead of the game.

2. They're self-motivated

Sure, being your own boss means no one can tell you what to do. But no one will call you out for slacking off when you should be putting in the hard yards, either. Entrepreneurs have to be self-motivated, driven and hungry to succeed; that's not negotiable.

3. They see the big picture

A successful business is more than just a product or a service. While it's great to be talented or a specialist in a particular field, to make a venture work it's important to see the big picture, too. That's why entrepreneurs need to act as their company's head of sales, marketing, finance, technology and strategy, as well as fully understand their industry, their own competitive advantages and the opportunities for growth.

4. They take responsibility

Entrepreneurs know their role doesn't have set hours or working conditions. In fact, they're on call 24 hours a day, 365 days a year. In your own business the buck stops with you, so it's crucial to be able to take responsibility.

5. They're organised

Business owners are spinning more plates than the nearest circus. A big part of an entrepreneur's role is to be organised, keep things running smoothly and make sure everything gets done.

6. They learn from failure

Everyone wants to succeed, but when starting something new, it's inevitable you'll come face to face with failure. There's an old adage used by many famous entrepreneurs: 'Fail fast, fail often' – in other words, know when to call it a day and always learn from your mistakes.

7. They don't follow, they lead

Entrepreneurs genuinely believe they can do things better and make a difference, and they're able to sell that vision to other people – employees, clients and investors. Toeing the party line is for people who pull in a salary, so get used to being a leader.

8. They make decisions

Have you ever noticed that successful people always seem to act quickly? For better or worse, they make tough decisions fast, because they know if they don't the world will move on without them.

This doesn't mean all business owners have to shoot from the hip or make rash judgements, but be prepared to back yourself and your opinions.

9. They control fear

Starting a business is a daunting prospect for anyone. But for great entrepreneurs, that fear is a good thing. It motivates them to try harder, innovate and strive to be better every day. As a business owner it's important to be able to control fear, otherwise it will end up influencing your actions and controlling the business.

Tick all the boxes? You could be the next great Aussie entrepreneur. So go for it.

THE SIDE HUSTLE

As you know, Lib and I decided right from the start that she'd be the homemaker and I'd be the breadwinner while bringing up the kids. It was a very personal decision, but it's one we've never regretted. Four kids, one income and a mortgage meant it was tough for Libby and me to balance the family budget, so for virtually all of our married life I've had a second job. The extra income I earned was invaluable in balancing the family budget.

It's the same for many Australian families. Stretching the budget is difficult at the best of times, but after periods like Christmas it can be downright impossible. For many there aren't any luxuries left to cut out to help pay the bills. The only answer is to earn more income. If your boss won't come to the rescue with a pay rise, it may just be the incentive you need to start that business you've always dreamt of while still earning a regular income. It could not only pay off the credit cards but also be a stepping stone to solving your financial crisis for the whole year.

Easing yourself in

Starting a business part time – also known as creating your own side hustle – is the first and most secure route to turning that dream into a full-time reality. It means entrepreneurs can get a taste of being their own boss without the sink-or-swim risks of diving in with big upfront costs to sustain.

For many, moonlighting with a part-time business is the perfect blend of security and adventure. People approaching retirement feel they can start a retirement venture while under the wing of another job, others start part time to learn the business and build a client base. Whatever the reason, testing the waters before taking the plunge is generally a good idea.

By starting a business part time, you learn whether the concept is viable and whether there are enough customers and a strong enough market to support a full-time business. That time can be used to fine-tune the venture, try new marketing techniques and build resources – all the time safe in the knowledge that a regular pay cheque is coming in whether the new business is doing well or not. You'll feel more secure with cash coming from an alternative source, and more confident in taking the step to full commitment in your own business if you know that the foundations have been established.

The alternative is to follow the riskier strategy of starting a business full time and struggling to meet the overhead costs of premises and equipment when your business income is still volatile. Mistakes under this scenario are also a lot costlier. Experimenting with new strategies when running a business part time is a lot less stressful than when you're depending on the outcome to feed your family and pay bills.

In effect, moonlighting in a part-time venture is providing the business with seed funding to get started. Banks know the success rates of start-from-scratch businesses and are reluctant to lend money, so it makes it a whole lot easier if you can fund that early establishment phase using the wages from a salaried job.

 *Banks are more likely to lend money if your business is up and running and you need the finance simply to expand the operation. The bank manager will be comforted by the fact that all those early mistakes were made with your money rather than theirs.*

Important side-hustle considerations

It's a difficult balancing act. Not only do you want to build a new business, but you don't want to put your existing job, and its pay cheque, at risk either.

Technology certainly works in favour of part-time businesses. The growth in use of smartphones and personal computers can give customers the impression of a fully fledged operation. The secret is to become a time-management expert. Most of the work for the new venture will have to be done after hours and at weekends.

But be aware that family life can suffer and the risk of divorce increases. The joys of life may have to take a back seat to the business. Annual leave and public holidays may have to be used to work in the business. That regular trip to the movies may have to abandoned. Weigh up these sacrifices before making your decision.

It isn't easy, but it can be done if you follow some simple rules:

* **Talk to your family.** It's essential to have the support of your family before starting a part-time venture. Discuss the idea with them and explain the pressures it will place on family life and free time.
* **Give family members tasks.** The best way to involve the family is to make them part of the venture. It may be that you and your partner can also be business partners. If not, give your family tasks that make them feel as though they're contributing.
* **Be a time manager.** Juggling the hours in the day for full-time work and a part-time dream means you have to take advantage of every minute of the day. Use lunch hours and free time to work on the business, but do it in a disciplined way.
* **Forget the luxuries.** Quiet nights in front of the TV or going out to the movies and restaurants may need to be sacrificed initially to spend time on the business. You must be prepared for this.

- **Confine business to one room.** The last thing you want is for a part-time venture to disrupt the whole household. Try to limit your office equipment and storage to just one room, or you'll be in constant turmoil and unable to escape the pressures.
- **Don't let the day job slip.** The performance at your full-time job is critical – it must not deteriorate. Remember, the job is providing that all-important financial security to allow you to try a new business.
- **Don't make business calls during your day job.** The number-one reason: you'll get fired.
- **Tell the boss.** There's no reason why you must tell your employer about the part-time business, but if you have a good relationship it would do no harm. You never know, they may become a customer.
- **Never compete with the boss.** Apart from being unethical, you can be accused of fraud for pinching ideas, systems or even clients. Start a totally different business or in a completely separate niche.
- **Don't use company equipment.** Unless you have permission from your employer and offer to pay for anything used, don't use your employer's photocopier or PCs for your business.
- **Understand the tax implications.** Any extra income earned will be treated as taxable income at your marginal rate. But you'll be able to claim back expenses incurred by earning that income. Get some advice from a good accountant. Be warned: the tax office has been taking a close look at digital platforms like Airbnb and Airtasker and whether income earned by users is declared. Even if something seems to you to be only a hobby, it's important to work out if the ATO thinks that way too! You will probably need to get an ABN and pay quarterly PAYG (pay as you go) tax. If your business turnover is large enough (more than $75,000), you may also need to register for GST and fill out a quarterly BAS (business activity statement). Talk to your accountant (to find one, see page 137).

> **TAKE THIS QUIZ: Hobby or business?**
>
> It's important to understand the differences between a hobby and a business for tax, insurance and legal purposes.
>
> Key questions to consider:
>
> 6. Is the activity being undertaken for commercial reasons? Y / N
> 7. Is your main intention, purpose or prospect to make a profit? Y / N
> 8. Do you regularly and repeatedly undertake your activity? Y / N
> 9. Is your activity planned, organised and carried out in a businesslike manner? Y / N
>
> If you answered yes to most of these questions, you're likely to be running a business, although it depends on your individual circumstances. The ATO website provides further questions, information and examples to help you understand the differences between a hobby and a business.

Some ideas for your side hustle

Start by thinking about your skills, both professional and personal. For example, you maybe be a bookkeeper at work but a great cook or handyperson privately. You may work in retail but love photography. Start thinking about how to turn those skills and passions into a money maker.

With the internet and digital collaborative platforms it has never been easier to find casual work that can adapt to your family and work schedules. And then there's the burgeoning field of collaborative consumption – the idea that, rather than buying things from conventional retailers, consumers swap, rent and share goods. From shared shed spaces to carpooling and renting clothes, setting up a collaborative consumption business can be sustainable for the environment and great for your own finances too. Imagine coming up with the next Airbnb!

And even if you don't have the big idea, you can still make a buck getting involved in these networks. Renting out your home, garden tools or car can bring in cash, and you can also save big bucks if you reciprocate and rent from others too.

Use your existing skills

Most often, part-time businesses are started using the personal expertise or hobby of the owner.

- **Blogging.** If you have a bit of experience or expertise in a particular field and can create engaging, sharable content, blogging and/or vlogging can be a great launching pad to an online career. Whether it's through pay-per-click or affiliate marketing, really good blogs can create a regular income. Write and video your opinions on your speciality and earn money from people and companies that want your endorsement.

  To make money you need followers, and to gain followers you have to be professional but quirky. You might blog about cooking, crafts, travel, make-up or car mechanics. Bear in mind, though, that it requires a lot of patience, hard work and a strong point of difference to stand out – it's no guarantee of riches.

- **Creative writing or graphic design.** List yourself on websites like Freelancer, Airtasker, DesignCrowd or Upwork and bid for jobs from around the world. From writing reports to designing logos, websites and EDMs (electronic direct mail), most of these jobs can be done remotely and after hours.

- **Share that unique talent by teaching others online.** It might be teaching a musical instrument, a language, a craft or even maths. Platforms like MyWebTutor, Udemy, Tutors Field and ClassCoach match you up with students online.

Use your passion and/or creativity

There are so many options here:

- **If you love animals.** Start a dog walking service, look after other people's pets when they're on holidays, or offer a washing and grooming service.
- **If your passion is fitness.** Turn that into personal training business for local groups or individuals before or after work or on weekends.
- **If you're crafty.**
    - Make things – furniture, accessories, toys, etc. – and sell them on Etsy, Gumtree or eBay. Or create patterns and sell them online (e.g. knitting patterns on Ravelry).
    - Set up a stall at the local markets and at school fetes. Specialty shops are sometimes on the lookout for handmade items to sell.
    - Think about starting evening craft classes at your house or the local community hall.
- **DJ service.** With a professional sound system and a decent music collection, this can turn into a $400 a weekend business. The secret is knowing your audience and having the range of music to cater for all tastes, from Australian Crawl for a 60th Birthday party to Justin Bieber for teenagers. You don't have to like the music, as long as they do.

* **Gift baskets and balloons.** You can start with less than $500 and a little imagination. The only problem would be deliveries if you have a nine-to-five job. But this could be overcome by making up the baskets after hours and organising courier delivery at the appointed time.
* **Instagram inspiration.** The photo-sharing app Instagram is free to download and doubles as a great marketing tool for budding business brains appealing to a younger market. From selling your own services to taking photos for other companies and hawking your endorsement of their products, hitting Insta-fame can be pretty lucrative. There are also opportunities for selling sponsored posts, running competitions and opening up dialogue with current and potential customers of an offline business.

  Adelaide personal trainer Kayla Itsines has used Instagram to full effect in promoting her health and training guide. She's accrued 16 million followers across all platforms along the way, and sells out stadiums around the world.

  If you're a social whiz, why not look into starting a small social media management business to serve other brands?

Use your labour

* **Apartment maintenance.** There maybe a lot of apartment blocks in your local community that could use someone handy. Contact the body corporate and offer your services for landscaping, gardening, window cleaning and minor repairs. The work can be done after hours or on weekends.
* **Be a jack- or jill-of-all-trades.** Airtasker enables customers to outsource a myriad of everyday tasks, from moving furniture and assembling IKEA furniture to tutoring kids or doing the shopping. So list your skills and start earning cash.
* **Babysitting.** That old faithful pastime is still a money maker. Even more so with the advent of two-income families. But rather than doing the sitting yourself, how about setting up a babysitter referral network, where you maintain a stable of reliable babysitters?
* **Laundry service.** Today's busy singles and two-income families don't want to spend their valuable leisure time bending over the washing machine. Come to the rescue with a pick-up and delivery service to wash, dry and iron clothes. Make sure you factor in the energy costs as well as your labour.
* **Be a virtual assistant.** VAs are the big thing for small business at the moment, doing everything from admin to answering emails and organising travel – all online. With plenty of companies looking to reduce their overhead costs and outsource administration, becoming a virtual assistant from home is quite straightforward. Email and Skype mean there's not much that can't be done from a laptop at home.

STEP 5: GROW YOUR INCOME

Depending on your background, VAing might involve simple tasks like setting up meetings, making travel arrangements and handling client enquiries. All you need is a bit of tech nous, time on your hands and sharp organisation skills.

* **Be a personal shopper.** Not just in Australia but for overseas clients. Big money has been made by Australians shopping here for Chinese customers – they're called 'daigous'. Not just baby formula, but all sorts of local products the Chinese love. Some people buy the products, then advertise them on a Chinese web platform like JD.com, VIP.com or Alibaba's Tmall.

Use your house

* **Bed and breakfast.** Why not take advantage of the boom in the tourist industry and open your home for visitors? You could restrict the hours to the weekend or when it suits you.
* **Rent out a room, your garden, your shed or even the couch.** Everyone knows of Airbnb, but there are also services like Spacer (renting sheds and garages), CouchSurfing (renting your couch to travellers) and Glamping (renting your lawn for campers to pitch a tent). It's probably worth a check with your local council and your body corporate (if applicable) to make sure you're not breaking any rules, because some are starting to crackdown.

Use your vehicle

Bear in mind that it has to be a vehicle you own, and not a work vehicle!

* **Be a part-time driver.** If your car sits at home more than it's on the road, why not use it to make money by driving for groups like Uber, Taxify or Ola? These platforms send you jobs and you have the flexibility of driving when you want.
* **Deliver takeaway food.** UberEats, Menulog, Deliveroo and Drive Yello allow restaurants to offer home-delivered food, but they need drivers and cyclists to do it. GoFetch is another sort of delivery service for 'things' rather than just food.
* **Rent your car.** Platforms like DriveMyCar and Car Next Door let you rent your car to strangers when you don't need it . . . and they make sure you have insurance cover.
* **Make your van or ute a taxi truck.** Haul garden rubbish, dirt or whitegoods. Put a sign up on the community noticeboard at the local shopping centre or online.

Use everything you have!

Camplify and RentMyCaravan let you rent out your campervan or caravan when you're not using it. LifeHacker and ToolMatesHire will rent your tools out to other people. And big platforms like Gumtree let you list virtually anything for sale or rent. The same goes for your free car spot (Parkhound) – though make sure you check with the body corporate – or pretty much anything you own, such as a lawnmower (Mobilise).

KOCHIE CALCULATOR: FINANCIAL CONSIDERATIONS WITH AIRBNB

ESTABLISHMENT COSTS

Furniture	$1000
Bedding	$900
Linen	$300
Total	**$1200**

DAILY EXPENSES

Cleaning	$20
Laundry	$10
Insurance	$5
Amenities	$2
Total	**$37**

EARNINGS

Studies of Airbnbs in Australia showed the average charge was $150 a night for a house or apartment, while a private room averaged $59 a night and a shared room $39.

The average number of nights booked was 20 a year; only 10% of Airbnbs hosted guests for more than 180 nights a year.

The median annual earnings of Airbnb hosts in Australia was $5200.

TAX OBLIGATIONS

The ATO recommends keeping aside 30–40% of what you earn to meet tax payments.

STEP 5: GROW YOUR INCOME

Some quick money earners

Everyone has a moment of financial desperation: an unexpected big bill, an opportunity too good to resist, a sudden overseas trip – the list is endless. Here are some options when you need money in a hurry:

* **Have a garage sale.** You'll be stunned how much a well-organised garage sale can raise by getting rid of your Aladdin's cave of unused stuff. But make sure it's professionally organised. Market in the area (schools, community noticeboards, street signage, Facebook community groups), organise the items into categories to make it easier to browse, have clear price tags, make sure you have enough change to settle purchases and be an animated salesperson.
* **Sell other assets.** Could you sell some of the equipment you bought when you decided it was a good idea to take up golf, surfing or sea kayaking?
* **Go on a savings sprint.** Create a completely streamlined budget and live frugally for just one month, taking out anything other than necessities. Spend the month exploring free options for entertainment, give up grog, take your lunch to work instead of buying it, then pocket the savings.
* **'Freeze' your gym membership.** Most gyms have a mechanism where you can do this for up to eight weeks a year. Exercise outside or at home instead, and put your gym money straight into savings.

WHAT HAVE WE LEARNT?

I hope you've been inspired by this chapter to:

* build your career and maximise its potential to earn more income
* take the plunge and ask for that pay rise
* develop a side hustle – it could turn into something very big
* implement other ideas to earn extra cash.

There are huge opportunities if you have a plan and put in the hard yards.

 **HOMEWORK**

KEY POINTS

- **Assess your career**
- **Consider things other than salary**
- **Start a side hustle**
- **Earn extra from what you already own**

HOMEWORK

- ☐ Find out your worth and meet with the boss to ask for a pay rise
- ☐ Work out the value of non-cash benefits that would suit your life
- ☐ Think about what personal skills or passions you could turn into a money maker
- ☐ Try renting out your home or a room for holiday-makers, or your car or equipment

NOTES

STEP 6: FUTURE-PROOF YOUR EARNINGS AND ASSETS

Write a will, and while you're thinking long term, turbocharge your super and sort out your insurance.

> **DO THIS NOW**
>
> * If you have a will: get it out and keep it next to you while you read this chapter.
> * If you don't have a will: fill one in online, sign it, and keep it at your fingertips as you read this chapter.

YOUR MOST VALUABLE ASSET IS . . . ?

I know that with all the immediate issues you have to deal with – relationship, kids, health, finances – you don't have time to think about what's happening next week, let alone next month, year, decade or even longer. But I'd be breaking the trust we've built together if I didn't gently remind you of the importance of superannuation, estate planning and proper insurance cover.

On second thoughts, bugger it, I'm not going to be gentle. You *must* read this chapter because it may just be the most important step in your financial life. If you're not looking after your will, superannuation and insurances, you're not financially healthy. Sorry if that's too blunt, but I'm passionate about this.

Your biggest assets are invariably your house, possessions, car – and you. Yes, *you*. You help earn the income, make the decisions, care for the family. Protecting your ability to earn an income is crucial. You need to future-proof your income streams and make sure you have control of them – even from beyond the grave.

Insurance is a waste of money – until you need it. Superannuation feels like fake money in an invisible bank account, but it will feel very real when you retire and it's your main source of income. And your will feels like something someone else needs, not you – but none of us is immortal! Now I don't want to be morbid, but whenever you're reading this chapter and think, 'It's all too hard', or, 'It's so far in the future', just glance over at that will I asked you to have nearby, as a gentle reminder that nothing lasts forever.

This chapter is all about protecting you from yourself – by protecting:

* your income and major assets
* your superannuation
* your right to distribute your wealth the way you want to when you fall off the proverbial twig.

STEP 6: FUTURE-PROOF YOUR EARNINGS AND ASSETS

INSURANCE: PROTECTING WHAT YOU'VE GOT

We all hate paying insurance premiums when things are running smoothly. But when a disaster happens and we need to make a claim, those premiums become worth every dollar. The trick is balance: having the right amount of insurance cover for your circumstances – not too much and not too little.

Home and car insurance

It's ludicrous to pay $600,000 for a house and then not insure it – it's too big a risk. If you can't afford to insure your house or car, you can't afford to own them. If you live in a bushfire- or flood-prone area, make sure you're covered for those.

To save money, contact your insurer and ask if you can reduce your house and car premiums by increasing the excess you have to pay in the event of a claim. You may also be able to cut the amount of car insurance you pay if you restrict your cover to two nominated drivers or if you ban people under 25 from driving your car.

If you're shopping around for a new policy, ask about savings from insuring your house and car with the same company. It's called 'bundling' your policies and insurers love it because it means they get all your business. Your bank is a good place to start, because they often do good deals for existing clients. Some insurers also offer discounts if you buy policies online.

Home and contents insurance

Think about how much all your furniture, electronics, jewellery, books and clothes would cost to replace if they were stolen or lost in a disaster. If you have contents cover, your insurer will pick up the bill.

You may get a discount on your contents insurance if you buy it with your home insurance. If you have an existing policy, make sure your household contents cover is up to date and your most valuable items are covered and noted. Most Australian households are under-insured when it comes to contents, so take some time to value everything.

Ask your insurer if you can save on both home and contents insurance by installing deadlocks, burglar alarms or smoke detectors.

Income protection

A family's primary breadwinner is its most important financial asset. Forget shares and property, if there's no money coming in to put food on the table or a roof over your heads, you're in trouble. A disability or income protection policy will pay up to 75 per cent of your income if you can't work due to sickness, injury or accident.

If you're struggling to fit income protection insurance into your budget, don't sacrifice the quality of the policy. Compromise in other areas and look for the following:

* **Policies with step premiums that increase according to age.** These are less expensive than policies with flat premiums.
* **A longer qualifying period.** Instead of choosing a policy that doesn't pay for the first 30 days, go for one with a 45- or 60-day no-payment period.
* **A shorter benefit period.** Choose a policy that will pay benefits for five years or even two years instead of one that will pay until you're 65. Most disabilities last two years or less.

But remember, you're trading off cover for premium savings, so be aware of how it increases your risk. And make sure you check the definitions in your policy, as they vary between companies.

Life insurance

Generally, the closer you get to retirement age the smaller the life insurance policy you require, because your costs are lower and your superannuation lump sum is higher. If you're younger, have dependent children, large debts and not much superannuation, your family will need a much bigger life insurance payout to get by. The good news is, the younger you are the cheaper the life insurance premium.

Look for a policy that will pay some money early if you're diagnosed with a terminal illness. That money will help cover the financial drain of specialist medical care and give you freedom to spend more time with loved ones. The cover provided by your superannuation fund could also be cheaper, so make sure you check your statement carefully (see page 130).

To work out how much cover you need, start with your total debt – that should be the minimum. Then add an amount your family would need per year to live a comfortable life without you earning an income, factoring in of course your partner's current income.

The premium on coverage, worth $500,000 for a 40-year-old non-smoker, would be about $7.14 a week ($371.28 a year) for a man and

$5.45 ($283.40) for a woman; naturally it depends on the insurer and your individual circumstances (age, occupation, etc.).

Health insurance

Since the year 2000, private health insurance premiums have increased on average by 5.35 per cent a year. That's more than *double* the inflation rate and more than *double* the average wage increases we've been getting. Private health insurance companies boasted that 2017's 3.95 per cent average premium increase was the lowest since 2001, but inflation and wage increases were both less that 2 per cent.

Is it any wonder average Australian families are shaking their heads at how much they're paying for health care, or that they're seriously asking why they need it at all? It's a significant household budget expense and it all boils down to you taking an interest. Never automatically renew any insurance policy, especially private health insurance, without checking you have the right cover for the right price.

When assessing your need for private health cover, find the answer to these three questions.

1. Do I need private health insurance?

With premiums rising so quickly, many people ask us if they should just cancel their cover. I understand why you might think that way, but I just don't recommend it.

First, private health insurance provides you with a broader choice of treatment options than Medicare, both for hospital treatment and common health services such as dental, optical or physio. And if you earn more than $90,000 a year for singles or $180,000 for couples (which rises $1500 for each dependent child after the first) and don't have private health insurance, you'll pay a Medicare levy surcharge of 1–1.5 per cent of your income – on top of the 2 per cent Medicare levy everyone already pays.

There can also be an extra cost for choosing private health insurance later. If you don't have hospital cover by the time you're 30, you'll pay a 2 per cent loading on your private health premium for every year you are aged over 30, to a maximum loading of 70 per cent. So the financial penalties for not having private cover can really mount up if you want to opt in later.

KOCHIE CALCULATOR: MEDICARE VS PRIVATE HEALTH INSURANCE

John and Judy, aged 35, earn a combined family income of $220,000 a year and decide not to have private health insurance.

So John and Judy's Medicare costs come tax time would be the 2% levy + the 1.25% surcharge = 3.25% of their income, or $7150.

But given that they would have to pay the 2% anyway, this brings their *extra* Medicare cost down to 1.25% of $220,000, or $2750.

Their health insurance premium for basic hospital cover, if they took it out now, would be $6864 + 10% (which is the annual 2% cumulative penalty on not having private cover for five years after age 30), or $7550 (less 8.5% rebate or $642).

So, based on this calculation, it's actually cheaper at the moment for them to stay with Medicare. But remember, that annual 2% accumulating penalty on private cover premiums keeps going up (to a maximum 70%) if they decide to take out private cover sometime in the future.

One of John and Judy's non-financial considerations for taking out private cover is the ability to reduce waiting times for some procedures.

2. How do I choose the right cover for me?

It's sometimes possible to save a significant sum simply by choosing a more appropriate policy. To do this, first make a realistic assessment of your health needs and how you expect them to change over the short to medium term.

If you have a few kids playing sport, and you're pretty active as well, it may be worthwhile paying for extras like physio. If you're planning on having a baby in the next couple of years you may well want to be fully covered for pregnancy-related services if you're not happy with the local public hospital (see page 168 for more on this).

HOT TIP *Not sure what cover you need? Speak to your insurer. They'll ask you a series of questions to establish your needs, and talk through your current policy in detail.*

3. How do I cut costs?

Your main options for cutting costs are dropping unused hospital or extra services, increasing the excess you pay, getting a discount by paying your premiums annually or switching to another insurer. As always, there are pros and cons for each.

Cutting cover down to the bare minimum will save money on premiums, but it often means you'll receive fewer benefits for the services you do claim on. And if you suddenly decide that you *do* need cover for a particular treatment – major dental, for example – there'll be a waiting period before you can access a benefit.

Raising your excess is another way to save money but, again, be careful. While the savings can look tempting now, if you were in an accident or needed treatment for an illness, could you afford the higher payment? And is that something you want to be worrying about in that kind of scenario? As a safety net, maybe put the savings from any lower premiums into an 'emergencies' account for any unexpected eventualities. Remember, while saving money on your premiums is great, if it puts you or your family's health or security in jeopardy, it's not worth it.

When it comes down to it, the simplest option is to review your current policy against your needs, then compare the market and see what else is out there. Before switching to another insurer, do a full comparison of your current policy against the new one, and be careful you're not losing important benefits. And remember, if you have a trusted service provider such as a physio or dentist, you might not get the same rebate from them with your new insurer.

Once you're fully informed, you'll be in a strong position to negotiate with your current provider for a better deal or more appropriate cover.

UNDERSTAND YOUR SUPERANNUATION

 *For most Australians superannuation is their second-biggest asset after their home.*

Yep, it's that important. As I mentioned at the beginning of the book, the average Australian citizen is among the richest in the world. Why? Because of the value of our homes and superannuation.

With life expectancy climbing and the government tightening its belt on age pension concessions, it's never been more important to ensure your superannuation is in good shape. And I'm not just talking to those approaching retirement. We all, no matter our age, should bear in mind that the current (relatively generous) age pension and associated government concessions will likely look very different by the time we reach retirement age. This means that having a healthy stash of super will be even more critical to enjoying a comfortable retirement.

Most people would have a rough idea of the value of their home, but do you really know what your superannuation is worth and whether your fund is delivering the best value for you?

Reading and understanding your superannuation statement

It all starts with that annual superannuation statement – it's one of the most important bits of paper you'll receive all year. While finance nerds like me run through their statements every year with a fine-tooth comb, I reckon that's not the case for most people.

If unit values, premiums and preservation status set your brain spinning, here's my jargon-free guide to help you decode your super statement.

1. Your details
Make sure you review your personal details to ensure your fund has up-to-date contact details on file. That way you won't end up 'losing' a super fund down the track.

2. The snapshot
One of the first things you'll see in your statement is a snapshot of your account.

Your account balance from the beginning of the statement period, usually 1 July on the previous year, will be shown on the statement. You'll then see a record of all the contributions and withdrawals you've made over the year, the total value of fees, insurance premiums and taxes you've paid, and your total investment earnings.

It's always worth double-checking your employer contributions to ensure they're paying in the right amount – currently 9.5 per cent of your 'ordinary time earnings' (generally your gross income minus any overtime payments). If not, follow up with your boss or the payroll officer in the finance department.

At the end of the snapshot, simple maths will give you a closing balance (hopefully much higher than where you started). While this is a handy reference, it's light on detail, which means you need to read past this page.

3. Preservation status

Super is classified either as preserved, meaning you can't touch it until retirement, or non-preserved, meaning you can (another classification, restricted non-preserved, may also apply to contributions made before 30 June 1999).

Your super will be preserved until you meet a condition of release, such as reaching your retirement (or preservation) age, or in a small range of other special circumstances, such as hardship.

4. Investments

This section provides important details on how your money is invested.

Remember, most super funds offer a number of different investment options that range from low to high risk, so make sure you're comfortable with where your money is invested. These different investment options also vary significantly in cost. Generally, the fees for more complex, riskier investment options will be higher to justify the higher expected returns.

The mix of investment options will depend on you: your age (how long to go until retirement), how much risk you're happy to accept and what other investments you have outside superannuation. For example, if you're close to retirement, you'll want to be in more conservative investment options, compared to someone locked in for another 30 years, who'll be able to overcome any market crashes.

In a confusing twist, you'll also see a 'unit value' and 'unit price' next to the balance of your investments. That's because super funds pool your money together with other investors before they invest it in the market. This pool of money is divided up into units, which you're allocated based on how much money you've invested.

Superannuation comparison websites such as canstar.com.au, chantwest.com.au and morningstar.com.au look at performance and fee levels between funds and offer a good benchmark.

5. Fees

High fees can have a huge impact on how well your fund performs over the long term, so this is another section that demands close attention. For some reason, most funds will hide this information after a long list of the transactions on your account. It's almost like they have something to hide . . .

All funds will charge some combination of an administration fee and an investment management fee (sometimes called an ICR or MER). You may also be paying a fee to an adviser, as well as a contribution fee, which can still be part of some old-fashioned super funds which haven't modernised their fee structures. At this stage it makes sense to compare what you're paying with other funds in the market (it's a good idea to calculate the total fees you pay as a percentage of your balance).

Remember, when it comes to fees, the lower the better. A general rule of thumb is that your total fees should be around 1–1.5 per cent of the value of the funds invested.

KOCHIE CALCULATOR: SWITCHING TO A LOW-COST SUPER FUND

Judy is 35 years old, earns $110,000 and has $50,000 in a balanced superannuation fund that charges a 2% contribution fee and an annual 1.3% fee. If she continues to earn the same income, she'll retire at age 67 with a balance of $373,295 and have paid $135,101 in fees (based on standard super calculation assumptions).

By switching to a low-cost fund charging an annual $50 plus a 0.3% annual fee, her retirement balance would be boosted to $442,413 and she would only have paid $65,984 in fees.

To do a similar calculation for your own situation, use an online calculator, such as the one on ASIC's MoneySmart site.

---

6. Insurance

Most super funds provide some level of insurance for their members automatically, known as default cover. This is generally any combination of life, disability and income protection insurance. It's important to review this cover on your statement.

Check the total benefits available to you and review the premiums you're paying to make sure they're appropriate for your situation. If you have your own personal insurance cover, check whether you have a better deal and, if so, tell your super fund you don't need theirs.

7. Beneficiary nomination

If you don't make a beneficiary nomination, your super fund will decide how your account is distributed in the event of your death, so ensure you nominate where you'd like it to go.

Will you have enough super to retire on?

It obviously depends on a lot of factors, including your income, but generally speaking, it's very possible that your employer's contribution alone to your superannuation fund will not be enough to fund the lifestyle you want, and you'd be well placed to make your own additional contributions. See more below.

This is one of the most common questions I get when it comes to retirement. My best suggestion is to play with the retirement calculator on your superannuation fund's website. Because the answer will depend on the lifestyle you want in retirement and the returns from your super fund.

But to give you a few general rules of thumb to get you thinking:

* If you want to retire on 75 per cent of your pre-retirement income, you'll need to have contributed roughly 12 per cent of your salary into superannuation each year for your working life. That's an extra 2.5 per cent a year on top of your current compulsory contributions.
* A 'comfortable' annual retirement income is seen as $60,604 for couples/$42,953 for singles a year. To achieve this you'll need to retire with a superannuation balance of $575,000 (couples)/$505,000 (singles) if you're eligible for a government age pension, or $1.23 million/$870,000 if you're not eligible for the age pension.

The ATO's top five super tips

1. Check your super statements

As we've seen, super statements provide important information about your fund, such as the balance, investment performance, fees, insurance and beneficiaries. Remember that super is your money, so take the time to understand it.

2. Make sure your super fund has your tax file number

If it doesn't have a record of your tax file number, the ATO will charge extra tax on employer contributions, won't accept personal contributions and you won't receive the government co-contribution (see below). So it's simple – make sure it has all your details on file.

3. Keep track of your super using myGov

The ATO section of myGov makes it easy to check all your super accounts, find lost super and also transfer super between accounts. Log in and see if there's anything that needs attention.

4. Consider government co-contributions

People earning less than $48,516 may be eligible to receive a government co-contribution when they make a voluntary contribution to super. If you're in this income bracket, it's certainly a healthy boost worth taking advantage of if you can afford to.

5. Put extra money into super

If you're worried about not having enough to retire on, the best thing you can do is be proactive. Salary sacrificing even small amounts of pre-tax income will not only boost your balance but will also reduce your taxable income.

KOCHIE CALCULATOR: SALARY SACRIFICING

Let's stay with Judy, who a couple of pages back switched to a lower-fee fund and will retire at age 67 with $442,413 in superannuation just from her compulsory 9.5% contribution from the boss.

If she salary sacrificed an extra 2% ($2200 a year or $183 a month) of her salary (remember it's pre tax), that retirement balance would be boosted to $509,102.

If she sacrificed 4%, her super would be $575,792; at 6%, $642,482; and at 8%, $709,172.

Four simple steps to supercharge your superannuation

To help you prepare for a smooth ride into the sunset, here are some ways to supercharge your retirement savings.

STEP 6: FUTURE-PROOF YOUR EARNINGS AND ASSETS

1. Choose the right fund

If you haven't been proactive about where your money is invested, a big chunk of it could be sitting in a fund that's not appropriate for your situation or, worse, is actually eating it up through excessive fees or poor investments.

Take the time to compare your fund against the market, focusing on fees and the range of investment options available to meet your long-term objectives. And don't forget to compare the insurance benefits provided by each fund as well. Many super funds automatically offer members some combination of life, disability and income protection cover.

2. Consolidate your accounts

People who've switched jobs regularly or haven't paid too much attention to super can easily end up with multiple super accounts. This means multiple sets of fees eating away at your money.

So once you've settled on a super fund you're happy with, it usually makes sense to consolidate money from any other accounts you may have into the main one.

To get a full view of every super account held in your name and kick off the consolidation process, visit the ATO section of your myGov account.

3. Maximise your contributions

As we've seen, salary sacrificing allows you to benefit from tax concessions, so see if you can afford to forgo some of your salary each month and send it to super.

You can make pre-tax contributions, called concessional contributions, up to the current cap of $25,000 per year, and benefit from paying 15 per cent tax on them rather than your marginal tax rate.

It's also possible to make after-tax contributions, called non-concessional contributions, to bolster your super balance, up to a cap of $100,000. And if, say, you come into a big inheritance, you can make three years of non-concessional contributions ($300,000) in the one year. As tax has already been paid on this money, no further tax will be withheld, and you could also benefit from reduced taxes on earnings in super.

Low- to middle-income earners may be eligible for a government co-contribution when making after-tax contributions, up to a maximum value of $500. And if your spouse is a low-income earner (earning under $37,000 a year), there are tax offsets (up to $540) available if you make a contribution to their super.

The tax implications of super can be confusing, so see point 4 over the page.

PRE-TAX AND AFTER-TAX SUPER CONTRIBUTIONS: WHAT'S THE DIFFERENCE?

These terms are relatively simple to understand.

Pre-tax (i.e. employer plus salary sacrificed) contributions are called *concessional* contributions because they are taxed at 15% when received by your super fund. Because this is generally lower than the marginal tax rate (the cents per dollar you pay), it's referred to as concessional (i.e. you get a concession on your tax).

After-tax contributions (i.e. paid from savings or income that has already been taxed) are called *non-concessional* contributions and can be claimed as a tax deduction. Those contributions will be taxed at 15% by the super fund so have broadly the same tax position as salary sacrifice.

4. Talk to a professional

Super can be a complex and challenging area to get your head around with constantly shifting goalposts and many strategies and considerations I haven't covered here. So if you're keen to supercharge your retirement savings but you're not sure how to go about it, speaking to a financial adviser can be a good way to go.

No matter where you are in life, partnering with a good financial adviser will help you set and achieve your financial goals.

According to the ASX Australian Investor Study 2017, 60% of all Australian investors use some form of professional advice (be it a financial adviser, accountant or lawyer, etc.) to help them with their investment decisions.

HOW DO I FIND A GOOD FINANCIAL ADVISER?

With more than 15,000 advisers operating in Australia, finding someone with the right combination of trustworthiness and expertise can be tough.

Where to start: professional associations like the Association of Financial Advisers (afa.asn.au) or the Financial Planning Association (fpa.com.au) can help you locate member advisers in your area. Banks and super fund advisers are also an option, but keep in mind that their recommendations can be limited to specific products and services from the bank or its partners. Recommendations from friends can be another great way to find proven performers.

Check out Adviser Ratings: it's the TripAdvisor of financial advice (adviserratings.com.au). It lists all advisers with their credentials and specialties, *plus* their clients rate them (which I love). So you get feedback from real customers on just how good they are.

Do your due diligence: you're trusting an adviser with your financial future, so it's crucial to have confidence in their abilities before making any commitments.

The first step is to call and ask for a copy of their Financial Services Guide. This will set out important information about their practice – their Australian Financial Services Licence, who owns the practice and if they're aligned to a larger organisation like a bank (they probably are). Professional qualifications like Certified Financial Planner show a higher level of education and ethical standards in financial planning, so look for a CFP after the adviser's name.

Once you're in a position to meet an adviser in person, treat the initial conversation like a job interview. Don't be afraid to ask questions about their experience and specialties, and if the practice is set up to cater to your specific needs. And don't agree to anything in the room – just get as much information as possible and take it home to do some research (including googling the adviser and their practice).

Remember, trust your gut, and don't feel any obligation to get involved if things don't feel right.

Check their fees: the key thing here is transparency, so make sure the adviser runs through in detail exactly what they'll be charging and how often. Ask if they'll also be receiving commission payments, fixed advice fees, or a combination of both, for the products you sign up for.

And, if you don't understand something, speak up. There are no dumb questions.

MAKE A WILL – AND MAKE IT RIGHT

If you've done your homework, you already have a basic will. Now that we've spent some time thinking big picture with your super, let's revise your will, shall we? It might not seem like your most urgent priority, but doesn't it make good sense to ensure that your assets are distributed according to your wishes when you die?

If you don't do it right, the law will step in and stipulate who is to receive your property. What's more, if this happens, the legal procedures are complicated, expensive and will cause unwanted complications for your beneficiaries. Don't give me that lame excuse, 'I won't be around to care'. No decent person wants to see their family potentially torn apart because they've been too lazy to get a will done.

A will is your most important investment, because it protects your other investments and ensures that your wealth is split exactly the way you want. The other excuse I often hear is, 'I don't have any assets to pass on'. You do: superannuation, equity in your home, life insurance. It's particularly important if you have a family to provide for, you're self-employed or you own a business.

Over the years there have been some very famous wills. For instance, Hollywood actress Joan Crawford used her will to make a statement about two of her children: 'It is my intention to make no provision herein for my son Christopher or my daughter Christina for reasons which are well known to them.'

As it happened, Christina did alright in the end. She later won an out-of-court settlement of $55,000 and also, in her anger, wrote the bestseller *Mommie Dearest*, which was made into a movie starring Faye Dunaway.

Harry Houdini, the great escapologist, made allowance in his will for the fact that he might be able to escape his after-life and come back to earth.

But back to the more mundane wills of people like you and me.

Here are some guidelines and checklist points for making a will:

* One will isn't enough for a lifetime. There'll be changes in your family relationships, in the assets you own and in the value of those assets. Review your will on a regular basis and be prepared to redraft it throughout your life. Don't forget that you can make alterations by adding codicils, but if you add too many, the will can be difficult to work out. Keep codicils for minor changes.
* Remember, marriage cancels a will but divorce doesn't.
* Be alert to capital gains tax on your estate when you sell assets rather than pass them on to beneficiaries. It can be quite complex so get the advice of an accountant to make sure it's done right.
* Nominate more than one executor for your will. I think it's one of the worst jobs you can give someone, so give them some help and

appoint a couple of executors. One can be a family member or friend, but make the other a trustee company, accountant or solicitor. This is also a good idea because, if you only choose one executor, they may die before you.
* Likewise, where the administration of a will is more complex and couldn't be completed easily and quickly, it may be preferable to nominate a trustee company or other professional administrator as executor rather than place a heavy ongoing burden on family or friends. This is a matter you could check with them before making the will.
* Bear in mind that an executor needs to have some knowledge of the law, accounting and financial counselling. They'll have to deal with listing and controlling assets, paying liabilities, a variety of taxes and selling properties, to name just a few tasks.
* Problems occur when a will can't be found. It's important to keep it in a safe place, but make sure you tell the executor and your partner where it is. Solicitors and trustee companies will keep wills in a safe place.
* Don't attach anything to a will. There have been many cases where a mark made by any attaching object, such as a pin or safety clip, has had to be explained by affidavit before courts have granted probate of a will.

Also remember that a number of events can affect a will. It's a living document and your actions can affect it. For instance:

* If you state in your will that you'll leave a property to one of the children but you later sell that property and buy another, remember to amend the will.
* A will must conform to legal requirements to be valid. The only safe way to do this is to have the will checked by a solicitor or trustee company. Outsiders like accountants or trustee company officers will probably be more objective in analysing your personal affairs than you would be. And don't hold anything back from the person helping with the will's preparation, or you could create more problems than benefits for your beneficiaries.
* If your will mentions your children by name, and then another child is born, remember to add the newborn's name to the will or you risk leaving one child out of the money.
* If you make a will and later marry, that marriage will normally revoke the existing will unless the will is made while in 'contemplation' of the marriage.

The secret to making sure your will and estate planning are right is linked to the amount of time and effort you put in. While some people look upon writing their will with great trepidation, it really isn't that hard.

TAKE THIS QUIZ: Is your will easy to administer?

1. Are your assets sufficient to cover all bequests? Y/N
2. Is the cash content of the estate sufficient to meet all the charges on it and still cover cash bequests? Y/N
3. If you answered no to the last question, can the executor administer the will without selling some of the assets? Y/N
4. Is part of the estate in a business where someone without with specific skills or interests would be able to administer it? Y/N

(If you answered no to question 4, consider giving a share of the estate to a capable employee who can keep the firm going for your heirs and stop the business going to the wall in your absence. Another option is to arrange for the favoured employee to buy the business at an agreed fair price. The problem here is that a 'fair' price could quickly become inadequate unless the agreed price is reviewed regularly and changed as appropriate.)

5. Have you made an allowance in the will for the cost of a funeral and other costs associated with dying? Y/N
6. If you've directed the executor to sell some of your assets, will the price be up to the expectations in the will? Y/N

If you answered no to any of these questions, you might want to have another look at your will to see if any of it can be simplified.

Make sure the will is fair to all your heirs. This is often a problem when comparing the value of very liquid assets (such as cash and bank investments) and less liquid ones (such as a house or a business). If you leave all the liquid assets to one family member and all the concrete assets to another, there's a potential for sibling jealousy, particularly if a boom or recession in the property market sends prices up or down. Despite the administrative hassles, it could be better to divide everything up equally.

STEP 6: FUTURE-PROOF YOUR EARNINGS AND ASSETS

WHAT HAVE WE LEARNT?

I know I got a bit terse at the start of this chapter but I hope that, as we worked through it, you realised how important it is to get these key long-term pillars of your financial life sorted early, namely:

* insurance to protect *you* from a financial crisis
* the best superannuation decisions to protect your retirement
* a solid will to protect your decisions about how you want your hard-earned wealth distributed to the next generation.

They are massive issues – but now you know how to get them sorted.

# HOMEWORK

KEY POINTS

- **Protect your earning ability**

- **Maximise your superannuation**

- **Ensure your will reflects your wealth and wishes**

HOMEWORK

- ☐ Take out life, income protection and private health insurance if you decide you need it

- ☐ Do the calculations: how much do you need in retirement, how much extra will you need to contribute to hit that target, is your current superannuation fund good enough?

- ☐ If you haven't made a will already, do it. If you already have one, review it to make sure it's right, and make sure you update it regularly

STEP 7: BUY YOUR OWN HOME – OR DON'T

How do you make the best decision possible one way or the other? If you do buy, what's the best approach? If you don't buy, what are your options?

> **DO THIS NOW**
>
> If you don't own your home:
> * Write down how much you currently pay per month in rent: _____
> * Go to any bank's online mortgage calculator, and use it to get an idea of how much your monthly mortgage repayment would be if you owned the home you live in, based on your particular circumstances (price bracket, deposit, etc. – if you don't know the value of your home, estimate based on other similar properties which have sold or are for sale in your area): _____
> * Calculate the difference between the monthly rent and the monthly mortgage payment: _____
> * Work out the repayments for a smaller property, perhaps in another suburb, that you could bear to live in. Calculate the difference between your current monthly rent and that monthly mortgage payment: _____
>
> Now read on . . .

THE BIGGEST FINANCIAL COMMITMENT YOU MAY EVER/NEVER MAKE

Your own home is a massive financial commitment, and one you might ultimately decide not to make. Home ownership is actually declining across the world:

- **In the UK:** home ownership peaked at 69 per cent in 2001, and is currently at 64 per cent, according to the Office for National Statistics.
- **In the US:** according to figures from the Department of Commerce, home ownership was at 69 per cent in 2006, but is currently at 63 per cent, the lowest rate in 20 years.
- **In Australia, New Zealand, Ireland and Japan:** home ownership statistics show similar trends to the UK and the US.

Now, there are myriad explanations – some of them contradictory – for why this might be happening. But, whatever the reasons, it should at least prompt all of us to ask ourselves: is home ownership for me? It might be, or it might not, but either way it's worth having a considered discussion about it to make sure you're doing what's best for you.

In this step we'll look at:

- whether the Great Australian Dream makes financial sense for you and what the alternatives are
- if you've committed to buying, how you can make it work for you
- how to protect yourself from a potentially devastating property crash
- how to get the best price when selling your home.

IS BUYING A HOME YOUR BEST OPTION?

It's the Great Australian Dream. Owning your own home seems an entrenched rite of passage for every Australian adult. It's engrained in us. Your grandparents told you to buy bricks and mortar. Your parents told you. Your aunts and uncles invariably told you. Even your friends ended up telling you, as they saw it as a badge of adulthood honour.

But this great dream is your biggest financial commitment and, if you get it wrong, can be your biggest financial nightmare and become a millstone around your neck for years. Sure, at the time of writing, some big capital cities (e.g. Sydney, Melbourne and Brisbane) have seen property prices stagnate or fall over the past year, but the property boom of the past decade has been enormous and prices have skyrocketed.

Eeek! The Great Australian Dream is now a bloody expensive one. Look at the facts:

* average capital city house price: $650,000
* average home loan: $480,000.

No wonder home ownership has dropped over recent years to an almost record low of 65 per cent of Australians. For 25–34-year-olds, home-ownership rates have dropped from 58 per cent in 1986 to 45 per cent today.

Should you keep renting?

The drop in home affordability because of rising property prices has been a critical issue for a number of years, particularly among young Australians wanting to buy a first home. Maybe the solution is . . . don't buy, but rent instead. The Kochie Calculator across the page shows you just one example of the buy vs rent conundrum.

Now that you're over the shock, think about it. It does stack up, but it needs discipline to work. I know it's easy for me to say as a homeowner, but maybe we Australians take our love affair with bricks and mortar a little too far. I must admit I've always thought we would have been better off renting rather than owning; we've never made a massive financial gain from any of our houses. We've loved each one of them, but none have generated a huge financial windfall.

In the end the deciding factors to own rather than rent were more personal than financial: being able to decorate the house the way we wanted and the security of not being turfed out at the whim of a landlord.

Having said that I can mount a very plausible case that renting is emerging as the most financially savvy move right now. It can be really hard to find a good rental property and a good landlord who wants a long-term tenant, but if you do, it can be a great way to live.

Rental growth is now near its lowest level on record, with average rents inching up to $450 per week (or $1950 a month) across our combined capital cities. Against an average capital city property price of $650,000, even a novice buyer would suspect a gap between rents and mortgage repayments. And they'd be right.

Running those numbers through a mortgage calculator, assuming a rock-bottom mortgage interest rate of 4.25 per cent, monthly repayments on the average property will be $2361. So mortgage repayments will be $403 *more* per month than renting the same property. That's more than $4800 a year before adding council rates, insurance and the huge costs of buying the property (stamp/transfer duty, legal fees, etc.). You probably found out the same thing when you did the exercise at the beginning of this chapter. If you did a second calculation on a starter property, how do those figures look? If they're closer together, you might have a chance to buy.

Of course, buyers build up equity as they pay off their loan, which can make up for higher monthly costs. In the short term right now, however, most people are better off renting. But, and this is a big *but,* renting is only a better financial decision if you invest (see Step 10) the difference between the cost of renting and what the repayments on a loan to buy it would be. If you blow the money saved from renting instead of investing it, you're better off servicing a mortgage and having an asset to show for it at the end of the day. Think of it as enforced saving.

In 2018, a survey by US blog RENT Café showed that, in 21 of the 30 most populous developed countries in the world, the percentage of people renting rather than owning their home was on the increase, though in 29 of the 30 countries homeowners still formed the majority. Switzerland was the exception: 56.6% of the Swiss population purportedly rents.

If you do have that financial self-control, then renting is probably a better option. I don't just say that because of the greater financial burden of a mortgage compared to renting in the current market, but also because of the less tangible benefits. The opportunity cost of a mortgage is significant. By that I mean that having your money tied up in a mortgage means you don't have it to spend on other opportunities – investing in a business, buying shares, funding further education. Renting also provides greater flexibility to move for work, upsize your digs for a growing family and find a neighbourhood that fits your lifestyle better.

There's also diversification to consider. Often people are so stretched in affording a deposit on a house that they end up with all their savings in one spot – their property. This is a risky investment strategy because if property prices fall in your suburb, so does your wealth. Smart investors reduce this risk by spreading their investments across different assets – shares, bonds and property – to ensure that if one market falls, there's a greater chance that fall will be offset by gains in their other investments.

But, and I'm going to emphasise it to make sure it sinks in, *this approach only works if you have the discipline to invest the money you save from renting into other areas.* The big benefit of buying has always been the way it forces you to save and, if you stick with it, wind up owning an asset.

So really, whether to rent in the short or long term all boils down to your self-discipline.

KOCHIE CALCULATOR: BUYING VERSUS RENTING

Jessica buys a three-bedroom house in East Brisbane that's valued at $816,000, which happens to be the median price. She buys it as an investment, with a 20% deposit ($163,200) and a 30-year interest-only home loan ($652,800) at 5.05% interest. Her loan repayments will be $2749 a month, while the rental return will be around $2340 a month. This would leave Jessica with a negative cash flow of $409 a month.

In other words, Jessica's tenant renting that property from her will be paying $409 a month less than if they owned it themselves. That's a saving of $4908 a year to them for renting the same property rather than owning it.

Renters, of course, don't get the benefit of any capital growth in the value of the property, which is why they need to invest the $409 a month difference into other assets.

EASING THE FINANCIAL PAIN OF BUYING A HOME

Okay, so you've decided to buy. It's the home of your dreams. It's everything you want for this stage of your life. But, like most property purchases, it's going to stretch your finances and you'll need to make significant lifestyle changes. One way around this is to start off buying it as an investment property (see page 152). Here are some other suggestions for making the dollars stack up so you can have the best of all worlds – a great home and a good lifestyle.

Do your homework

Borrowers have never had more access to information, or more power, to find the very best deal. A large number of real estate websites analyse every property, suburb and financing option. It's incredible the amount of information available from sites like realestate.com.au and domain.com.au, so there's no excuse not to have everything covered. It's up to you to put the effort in – and it's worth it because of the size of the financial commitment you're making.

You should also investigate, and ask your real estate agent about, assistance schemes and other incentives, as they can have a significant effect on your bottom line.

WHAT ABOUT FIRST HOME BUYER'S SCHEMES?

All states have a different incentive scheme to help first-home buyers into the market, and they can be pretty attractive. Your mortgage broker and banker will have all the details of the one in operation in your state.

As an example, in New South Wales first-time property buyers can be eligible for a transfer (stamp) duty exemption on homes valued up to $650,000 and vacant land valued up to $350,000, or a concession on homes to $800,000 and land to $450,000. If the property is a new build, there's also a grant of $10,000 towards the purchase.

At least one eligible purchaser needs to live in the property for a continuous period of six months, starting within 12 months of completion of the purchase. Some people work this to good effect by making their purchase an investment property on either side of their six months' residency.

Find the right real estate agent

Always remember that real estate agents are working for the vendor. The higher the price they can get out of you, the more they receive in commission from the seller. Having said that, finding a good real estate agent who understands your needs can pay large dividends in the long run. Reach out to friends for recommendations, and interview several options to determine their level of experience and expertise in the suburbs you're interested in.

Buyer's agents are becoming popular. They act for you, doing all the legwork of finding the perfect home and dealing with real estate agents – for a fee, of course. It can be a flat fee or a percentage of the value of the property.

You can also hire a buyer's agent simply to bid at an auction on your behalf.

Lock in a low interest rate

If the Reserve Bank so much as nudging interest rates upwards would send your perfectly balanced (and stretched) budget into disarray, then a long-term fixed-rate home loan could be the answer. A fixed-rate loan starts off at a slightly higher interest rate, but it means your repayments won't change no matter what official and variable rates do, so it's easy to work out exactly how much you'll have to sacrifice to repay your loan with no nasty surprises. If you're happy to do it tough for a few years (we have a famous cheap dinner recipe for such periods) for the pay-off of having a place to call your own, this could be a good option. Many loans have a fixed rate for a set period that then automatically reverts to the variable rate.

At the time of writing, interest rates are at historically low levels and are very unlikely to fall any further. All the experts agree that the next rate move will be up. The only debate is about when.

> **KOCHIE CALCULATOR: FIXED- VERSUS VARIABLE-RATE HOME LOANS**
>
> Let's stick with Jessica's three-bedroom house in East Brisbane, valued at $816,000 and financed with a loan of $652,800.
>
> At an average variable home loan rate of 4.5% the monthly repayments would be $3307.
>
> Financed with a five-year fixed-rate loan of 4.85%, monthly repayments would be $3445.
>
> But if home loan interest rates rose 0.5% the variable loan monthly repayments would rise to $3504 (i.e. an extra $197 per month), while the fixed-rate loan repayments would stay at $3445.
>
> If home loan rates rose 1% then the variable loan monthly repayments would rise to $3706 – that's $399 a month more than the original 4.5% rate – while the five-year fixed-rate would stay the same.
>
> **Be aware:** the reverse happens if interest rates fall. The variable home loan repayments will drop but the five-year fixed-rate loan repayments will stay the same.

Control your mortgage

For tips on minimising your interest rate and repayments – and otherwise getting ahead of your mortgage – see page 56.

Find a guarantor

A friendly guarantor can help you buy a place you couldn't otherwise afford. Banks look much more favourably on loan applications with a guarantor attached, as having two parties responsible for repayments dramatically reduces the risk that the debt will go bad.

Apart from increasing the amount you can borrow (although I'd generally recommend sticking to a house you can afford or waiting until you can afford the place you want), having a guarantor also usually means it's possible to access a lower interest rate and avoid paying lenders' mortgage insurance.

Be appreciative of the help the guarantor is providing you. As I've said in Step 3, I generally advise people not to go guarantor for anyone because of the risk. They're trusting that borrower to meet the commitments of their loan so the financier won't call on them to make it up. In this instance, *you* are the risk to the guarantor. They're trusting you to fulfil your commitments. So it's up to you to do the right thing.

Get serious about your career

A mortgage is the largest financial commitment most people ever make, and if it goes wrong you could find yourself in severe trouble, financially and personally. So if you're borrowing big, it's time to get serious about how you're going pay for it. Step 5 contains loads of tips for getting the most out of your career (page 94), including how to ask for a pay rise (page 105), and other ways to earn extra money (page 111).

NOTES

INVESTING IN PROPERTY INSTEAD – OR AS WELL

One much more affordable way to enter the market is to buy an investment property, renting it out until you can afford to live there yourself. While you rent somewhere much cheaper, your tenants will be chipping in a big chunk of the mortgage repayments, meaning you only have to pay the difference. You should also be eligible for negative gearing tax deductions on expenses associated with owning the property, and potentially depreciation benefits too.

A few years and a couple of career promotions later, your financial situation will hopefully have improved to the point where you can move in yourself. You'll lose the investment property tax advantages, but any future capital gains (from selling the property) will be tax-free because it's your home.

Talk to an accountant to ensure you make the transition from investment property to principal place of residence correctly.

It's amazing what a few relatively cheap renovations can do for your property's rental return and even the value of the home. Simple things like fixing leaky taps, replacing broken blinds, a bit of painting and a thorough clean can also work wonders.

The pitfalls of investing in property

It does worry me sometimes the number of people who double down by adding an investment property to their own home. In fact, 15 per cent of Australians have at least one investment property. A few years of stellar returns have convinced many people that investing in property is a sure thing. Just buy a reasonable place in a suburb close to a capital city, then sit back and watch capital gains accumulate – or so the thinking goes.

But before you start counting your money, be warned that being a property investor may not be all it's cracked up to be. Not only is it foolish to believe that prices will always appreciate, but any number of issues can spring up and turn your goldmine into a sinkhole.

Here are five things to be aware of before jumping into the property market with both feet.

1. Expect the unexpected (expenses)
Before investing in property, the vast majority of people sit down and do their sums to work out whether they can actually afford it. But even with the best planning, it's difficult to account for all of the unexpected expenses that inevitably pop up. From fixing a leaky roof to replacing the oven,

or landlord insurance premiums increasing, the unexpected costs of owning an investment property can quickly add up.

2. Top tenants are hard to find

The dream for property investors is to find a long-term tenant willing to pay a reasonable rent and treat the property well while living there. Of course, sometimes the dream is just that – a dream.

In some cases, you may have to accept a lower rent to fill the property, and tenants might move out unexpectedly or cause damage, intentional or otherwise. In slower markets, your property may sit empty for an extended period of time, meaning that you'll need to stump up for the entire mortgage yourself.

3. Your time is money

Your time is money. Managing a property and dealing with the potential issues I've just outlined is a very time-consuming process. Of course, it's possible to pay other people to help you with many of these tasks, but that's another expense that will eat into your overall return.

4. Property isn't a sure bet

Those headlines about the property boom up and down the eastern seaboard of Australia have quickly changed to concerns about falling prices.

No one is ever happy. When property values are rising the headlines scream about locking first home buyers out, housing affordability and record sale prices. When property values fall the headlines scream about losses being made, governments being hit by falling stamp/transfer duty revenue and low auction clearance rates.

Always remember that property can go down in value as well as up.

5. Negative gearing means making a loss

Despite the generous tax breaks you receive, negative gearing isn't a guarantee of making money. In fact, negatively gearing a property means you're making an ongoing cash loss on the investment. So the money you earn from a tenant doesn't cover the cash going out on loan repayments, maintenance costs and insurances. To make sense as an investment strategy, a loss-making property must appreciate in value over time to cover these losses. But as we've just seen, there's no guarantee that this will happen.

How to make it work

Of course, it's not all doom and gloom: property can be a great long-term investment when approached sensibly. It's secure, tangible, offers great tax benefits and can produce a fairly stable income. But before investing in any property it's important to:

- do your research
- consider the risks I've outlined above
- factor a rate rise of at least 2 per cent into your repayment calculations to make sure you don't borrow more than you can afford
- look for a reasonably priced property in an area you believe has strong potential for capital growth and is attractive to tenants.

And if you do plan on managing it all yourself, be prepared for some hard work. Good luck!

KOCHIE CALCULATOR: THE COSTS OF AN INVESTMENT PROPERTY

Let's stay with Jessica and her $816,000 three-bedroom house in East Brisbane. As we saw on page 147, her loan repayments would be $2749 a month while the rental return would be $2340 a month, leaving her with a negative cash flow of $409 a month.

But there are other costs apart from the loan, adjusted here to monthly figures for ease of comparison:

Council rates	$204
Insurance	$129
Repairs and maintenance	$102
Water rates	$136
Property management (5.5% of rent)	$129
Total:	**$700**

That's a lot of money going out. But remember, there is tax and capital growth to add into the calculations.

As I explained back a page, the 'negative' in the term 'negative gearing' means there is an income outflow: the difference between the rent and loan repayments plus the expenses.

That negative income (the costs) of the investment property can be offset against Jessica's other income – wages, income from investments, etc. – to lower her overall tax rate. Plus there is the prospect of the property rising in value and providing a capital growth return. Finally, the tax concessions on owning an investment property are quite extensive. All of which is why it's best to seek professional advice from an accountant or tax agent to make sure it's done right.

RIDING OUT A PROPERTY CRASH

After a decade of booming property prices, values have been stagnating and even going down. Like any investment, property goes in cycles. The critical issue is that no one wants a property crash, and no one wants to be forced into selling during a downturn and copping a big loss on the value of their house. A soft landing in the housing boom, rather than a crash, is the desired outcome. But that's the tricky bit – making sure it's a controlled slowdown.

While some experts, particularly from overseas, are suggesting that we're now at the start of a well-overdue crash that will bring our housing bubble back to reality, other local experts say these dire predictions just don't take into account the nuances of the Sydney and Melbourne markets, which are driven by strong immigration, a shortage of supply and intense investor interest.

Both sides have strong arguments, so it's virtually impossible to know what the future will hold. There are certainly no current signs of a market crash but, as investment history shows us, things can change quickly.

Watch for the early warning signs of a crash

There are three key early warning signs of a property crash:

1. **Falling auction clearance rate.** This measures the number of properties sold at auction. During boom times the auction clearance rate can be up around 80 per cent. During crashes it can be under 50 per cent. So beware when the clearance rate starts tumbling.
2. **Falling off-the-plan settlement rate.** During boom times buyers will pay a deposit on an apartment that hasn't been built yet, in the hope that by the time the block is finished (in a couple of years) the value of the unit will have gone up. But if values have fallen in that time the buyer might opt not to settle the remaining 90 per cent on completion and cut their losses. This is a sign that the market is poor.
3. **Rising vacancy rate.** If rental vacancies start to rise significantly it means rental income could dry up, forcing many investors to sell because they need the income to meet the loan repayments. Or they'll need to lower rents to attract tenants.

Ask yourself if you want to live there for the next five years

If you're an existing homeowner, this is the most important question to ask yourself right now. Because a downturn in values really only affects you if you want to sell during the downturn.

If you're happy to stay in your existing home for the next five years, and it's perfect for you, you don't have a care in world. You can happily ride through a downturn with no problems at all and wait until the next recovery is well under way.

But if your plan is to trade up or down in the next five years, it might be worth taking advantage of the peak of the cycle and selling, then maybe renting until the cycle gets to the bottom and you can buy back in. You must be disciplined in this situation, though, and not spend the next five years chewing through the money. And you have to make sure your money is well invested, so that you can afford to buy in again.

Libby and I went through this process about a year ago when signs of peaking in the property cycle started to appear. We decided that the house we have now is a keeper and we'd stay, but the discussion was revealing!

Ask yourself if you have too much debt against your home

When property prices start to fall, financiers become nervous. They look at what's called your 'loan-to-valuation ratio' and, if it falls below a certain level, they start to examine your borrowing closely.

Start looking at it yourself before they do. As valuations fall, the level of equity in your home falls as well. If the valuation falls below the level of your debt, you have what's called 'negative equity'. Banks hate that.

If interest rates start to rise then that adds an extra layer of nervousness. Rising loan repayments on falling equity can be dangerous. So start getting your home loan down and increasing your equity while the going is good. See Steps 3 and 5 for tips on how.

KOCHIE CALCULATOR: NEGATIVE EQUITY

Jessica's $816,000 three-bedroom house in East Brisbane was acquired and financed with a 20% deposit and a home loan of $652,800.

But let's say that over a period of time the property market falls 21% in value, so that the property is now worth only $644,640. This is $171,360 less than when she bought it and $8160 less than the value of the home loan. That's negative equity. Jessica has no equity in the property because the value of the loan is larger.

Most banks will get nervous if the owner's equity drops below 10% – in Jessica's case, that trigger would be when her property value falls 10% to $734,400 – and may ask for her to put in more cash to boost her equity back to the level at which the loan was approved.

Never, ever buy before you sell

In this market at this stage of the property cycle, it's just crazy to buy before you sell, and doing so will add to the pressure to sell your existing property quickly and cheaply. While at the time of writing auction clearance rates in Sydney and Melbourne are weakening, there's also an increase in negotiated offers after a reserve isn't reached at auction.

We have a mate who came across a 'bargain' in the next street selling for the same price it was four years ago. He snapped it up and now finds that his existing house isn't getting the interest or the offers he was expecting. But he's committed to the bank and he's starting to sweat. He needs a buyer.

You don't need that pressure, so sell before you buy.

Set a realistic price

If you do want to sell, make sure you price correctly because, in a falling market, time can be your enemy. The longer a mispriced property stays on the market, the harder it gets to sell. If you set the price too high you may discourage potential buyers, but you don't want to sell it for too little. Take the time to research what similar homes, on similar blocks, have been selling for in your area.

Set the maximum price you expect your house to go for. In these times buyers know they're in a better bargaining position and will be keen to negotiate. We know it can be a bitter pill to swallow but, if you're trading in the same market, you'll probably pick up a bargain on the other side.

SELLING YOUR HOUSE: HOW TO ADD VALUE

If you're already a homeowner, your house is your biggest and most important asset: the family home is your investment castle. For years you've had a rough idea of what the house is worth, but the real crunch comes when it's time to sell. What someone else is prepared to pay can either make you big money or lead to disappointment and financial loss.

But you can make a difference. The way you prepare a home for sale could add thousands of dollars to the eventual sale price and may not cost a lot of money to achieve. In fact, spending as little as $500 could add more than $10,000 to the value. You rarely see a used car for sale that hasn't been washed and polished, the chrome buffed, the tyres blackened, the upholstery cleaned and the windows sparkling. Detailing is a vital part of selling cars, and so it should be with your house.

Although improvements, and even wholesale renovations, will add to the value of a home, don't think that because there's a great new timber deck out the back, a new kitchen or a swimming pool, that these are the only features that will make a difference. Inside and out, there's a long list of things you can do to spruce up your home and entice buyers to dig deeper in their bidding. A good agent will help you go through those aspects of the property that need attention.

First impressions

The three most important aspects of attracting buyer interest in a house are kerbside appeal, kerbside appeal and kerbside appeal. In other words, the key for a house is the front yard, and for an apartment it's the common areas. Home buyers are looking for prospects that are neat, clean and tidy, so start at the front fence and work backwards:

* **Tidy up.** The lawns are the first thing to look at, making sure they are mown and the edges trimmed. If your apartment block common areas aren't as neat and tidy as they should be, talk to the owners' corporation about what can be done. Remind them that if you get a good price, they will too! Don't have the hose sprawled across the lawn – roll it up or put it away. Make sure there's a clearly visible letterbox with a number on it and give the house a name.
* **Paint the front wall.** If you have a house, a quick lick of paint on the front wall can make a huge difference. Don't change the colour or it will need three coats.
* **Spruce up the garden.** Have flowers in bloom and a well-manicured garden – but don't over-manicure or you'll give the impression that the garden needs a lot of maintenance. In summer, cheap seedlings in cool colours will give you instant welcoming colour. In winter, buy a

winter-flowering shrub like an azalea, magnolia, camellia or grevillea (check the label for flowering times) for $30–50.

If the front garden is really out of control, find a local horticultural apprentice through a technical college or the local nursery who can prune it all back for you.

Inside the home

Now that prospective buyers have stopped and walked through the front gate, the house itself will come under scrutiny.

* **Put in the effort where it matters.** Surveys of home buyers show that the kitchen, family room, bathroom and master bedroom are the most important rooms in a house (yes, in a one-bedroom apartment this is the whole flat!).
* **Create an atmosphere of light and space.** Make sure light passes through every window. Pull back the curtains and, if you can, trim any trees or bushes overhanging the windows. If the curtains or blinds are drab and dark, it might pay to replace them with brighter ones.
* **Freshen up with some paint.** A fresh coat of paint on the walls or the doors can freshen things up immensely, but stick to neutral colours to please the widest possible range of buyers. You're trying to sell the house, not show off your decorating skills.
* **Look at the floors.** Floors are also an area deserving special attention. The kitchen, bathroom and laundry floors often show up wear and tear more than anywhere else. If they're really bad, a new, cheap vinyl floor covering may look better than the old.
* **Do those little repairs you've been putting off.** You might have got used to them, but they'll stand out to someone else. Cracks in the plaster usually aren't structural faults but are unsightly and make the house look rundown. A bit of filler and paint will make a huge difference. The same goes for watermarks on the walls or ceiling.
* **Do the housework.** Tidy up the house – make sure the beds are made, the dishes washed and the toys, papers, shoes and socks put away. But don't be too tidy. A home has to look like just that – homely and lived in.
* **Don't rely on bells and whistles.** Many people like to have a fire going, soft music playing and the smell of brewing coffee wafting through the house. This creates atmosphere but really doesn't fool anybody if the rest of the house isn't up to scratch.
* **Give yourself enough time.** Although all these things are relatively minor details and cheap to fix, they will take some time. You could get a shock if you set aside one weekend thinking it will be enough. It may well take weeks to get through it all, so be prepared.

WHAT HAVE WE LEARNT?

Your house is your biggest investment, and one you might choose not to make. If you do decide to take the plunge, where you buy your home, how you finance it, what you do to protect it and when you sell it can have an enormous impact on your wealth.

In this chapter I've demonstrated how to:

* make a decision on whether to buy
* make buying as painless as possible
* invest in property wisely
* protect yourself in a volatile housing market
* sell your house for the best price.

Once you own a home, it's the asset you must pay the most attention to, so never treat it lightly.

 **HOMEWORK**

KEY POINTS

- Work out if you're better off renting

- Understand where we are in the property cycle

- Insulate yourself from a property crash

- If selling, work on maximising the price

HOMEWORK

☐ Do the numbers on what it would cost to buy a property and the cost of renting the same place

☐ Examine the region where you intend on buying, determine where it is on the property cycle, and work out how long you intend being there

☐ Look out for the signs of a downturn and react wisely

☐ Improve the appeal from the street, understand the tricks to attract buyers, and set a realistic price

NOTES

STEP 8: MAKE MONEY A FAMILY AFFAIR

Yes, you can afford a baby: draw up a baby budget. Doing this will show you how you can afford it and put your mind at ease, while also showing you strategies for minimising costs and teaching your kids about money.

> **DO THIS NOW**
>
> If you're considering having kids, sit down with your partner, if you have one, or a friend if not, and make a list including all the things you'd be excited about and all the things you're worried or scared about. Talk through each one and see whether you can decide that at least some of those fears are irrational. Keep this discussion in mind as you read on.

KIDS: GREAT JOY BUT BIG COST

'We just can't afford to have a baby.' It's an increasingly common lament, and sadly one we often hear from friends of our adult children, and our nieces and nephews – young Aussie couples excluded from the joys of raising a family purely because of cost. But it doesn't have to be that way. Careful planning and a rearrangement of priorities can achieve the best of both worlds.

In this chapter I'll talk through:

* making the decision to have children
* the financial realities of having children
* how to plan for and manage the financial impact
* the cost of child care
* possible government assistance
* some great tips on cutting the cost of raising kids
* teaching your kids about money – good financial habits are some of the most important life skills a parent can pass on to a child.

 *According to the ABS, 309,142 births were registered in Australia in 2017: that's nearly 900 per day.*

TRUST YOURSELF TO GET IT RIGHT

Having kids should be such a personal, rather than purely financial, decision that there's no rule-of-thumb 'right' time to have them. You just know when you're ready.

Libby and I were over the moon when we found out she was pregnant with Samantha. We were so excited, and busting to tell anyone who listened. Our first stop was Libby's parents, who were thrilled, but her very sensible father chipped in with 'Can you afford it?' Our euphoric bubble deflated a little. In fact, we hadn't really thought about it that much, knowing we'd just cope somehow.

When we told our friends, the reaction ranged from excitement to horror that we were throwing away our life: 'You won't be able to travel', 'There goes the partying', 'You'll have no freedom'.

It was amazing – that euphoria evaporated and we started to have serious doubts. But we quickly decided it was our life, our decision, and we were going to do what would make us happy.

You decide when to have them

It really annoys me when people say you 'must' have kids when you're young, or you 'must' have them when you're older and more experienced. It's just as stupid as when people say one parent must always be home-based for the 'good of the kids'. Everyone is different and is coping with different family situations. I know some terrific parents who are just wonderful with their children even though both parents work. Equally, I know terrible parents where one has stayed at home full time to look after the children.

Libby and I were pretty old-fashioned and decided to have children while we were young. I suppose your own individual family environment plays a big part, because we both come from reasonably large, happy families and our own parents started young. Our theory was that we'd grow with our kids, that we'd be active and young enough to relate as they grew. We also made the decision that Libby would be a stay-at-home mum, to look after our most important assets, while I'd try to work just as hard as her to earn enough to make ends meet.

In retrospect, I think, for us, that theory worked pretty well. We did without a lot of material things early on, which was fine because we have four wonderful children (and now five grandchildren) and we're a very close family. They haven't hindered us from achieving our goals. We've travelled extensively and worked overseas, all with the kids in tow, and haven't missed a beat. In fact, I reckon the kids travelled better than we did. We'd worry about them starting a new school and within a week they'd be off to birthday parties with their new friends while we struggled to settle in.

But it hasn't been perfect, it never is. Building a reasonably demanding career in the media and a family business plus having a young family needed maturity, and I think, at times, I didn't have it. Having said that, I reckon a lot of parents take their role far too seriously. Before you howl me down and call me irresponsible, I think parents rely too much on other people's advice rather than simply thinking it through for themselves and using their own common sense.

You decide how to raise them

So many of us buy books on parenting, each of which seems to take a totally different stance on what you should be doing. We slavishly concentrate on what they say rather than whether it's right for us.

It just shouldn't be that hard. Parenting is all about being sensible. You instinctively know what's right and what's wrong. Libby and I were lucky to have such good role models in our own parents. But even so, most people know what to do and it's simply a matter of having the confidence to make a judgement, and not having your instincts coloured by counterarguments from the kids or gratuitous advice from relatives or friends.

When it comes to children, everyone has an opinion on how they should be reared and they're not afraid to express it: on everything from the age your children should be toilet-trained through to what you feed them for dinner and their bedtimes. It all works to sow doubt in your own mind, but stick to your guns.

You decide whether to work or not

Parents who both work are particularly susceptible to taking this criticism on board because they generally have an unfounded sense of guilt about not being the perfect parent and not spending enough time with their children. Stay-at-home parents can be particularly scathing in their criticism of working parents out of some sort of self-righteousness. And vice versa.

It's all absolute hogwash.

Whenever we discuss working versus non-working parents on *Sunrise*, it's open warfare on the soapbox. We're absolutely inundated with emails vehemently defending their individual decision and attacking the opposite view. Why? My theory is that both sides secretly desire the opposite – a case of the grass is always greener on the other side of the fence.

Working parents feel like they're missing out on those special unexpected joys that come from being with their children and that stay-at-home parents are more likely to experience. Meanwhile, stay-at-home parents really would like the challenge, adult company, career experiences and income that come from working.

This happened to Libby and me. One of the most common causes of our arguments was my jealousy about not being around for many of those special moments, moments that aren't scripted and only happen once. Libby would be excited to tell me about that first step or cute comment, and I'd be pretty subdued, hating the fact that I wasn't there too.

There were times when I would gladly have swapped with Libby, and I'd often talk about her going back to work and me staying home. Then I'd get over it and realise I was best placed to be the breadwinner and I really didn't have it so bad.

NOTES

PREPARING FOR CHILDREN FINANCIALLY

I admit I can get a bit carried away with the non-financial reasons for having children, mainly because I reckon people stress way too much about the financial challenges. Having said that, the financial challenges can be daunting if you don't have a clear plan of attack.

The financial pain

This is the bit that spooks everyone. The sticker shock can be a bit scary.

* Out-of-pocket expenses for a private health pregnancy and birth are $2500–8500. Luckily, our public system is perfectly good.
* Research has calculated that raising two children to adulthood will cost $500,000 to $1 million, depending on your income, housing, education choices and lifestyle.

Yes, it's a lot of money, but the average full-time gross salary is $75,000 (per person) and the wealth of Australians has never been higher. With a sensible plan and a disciplined approach, you'll find you can manage having a family more easily than you might think.

DO I NEED PREGNANCY INSURANCE?

For many people, the thought of having a baby is what tips them towards private health insurance. You can access world-class pregnancy and birthing care through our public system without paying a cent, but if you want to choose your doctors and have a private room, you may opt for going private.

Bear in mind that if you want to use private health insurance for pregnancy and childbirth, you need to have already been in the fund for 12 months.

The financial plan

Before you and your partner even tackle the question, get a rough sense of your costs, which may not fall neatly in line with the national average. You don't need to calculate the next 18 years of expenses, but you can at least focus on the short term.

US website BabyCenter has a great calculator to help you get started; you can modify it for your own particular situation. Yes, it's American, but it's a nifty calculator. It factors in prices for one-time buys like a 'crib' (cot) as well as recurring expenses like 'diapers' (nappies). Use it to get a rough budget estimate, bearing in mind that some of the prices might be higher here. ASIC's MoneySmart website also has a budget calculator with a good section on the cost of children.

Remember that while a baby adds some major new expenses, it also cuts spending in other areas, like entertainment and dining out. And make sure you look into the maternity and paternity benefits your employer offers, because that will affect the extent to which your income could take a hit.

If you have friends who've recently started a family, ask them about the costs they've incurred, and especially any surprises.

> **DO THIS NOW**
>
> * **Jump online and start looking at baby cost calculators like BabyCenter or the 'children' section of ASIC's MoneySmart budget planner to get an idea of how your baby financial plan might look, factoring in the costs for the first two years.**
> * **Pull out your monthly budget from Step 2 but now modify it for those first two years, taking into account what you've learnt from these tools.**
>
> Remember to include costs for maternity clothes, baby clothes and nappies, bottles and formula, bedding (cot, mattress, sheets and blankets), and equipment (change table, car seat, pram).

The talk

You'll have had plenty of talk about having a baby, but have you had a financial talk? Tell your partner about any financial anxieties you have about starting a family and ask whether they share them, or have different ones. For many couples, the greatest anxiety comes from not understanding their current habits, so go through your budget, track your spending and understand what you could give up.

Here are some of the questions that might come up:

* **Is there anything we want to do before we have a child?** Do you have any other goals – travelling, going back to study, paying off the credit card debt – you want to achieve before you have a child? You may be

able to reduce some shared anxiety by talking in terms of 'when' rather than 'if'. Separately, each list three to five things you want to accomplish that could derail your family plans. Then talk through them together to prioritise each item and create a time line. But if having a child is a big priority, don't set up so many roadblocks that you delay it indefinitely.

* **How do you feel about me taking time off work?** Spouses start out with different assumptions, so share your own childhood experience, outline what you'd ideally like to do – and then ask the same of your partner. If one parent stays at home, at least for a while, you'll need to discuss both the short-term hit to your income and any longer-term effect on career goals. If both parents continue to work, you need to think about both the logistics and cost of child care, which can be huge even after the government rebate (see pages 173 and 174).
* **Do we really need all this baby stuff?** Once you start looking at costly baby supplies, it's easy to feel overwhelmed. Plenty of retailers are happy to make you think you need the latest of everything to be successful parents, but you don't. Focus only on the necessary – a car seat, clothes, feeding equipment and cot. Your baby will never know that your stroller or cot is second hand or that you bought all the toys on Gumtree.

NOTES

STEP 8: MAKE MONEY A FAMILY AFFAIR

FINANCIAL STEPS ONCE YOU DECIDE TO HAVE CHILDREN

Your life changes in a big way when you have kids. Sleep becomes a luxury, changing nappies a daily ritual, and seeing your children grow each day gives you more joy than you ever imagined possible. Alongside these daily ups and downs come some pretty big financial changes too, as you make sacrifices for your little ones and start planning for their future as well as yours.

We had the same cheap cane lounge and dining furniture for all of our kids' first steps, which was just part of starting a family of six on a cadet journalist's wage.

Immediate financial steps to take

With the benefit of hindsight, here are some smart financial steps to take when you have kids.

1. Budget for a more modest lifestyle

You probably don't need to be told that your free and easy weekends are over for the time being, but that doesn't mean you have to be homebound all the time. Spend some time redoing your budget to factor in your new family's everyday expenses and household essentials, which will involve adjustments to your old lifestyle. This can be a bit of a shock, but will ensure you recognise any shortfalls before they become big problems. Then see how you can arrange social and family engagements around a tighter budget, because mental health is just as important as financial health in a young family.

2. Review your insurances

While it may seem like an unnecessary expense, insurance protects you and your loved ones financially if something goes wrong. So go through your insurance policies, including any held within your super, and ensure there's adequate life, income protection, trauma, health and home insurance to protect your family if a crisis happens (see Step 6 for more).

3. Get your estate in order

Updating your will is crucial when you become a parent – or making one, if you haven't done so yet. One of the major decisions is naming a guardian for your child if both parents die together. See Step 6 for more on making a will.

4. Build an emergency fund

Setting up your will and adequate insurances is essential to guard against big, unexpected events. But it's also important to be prepared for the smaller financial headaches that life throws up. So, as I've suggested before (see page 99), start setting aside some money in an 'Emergency Fund'.

Ideally this will be six months' worth of living expenses to cover your bases, but whatever you have now, the most important thing is to start adding to it today.

5. Set up a savings program

Setting your kids up with the opportunities you want for them starts the day they're born. And there's no bigger help in funding their future education, sporting or social pursuits than compound interest. You'll need to shop around for a savings account with a good interest rate – visit canstar.com.au and/or finder.com.au as a first step to compare accounts. Look for the best combination of base interest rate and bonus interest rate. The bonus rate may only kick in with a certain amount deposited each month, so choose an account with a monthly deposit you can actually make.

Try to factor into your family budget a regular small deposit that goes into an account for your kids to access later. Then, rather than baby toys or bibs for their early birthdays, you can ask your family to chip in to their little future fund instead.

KOCHIE CALCULATOR: HOW SAVINGS FOR YOUR CHILDREN CAN GROW

* **Strategy 1.** Michael deposits $500 in an online savings account for his son and adds $20 a week. Assume an average interest rate of 2%. It will grow to $31,492 by the time his son turns 18.
* **Strategy 2.** Ashley deposits $500 into a balanced managed fund (see Step 10) for her daughter that invests across property, shares and fixed interest, and adds $100 a month. Assuming an average return of 6.5%, the balance when Ashley's daughter reaches 18 would be $42,440.

If you were to save in a bank account, it would have to be opened in the child's name, or in a trust, and the interest would be taxed depending on who uses the funds.

A good alternative, once you have the confidence and know-how (see Step 10), is putting some money into big reliable blue-chip shares or investing in a managed fund. There are also a number of education and 'scholarship' funds available that can be a good option. My only problem with some of these is their flexibility – if your child doesn't go to university you get back only what you've invested, without any return.

Also be aware that the ATO has tightened legislation to stop parents using their children as a tax dodge, so there could be big implications if you think you won't be up for an unexpected tax bill. This is where it's important to get some financial advice (see page 137 for information about finding a good adviser) and determine whether it's better for you to open an investment in your child's name or a trust account.

The costs of caring for children

Once the children arrive, there are ongoing costs you need to budget for.

Child care

Blimey, the cost of child care can be horrendous. My daughters tell me how much they pay for my young grandkids and I'm constantly stunned. They hate it when I do the calculations and show it's way more than private school fees. Given the lack of options, I suppose it should be. And after all, aren't these precious little things the greatest treasures we have? But having said that, if it costs more for your child to be cared for than you make at work, you need to weigh the pros and cons to decide if it's really worth it. Depending on your field, you may need to keep working to keep your career on track, so you'll need to factor in the potential impact that not going back to work for at least five years could have on your career and future earnings.

CHILD CARE SUBSIDIES: HOW MUCH ARE THEY?

The best way to work out your own entitlement for childcare subsidies is to visit humanservices.gov.au and put your details into the 'Payment and Service Finder'.

But as a general rule of thumb:

* Families on a combined income of less than $65,000 will have 85% of their childcare bills paid.
* This will taper down to 50% once you are earning $170,710.
* There will be no subsidies for those earning more than $350,000.

Grandparents and relatives and friends have long been the traditional carers, and as the professional carers charge more and more, we're seeing a swing back to that kind of arrangement. Some people don't have the luxury of besotted grandparents who'll drop everything to mind the grandchildren, though, and it's possible that both grandparents are still working professionals themselves or out of town. The only answer for some young parents, if they both still want to work, is professional child care.

With childcare costs so high, the great dilemma for most parents is whether it's worth going back to work. There are so many financial and, importantly, non-financial considerations to take into account. There are no right or wrong answers; your answer is right for you but may not be for others.

KOCHIE CALCULATOR: HOME CARE VERSUS CHILD CARE

Yao earns $72,000 a year and Amelia earns $72,000 for a combined income of $144,000, or $114,106 after tax. They have a baby daughter, Chen. Until Chen is two years old, Yao stays home to look after Chen. This means that:

* their income from employment is $72,000 ($57,053 after tax)
* they are also eligible to receive 18 weeks' government paid parental leave at the minimum wage, totalling $12,948
* their outgoing costs for child care are $0
* with only Amelia working, their net income in the first year of Chen's life, after tax and leave, is $70,001. (In the second year, with the government paid parental leave used up, the net income reverts to the $57,053.)

Note too that Yao and Amelia may also be eligible for Family Tax Benefits, which I've outlined briefly just a couple of pages on.

When Chen is two, Yao returns to work full time and Chen goes into day care five days per week. This means that:

* Yao and Amelia's income from employment is back up to $144,000, or $114,106 after tax
* their childcare costs are $10,080 a year or $210 per week, because:
   * the average cost of child care per week is $525 (or $105 per day), but minus
   * the rebate/subsidy of 60% or $315 per week.
* with both parents working full time, their net income after tax, childcare costs and rebates is $104,026.

This will give you some idea of the pure financial equation. Obviously there are other considerations (time with your family, career trajectory, etc.) to take into account.

If you are taking the childcare route, you'll need to find the right place for you and your child. My daughters treated the search for the best childcare facility like a military exercise. This is what was important for them:

- accreditation with the National Childcare Accreditation Council
- flexibility of hours
- a centre that takes less than 30 children
- enough carers: regulations stipulate that there should be one carer for every five children under three and one for every 15 children over three
- a centre that charges only for the hours the child is there
- an open-door policy, where parents can come and go as they wish
- excursions included
- good qualifications for all staff
- education activities and programs specifically suited to the children's age
- being able to visit the centre and check out its amenities
- nutritionally balanced meals, with allergies and special needs catered for
- toilet training and other life skills
- acceptable punishment regimes and attitudes to particular behaviours
- nappies and linen included.

I reckon that's a pretty comprehensive starting point, and they were happy with their decisions.

You may qualify for the federal government's Child Care Subsidy to help pay. Eligibility is quite complicated and is dependent on a range of factors, from income and assets to where you live and whether you're facing special circumstances. There is also a Child Care Rebate on tax, which isn't means tested.

HOW CAN THE GOVERNMENT HELP?

There's a range of federal government benefits to support Australian families. In fact, about half of all Australian families receive more in government assistance than they pay in tax. As many as 85% of single-parent families contribute no tax, once welfare benefits are deducted. For couples with children, with at least one adult more likely to be working, one in four families pay no tax.

Visit humanservices.gov.au for a full list of entitlements, but a quick snapshot of the major ones are:

* **Family Tax Benefit (FTB).** The broadest level of government support for Australian families comes in the form of Family Tax Benefits Part A and Part B. FTB Part A is a payment per child. The amount paid depends on how many children you have, whether you share care, your family income, and the number of days you were eligible for FTB Part A. FTB Part B depends on the age of your youngest child and the primary earner earning less than $100,000 a year.
* **Child Care Subsidy (CCS).** This is based on combined family income and hours worked or otherwise 'active' (e.g. study, volunteering, job searching). The subsidy is on a sliding scale, from a maximum 85% subsidy for those with a family income up to $66,958, and capped at a family income of $351,248.
* **Newborn payments.** You're possibly eligible for a Newborn Upfront Payment and Newborn Supplement when you start caring for a baby or child that's recently come into your care.
* **Parental Leave Pay.** Eligible working parents will receive payments for a maximum of 18 weeks to help with the cost of a newborn baby or adopted child. The payments are made to the primary carer of the child.
* **Dad and Partner Pay.** Up to two weeks' pay may be available if you're caring for a newborn baby or adopted child and you're on unpaid leave or not working.

As noted on page 173, you can use the government's 'Payment and Service Finder' at humanservices.gov.au to check what your payments might be.

Our top seven ways to cut the costs of having kids

See Step 4 for how to be a savvy spender and stretch your budget. This will help cut the cost of having children, but here are a couple of specific tips that Libby and I swear by.

1. Establish a babysitting club

Get together with friends who have children around the same age, and babysit each other's kids on a regular basis so that couples can have a date night without it costing the earth.

2. Buy their textbooks second hand

Target families with children in the school year above your own and buy the books they no longer need.

 *Always choose bright kids because they leave useful highlighting and great notes in the margins*

3. Have regular clothes swapping parties

Get together with a group of families with similar-aged children every three to six months, take all the clothes your kids have grown out of and trade them. Add a few glasses of wine and it can be a fun social event for parents as well.

4. Pack school lunches

This is so much cheaper than forking out for the school canteen every day. We used to mix up the usual sandwich routine by cooking a bit more soup or spaghetti bolognese at dinner and whacking it in a thermos for the next day's school lunch.

5. Choose sports wisely

For weekend sport we'd register each of the kids in a summer sport (Little Athletics, Nippers, cricket) and a winter sport (netball, hockey and soccer). Sport registrations are expensive so we'd weigh up bang for buck. Little Athletics and cricket, for example, take a few hours extra each week so the kids are occupied a lot longer. Having said that, if your kids are especially talented at sports, you might need to spend a bit more to develop those talents.

6. Be tactical in school holidays

Most museums, local councils and libraries have cheap/free fun activities over holiday periods, which our kids loved – and now our grandkids do too. Keep an eye out for programs in the local newspaper or online directories.

7. Get them reading

One of our best achievements was passing on a love of reading to all our kids. The hours of entertainment consumed with their noses in a good book was incredible – and cheap, especially if you use the local library.

> **DO THIS NOW**
>
> **You should have already got out the household budget and worked out the financial impact of having a child, factoring in the maternity and paternity leave benefits provided by your employer, the amount of time you actually want off and the reduction in your income.**
>
> **Here's the important part: start living your life to that budget *now*. It will help ease you into a changed lifestyle and also help you to build up a financial safety buffer before getting pregnant.**

Once your kids reach school age you'll be in the swing of managing your finances with kids. Caring for them financially is a major achievement, but as they grow there comes a new challenge – making sure they understand the value of money and learn to use it wisely.

Since opening in 1965, the Royal Australian Mint has produced over 15 billion coins. And despite our digital cashless society, there is a record number of bank notes in circulation: the most common note is the $50. You can use fun facts like these to get your kids interested in money.

TEACHING YOUR KIDS ABOUT MONEY

Parents usually think saving is the first lesson, but it only forms part of the big picture of managing money. Learning how to spend properly is as important as learning how to save.

For the record, according to the most recent research, 80 per cent of parents give their children pocket money. For 4–10-year-olds the average amount is $7–8 a week, for 10–12-year-olds $12, and for 13–15-year-olds $15. So the stats show we're generally using the $1 per year of age method.

What to teach your kids, and when

Use this guide to inspire and coax your child into saving for the things they want.

Starting off

Start teaching as early as possible. Managing money is a skill just like riding a bike or making the beds, so don't make it any more scary or boring than these activities. Start by explaining what saving is: putting something away in a safe place to be used when needed at another time. Inevitably your child will ask why. Explain that there are three basic reasons to save money:

1. to buy something we want at a later date when we have enough money
2. for protection against an emergency
3. for retirement.

Younger children aren't interested in the last two but they're worth mentioning to teenagers and young adults. The key is to emphasise the first reason and use examples that will appeal to them.

The next time you take your child shopping, let them choose an item and set them a goal of buying it for themselves. Even though they may find the amount of money daunting, explain that by saving regularly they'll soon have the required amount. In this way parents can help their children learn to save by emphasising the fun of saving money. Children, like adults, feel a great sense of satisfaction from being able to use their own money to buy something. It makes them feel 'grown up' and independent.

Don't rely on your child's self-discipline at this early stage, as it often fails. It's important to give them your support. Take an interest and make it a cooperative effort. Maybe match their saving with a contribution from you as they pass certain milestones. Reaching halfway to a savings goal, for example, should be a reason to celebrate and to remind your child that they're on the home stretch.

The key to saving is regularity, so set aside a particular time each week when you and your child deposit money into a piggy bank or a bank account. Buy them a fun moneybox and make sure it stays in a safe and accessible part of the house. Putting a picture of their savings goal on the moneybox can also be an incentive.

Saving is simply collecting money – there should be no mystique attached to it. So encouraging stamp, marbles or sports-card collecting can be a fun way to teach the notion of saving. Use the example of the swap market, where the number of cards in a collection have a value (just like money), but the value changes with respect to their individual worth (like money). Our grandchildren were avid AFL card collectors. It's healthy as long as it's kept under control and doesn't become a financial burden.

Ages two to four

It's never too early to teach children about money. For the very young it's a case of explaining what money is and making them familiar with the various shapes and sizes of coins.

To a very small child, 'big' means more, and the fact that the 50 cent coin is three times larger than the $2 coin can be confusing. Explain the different types of coins and use the tails pictures to make them interesting. For example, show them the kangaroos on the $1 coin and the Aboriginal man on the $2, and build stories around them.

At this early age, playing games can be an effective way to teach an understanding of what money is and what it looks like. Draw circles around the coins on a piece of paper and ask the child to match the coins to their circles. It's similar to fitting shapes into holes and a good way to teach them that small coins don't equal low value. Call out a particular coin and see if your child can select the right one to fit into the right circle.

Be careful to ensure that money itself isn't treated like a game. Children at this age should be told that money is important and they need to look after it. They must also learn not to help themselves to anyone else's money.

Ages five to six

At this age children are old enough to save regularly with a piggy bank. Get them to feel how much heavier it gets the more they save. We've found that a clear Perspex piggy bank can provide a child at this age with a sense of achievement because they can literally see the coins build up.

It's also an appropriate age to start teaching children about the value of notes. It often seems strange to children that something as flimsy as our polymer notes can be worth so much, especially when it looks like the paper they use for drawing and colouring. Use the stories behind the famous people on the notes to make them interesting. This is also the time to start giving them pocket money for a small household job performed regularly (more about pocket money in a tick).

The small change game is a good one for this age group. The aim of the game is to collect all the small change in the house and make as many different piles of coins as possible to equal one dollar. Its purpose is to make children realise how coins relate to each other. When all the money is stacked up, emphasise how much a dollar is worth.

Check out the program called Money Savvy Kids (moneysavvykids.com.au), which sells a clear, coloured Perspex piggy bank divided into four chambers – save, spend, donate and invest. It also comes with money management lessons and material for children and their parents to go through together.

Ages seven to 12

Now's the time to open a savings account for your child. Choose a children's account that has newsletters and a special club for the kids to join. We've been very impressed with the creativity and information offered by a number of accounts. Make sure you spend time with your child reading through the information and helping them understand what's available to them.

Now that they know why saving is important, you'll need to explain why we put our money into a bank, credit union or other financial institution. Here's a suggested explanation: *A bank is a safe place to keep your money. The bank uses that money to lend to other people, and as a reward for you keeping that money at the bank it pays you interest.*

It's probably worth a trip to your local bank branch so they can physically see what a bank is and then relate the branch and staff back to your online banking. The visit will put everything in context.

When the initial interest of opening an account has worn off, get the children to save for something they want, so that they can see how savings accounts work. Suggest they start with something not too expensive so they can save quickly. We encouraged our kids to save for a book or a special piece of clothing or basketball cap. We discouraged them from saving for a toy and restricted that to Christmas or birthday requests. They get excited when they see their balance grow, and learn quickly how money adds up with regular saving.

Saving for a goal is the only way to make kids understand why they're saving.

> **KOCHIE CALCULATOR: SAVING FOR THAT SPECIAL SOMETHING**
>
> Twelve-year-old Ava is saving for a surfboard. Her saving plan might look something like this:
>
> * Ava's savings goal: surfboard, $150
> * Ava's savings plan: $12/week
> * weekly contributions from Ava's parents: $13/week
> * time for Ava to reach her goal: six weeks.

After our kids had made a large withdrawal for spending money on a family holiday, we found they were keener than ever to keep on saving for the next goal. We also found with longer-term savings goals that when the money has been saved, the item or piece of clothing has often gone out of fashion. It's an important lesson in consumerism: time can determine how much you really want something and whether or not it's a short-term fad.

In our family one of the most valuable activities in learning the money game is 'playing shops'. Every child loves being the shopkeeper or dressing up and being the customer. One of our longest-lasting toys is a cash register with fake money. It has offered hours of amusement for all our four children and now our grandchildren. This role-playing is an important part of a child's early financial development. In the seven to 12 age group, children start to shop for themselves, so they need to know how to pay and receive change.

Set up a shop counter at home with the aim of showing children how to work out what change they should receive from shopkeepers. Take $5 play money and ask the child to purchase one of the items in the shop (which you'll have set up with clearly marked labels). Pose as the cashier and encourage the child to check the change they receive after payment. Take turns being the shopper so the child sees both sides of money at work.

This is a good time to introduce the idea of personal morals. What do you do if you get too much or too little change at a shop? Teach them to check their change and give back money if they've been overpaid. And explain that otherwise the cashier may have to make up the difference personally. Conversely, encourage your children to speak up if they've been short-changed. Children are usually shy about confronting adults, but they need to realise that adults make mistakes too.

Ages 13 and up

This is a critical age. Teenagers are targeted by marketers because they are seen to have a large amount of disposable income. Just consider how much television, press, radio and online advertising is aimed at your teenager.

It's also the time when they're at their most vulnerable to peer pressure and to the lure of expensive fads to stay 'cool'. It's difficult for them to comprehend the cost of brand-name clothing and sneakers, and the pressure to have them is immense. This is also the time when entertainment expenses start to grow as kids begin to form relationships. Movies, music and mobile phones are a fact of life for teenagers. All these things place more pressure on funds, and the savings goals become bigger. Inevitably, parents are courted for more pocket money, and part-time jobs loom.

At this point, consider giving your teenager management of their own money, particularly when they begin a part-time job. But remain active in their financial affairs so you can keep an eye on them.

Have a look at the teen money program called Spriggy (spriggy.com.au), which is a pre-paid card and app that helps parents and their children manage money together. The Spriggy app allows parents to allocate money to their child's pre-paid Visa account to encourage saving, and to follow their transactions.

The big spender

The biggest problem is the spendthrift child who, despite much help and encouragement from you in developing a savings habit, still doesn't manage to save. One school of thought says you should let an excessive spender be pulled into line by their peer group. They'll soon find out that showing off with big spending habits doesn't impress friends, while they also run the risk of being left short on other occasions.

At the same time, carefully use parental criticism and guidance to turn them around. Find out why they're always dipping into their savings. If it's simply excitement at the idea of having money, you must nip it in the bud quickly before it becomes a habit. For younger children, consider putting the piggy bank in a drawer or cupboard so it's not such a temptation.

For older kids, you'll have to become the banker. This means they have to come to you to justify their purchases. If you think the purchase is unwise, impose a week's moratorium on the account to avoid impulse buying. If, after this time, they still wish to buy, you have the right of refusal. Remember, you're the parent as well as the banker, and children need to learn that some things aren't worth buying just because they can afford them. But to help them understand your decisions, it's important to explain them. Let them know that spending now could mean they're left short in the future.

If these methods don't work, try a pay-deduction scheme. This is a bit like superannuation, where you put away a percentage of their pocket money. Show them the sum as it grows to encourage their saving habit. The other way to provide an incentive to save is to match the child's savings dollar for dollar over a set time frame for a mutually agreed goal.

We all have moments of uncontrolled spending or saving, much like eating too much chocolate cake when we're on a diet. Balance is the key to a good savings routine, so don't overreact if your child makes a mistake.

The scrooge

The flip side of the spendthrift is the scrooge. As strange as this may seem, compulsive savers can also be bad news. They can become effective at avoiding payments or manipulating relatives and friends into giving them money. They may eventually make terrible partners in marriage or business. This scrooge mentality is usually born out of a fear of spending and of being taught that spending is bad.

Explain to your child that a proper balance between saving and spending is the key to wise money management. Encourage responsible spending and show them the rewards of spending hard-earned money.

Pocket money rules

When it comes to pocket money, it's not the amount but the way it's used that teaches kids money lessons they'll keep forever. We followed these five rules for own children and now we implement them for our grandchildren. Thankfully their parents are strong advocates as well.

1. They must have a savings plan

For each of our kids, getting their pocket money was contingent on them having a plan about what they were going to do with it. Our rules were always the same: save 50 per cent and spend 40 per cent (don't worry about our maths, we'll get to what we did with the last 10 per cent soon).

The key is to agree with them on what to save for – saving for nothing is boring. We'd sit down with our kids and dream together – a new doll, skateboard, footy, etc. Then we'd work out how long it would take to fulfil their dream, and we'd draw a little bar chart so they could see the tally rising each time they received their pocket money. We'd turn it into a game so it was fun, and make a big deal of it when they reached their goal.

2. Teach them how to budget

One of the best ways to teach kids how to budget is to give them their pocket money monthly rather than weekly. This is particularly important with teenagers. That's on average four and a bit weeks when your kids will have to prioritise, improvise, scrimp and save to get by. It's a great introduction to the pressures they'll face once they swap the family home for the real world.

Just remember not to cave in if they blow their budget early. A week without visiting the school canteen won't hurt them, and they won't forget the experience. But paying them extra can undo many of the lessons you're trying to teach.

3. Show them the value of money

Yes, that means they need to work to be eligible for their pocket money.

This doesn't mean 'family' jobs like cleaning up their room or a mess they've made (which should be done for free for the privilege of being in a family), but jobs that save you time, like folding washing or unpacking the dishwasher. If they don't finish their jobs, they don't get paid until they do. Just like in real life. It's a great lesson, reinforcing that you never get something for nothing.

4. Encourage a part-time job as soon as they're old enough

Jobs at home are great for younger kids, but there's no substitute for the real thing. So, at 14 years and nine months, all four of our kids were shipped off to the local McDonald's. Whether you like the food or not doesn't really matter – it's a wonderful training ground for customer service and the process of work.

Not only was it a structured and positive introduction to working, it was a great way for them to meet other kids in the local area. And it was always interesting to see their reaction to their first pay slip – when they worked out how much of their hard-earned cash went to tax!

5. Give them a sense of community

I said we'd get back to what we did with the final 10 per cent of our kids' pocket money – it was used to give them a sense of community. One-tenth of their pocket money was saved up and donated to a charity of their choosing, and we matched it dollar for dollar. We know they felt empowered by this simple gesture, and learnt important lessons about social responsibility.

As you can see, pocket money is the perfect way to start your kids' financial education and develop their life skills. Use it wisely, set ground rules and join them on their financial journey. You'll see the rewards once they're all grown up.

How open should you be with your children about money?

Parenting today is a lot more open than previous generations, even when it comes to family finances. Far from the 'children should be seen but not heard' position of previous generations, modern families are lot more democratic and transparent in family decision-making. But there's a fine line between including children in so-called 'adult decisions' to help with their personal growth, and protecting them so they can enjoy a stress-free childhood.

Household finances are a classic example. In the past, any discussion about money was seen as grubby – it was one of those taboo topics never to be discussed. It produced young adults who were ill prepared in simple matters of money management, which often led to some very expensive mistakes.

My fear is that the pendulum may now have swung to the other extreme, where children are too exposed to the strains of the family finances, with the risk that they'll grow up to fear money and making mistakes.

Naturally, how much you reveal to children depends on their age.

What to share

- **Setting goals.** It's great to let children see that you're saving for something that will benefit the whole family. It could be a car, a family holiday or even new clothes. It's a good life lesson that you can't have everything you want without a bit of planning and a little sacrifice. When the goal is achieved and you're sitting under a palm tree sipping a cocktail, remind the kids what it took to get there and point out that it was worth the planning.
- **Paying bills.** We took each of our kids through our weekly supermarket bill and compared it with their pocket money. This teaches kids that day-to-day items, which they often take for granted, do have a value and shouldn't be wasted. We'd also break down the cost of an item into how many hours they'd have to work at McDonald's to pay for it. The message really sank in.
- **Making good consumer choices.** Drag them along to the supermarket and show them that consumers have choices. That big brand names are often more expensive but not necessarily better. That supermarket prices are usually more expensive at eye level on a shelf than above or below. Treat it like a field trip and pass on your canny shopping tips.
- **Everyday financial experiences.** Go through your online banking with the children and explain what a financial institution does, the concept of earning interest and the differences between the range of accounts. Do the same with the credit card statement. Explain that bit of plastic isn't a

money tree and that it has to be paid back, often with interest. Whip out the debit card and explain the difference.
* **Making charitable donations.** We'd always talk about our donations (not the amount but the organisations) because we wanted to show our kids that everyone has a community responsibility to help others.

What not to share

* **How much you earn.** All a child wants to know is that you're able to look after them. They want that security. Dollar amounts are often confusing, and they have no concept of what that figure needs to cover. So it's better to avoid exact amounts and just say, 'Enough to make sure we're okay.'
* **Your level of debt.** A 25-year home loan is an incredibly scary prospect for a child of any age – to them 12 months is a long way off. Instead, explain the concept of debt and how we can use it properly to acquire things that will hopefully appreciate in value. Avoid talking numbers or whingeing about how long it will take to pay off.
* **Investments.** Wait until children are studying commerce at high school or they show an interest in investing. When you do start talking about it, there's no need to use dollar amounts, but do explain what investments you have and how they operate. For example, tell them why you bought your shares and what moves prices. Relate the shares to companies and brands that children use every day, like retailers or clothing/technology brands.
* **Wills and life insurance.** Most children hate the thought of losing their mum or dad and being alone, so don't even attempt to explain wills or life insurance until they're old enough to cope emotionally with the prospect. Simply say that whoever your executor is will look after them.

WHAT HAVE WE LEARNT?

Having children can change your life in so many wonderful ways, but they can add financial strains and challenges as well. With a bit of planning, understanding the government assistance available and adopting some savvy money strategies, any financial pressures of raising children can be significantly reduced. Easing the money burden also lets you get on with loving your kids and enjoying all those memorable experiences they provide.

While you do so, remember that setting up your children with the right financial habits is a powerful responsibility of every parent.

HOMEWORK

KEY POINTS

- Plan early for a newborn

- Understand the financial assistance available

- Teach your kids good money habits

HOMEWORK

- ☐ Complete a 'baby budget' as soon as you consider having a child, then live to that budget in preparation

- ☐ Visit the government's Human Services website and work out the family assistance and Child Care Subsidy you could be entitled to

- ☐ Work out a pocket money program with your children, take them on a money field trip, and share some of your financial experiences with them

NOTES

STEP 9: SORT OUT YOUR TAX

And do it now – for peace of mind, to make sure you're paying what you should and not MORE than you should, and to avoid attracting ATO attention.

> **DO THIS NOW**
>
> If you're behind in lodging your tax return (or worse, tax returns!), I want you to make an appointment right now with your accountant to do so. (If you don't have an accountant, you'll see my suggestions for how to find one when you turn the page.) Make it in two weeks' time, which will give you the chance to read this chapter and get yourself organised before your appointment: the deadline of the booked appointment will motivate you to do it!

TAX – IGNORE IT AND IT *WON'T* GO AWAY

Look, I know tax isn't the sexiest subject to get your teeth into, *but* consider this. So far we've gone into the major elements of your financial life to make sure you're getting value for money and that you're not wasting money – so you can spend it on fulfilling your dreams. Properly managing your taxes is another important step towards achieving those dreams.

Every working Australian pays tax on their earnings. But what if you're paying too much tax? What if the government is keeping more of your money than necessary because you haven't focused on your tax and haven't claimed the deductions you're entitled to? It could be hundreds, even thousands, of dollars of your money that the government is keeping. They're just waiting for you to ask for it.

 *Would you believe Australians pay at least 125 different taxes each year? Of these, 99 are levied by the federal government (including 67 agricultural levies), 25 by the states and one (council rates) by local government.*

This chapter is about nudging and nagging you to get your tax right and get your money – and showing you how. I'll take you through:

* my Ten Tax Commandments
* how to prepare properly so tax time isn't a chore
* where to find expert help
* which expenses to claim
* what annoys the ATO and how to stay on its good side.

PAYING THE RIGHT AMOUNT OF TAX

Legendary media mogul Kerry Packer once famously castigated a bunch of politicians while being grilled in a Senate Committee hearing on tax, saying, 'I pay the right amount of tax and not a dollar more than I have to.' I reckon that's not a bad philosophy, but it also means you have to take an interest in your tax, to ensure you pay the right amount.

It can be incredibly complicated, so it can really be worth your while engaging a professional to help you through it. Yes, you have to pay them, but a good accountant should be able to save you more than they invoice you (plus, at least some of their costs may be tax deductible come tax-time!).

WHAT IS A TAX AGENT AND HOW DO I FIND ONE?

Registered tax agents are the people who are qualified to help and advise you with your tax. Many accountants and financial advisers are tax agents as well.

Just as you build a relationship with a GP to look after your health, building a relationship with an accountant or adviser to look after your financial health is a good idea. Like a GP gets to know you medically, an accountant/adviser gets to know your financial history and so can make informed, helpful ongoing suggestions on how to streamline your tax. They can take the hassle out of tax time – and their fees are tax deductible.

Start by asking friends and relatives whether they can recommend someone they use (and take a look at page 137, too).

My Ten Tax Commandments

The end of the financial year comes around at the same time every 12 months but always seems to catch us unprepared. Tax time is always a mad scramble.

Naturally, as good citizens, we don't mind paying the right amount of tax but, like Kerry Packer, we're damned if we're going to pay a dollar more than we have to. So here are my Ten Tax Commandments for you to think about now, to make sure you make the most of tax time:

1. Split your income.
2. Have your tax adjusted.
3. Consider your self-education expenses.

4. Keep accurate records.
5. Delay income until next financial year.
6. Top up your superannuation.
7. Offset capital gains with losses.
8. Pre-pay eligible expenses.
9. Work out any negative gearing implications.
10. Claim work-related expenses.

Let's go through each of these in more detail. But before we do, here's the most basic step of all:

Lodge your tax return

Ground zero. Before we get into the Ten Commandments, the most obvious thing to do, and the one so many people forget, is *lodge your tax return*. Just get it done.

1. Split your income

It's easy. Put all the bank accounts and other income-producing investments in the name of the spouse in the lower income tax bracket. With joint accounts, the ATO splits the interest earned and applies the tax rate of each individual partner to their share. The partner on the highest tax bracket pays the most tax on their interest. So do something about it.

Income splitting is very attractive in a family where there's one primary income earner, because the other spouse can earn as much as $18,000–20,000 tax-free.

KOCHIE CALCULATOR: INCOME SPLITTING

Sam and Toby have a combined family income of $180,000 a year. Sam earns $110,000 and Toby $70,000.

Sam takes home $79,603 (after paying $28,197 tax and $2200 Medicare Levy) and is in the 37 cents per dollar bracket.

Toby takes home $54,303 (after paying tax of $14,297 and $1400 Medicare Levy) and is on a 32.5 cents per dollar tax rate.

Say they earn $2000 a year from income-producing investments. If those investments were in Toby's name they'd pay an extra $650 tax ($2000 × 0.325) on that income. If the investments were in Sam's name they'd pay an extra $740 ($2000 × 0.37) in tax.

By making that simple income-splitting decision and putting the investments in Toby's name, they save $90 in tax a year.

2. Have your tax adjusted

If you think your withholding rate (the tax subtracted from each income payment) is too high, apply to have it adjusted. With interest rates at record lows, many people, particularly retirees, have seen their interest income cut sharply. You can approach the ATO for a withholding variation.

Talk to your accountant and tax agent, or check out the forms on the ATO website (ato.gov.au/Forms/PAYG-withholding-e-variation).

3. Consider your self-education expenses

As a rule of thumb, you can claim a tax deduction for the costs of self-education, provided it's related to your income-earning activities.

Generally, self-education is associated with courses run by schools, colleges and universities that end in you gaining an award such as a degree or a diploma. But you don't necessarily have to come out with a bit of paper to claim a deduction. You've just got to be able to prove the skills or knowledge you gained are sufficiently related to your job, the idea being that the completion of the course will help you get a pay rise or promotion – and pay more tax.

4. Keep accurate records

The reason you receive your tax refund so quickly is that the ATO takes your word for it. Hard as it may seem, the ATO accepts your calculations at face value and pays the refund.

All your calculations are matched against the average of other similar taxpayers like you, but the ATO computers will put a red flag next to you if you're out of step with the others. Then they come knocking.

So make sure your records are right to avoid any penalties.

5. Delay income until next financial year

Every dollar of income we earn, whether it be from wages or investments, is taxed at our marginal rate. But if you expect to earn less income next financial year, and therefore be in a lower tax bracket, delay receiving things like investment income, dividends, money from a side hustle or contract work until July. That way it will be part of the next year's tax return when you're in a lower tax bracket. For example, delay billing customers until July, or invest in term deposits which mature in July.

6. Top up your superannuation

Pre-tax superannuation contributions (up to $25,000 a year) reduce your taxable income, so less money goes to the ATO and more goes into your super savings. After-tax contributions (up to $100,000 a year) are also worthwhile because returns are taxed at a maximum of 15 per cent, not your regular income tax rate (see page 136).

7. Offset capital gains with losses

Profits on selling investments like shares, property or managed funds purchased after 1985, will be charged capital gains tax (CGT). While calculating CGT can be complex, it's roughly based on your marginal tax rate being applied to 50 per cent of the gain. But any losses made on these types of investments can be offset against your returns from other investments.

So if you've made a big profit on one investment, sell some of your disasters. You can then offset your losses from on the 'dogs' against the profits from the winners and cut your CGT bill.

KOCHIE CALCULATOR: CUTTING YOUR CAPITAL GAINS TAX

As a very simplistic illustration of this, James sells shares in a listed company, earning a capital gain (i.e. a return) of $2000 but he also sells a different set of shares that produce a loss of $1000. Instead of paying CGT on $2000, he only has to pay it on $1000.

It can be quite a bit more complicated than this. Make sure you get a tax agent to do the proper calculation to make sure the right cost base is worked out.

---

8. Pre-pay eligible expenses

Talk to your accountant about pre-paying eligible expenses into this financial year to reduce taxable income. For example, interest on an investment loan attached to a property can be paid 12 months in advance.

Investment property owners should also be getting those maintenance jobs done, and paid for, now to be claimed in this year's return. Also make sure the depreciation schedule on a newly built property is correct and being claimed.

What you're doing is bringing forward expenses to reduce this year's income and pay less tax. Next year you may not earn enough income to make it worthwhile and won't need to do it; it's all about planning ahead.

9. Work out any negative gearing implications

Australians seem to have a passion for negative gearing as the answer to all their tax problems. As I noted on page 153, I think the advantages are exaggerated by most people. Negative gearing works best at a time of high income tax rates, high inflation and high interest rates. But today we have lower tax rates, low inflation and interest rates have dropped. For most people, in this economic environment, negative gearing simply doesn't stack up.

That's not to say don't borrow to invest, but do it because of the investment potential, not just for tax reasons.

10. Claim work-related expenses

Many jobs require money to be spent on unusual items that are necessary for earning an income. The cost of these items can be claimed against tax and are called work-related expenses.

WHO MAKES CLAIMS FOR WORK-RELATED EXPENSES?

Australians claim an average $3000 in tax deductions a year. But those in some professions claim more than others. According to the ATO, the highest work-related claims come from:

Real estate agents	$8634
Lawyers	$7156
Truck drivers	$5059
Tradies	$4871
Farmers	$4428
Engineers	$4415
Accountants	$3324
Teachers	$3164
Nurses	$2622
Bankers	$2223

But be careful, because the tax office studies these closely. You must keep receipts and the expenses must directly relate to earning an income. For example, funeral directors can claim the cost of their black suits and professional dancers the cost of leg waxing. Hard to believe but true. Also, take a look at what I have to say about 'benchmarking' on page 200.

> **DO THIS NOW**
>
> Check out the ATO website, which lists the eligible work deductions for a whole range of occupations, to make sure you get it right (ato.gov.au/Individuals/Income-and-deductions/Deductions-you-can-claim/Deductions-for-specific-industries-and-occupations). This website is a terrific resource for every family and is pretty easy to understand.
>
> Then download the ATO app or another receipt app, or simply buy a folder, and file all your relevant work-related expenses. Add your new receipts at the end of every week.
>
> At tax time, make sure you talk to your accountant or tax agent about how to maximise your deductions.

Early tax preparations

The key to getting your tax right and not paying too much is to avoid the hectic new financial year chaos by doing a little early thinking and tax preparation well before the end of June.

Tax time will be a whole lot easier if you file all your tax-related documents together throughout the year. I'm talking about payment summaries, bank and dividend statements, investment property accounts, receipts for tax-deductible work or education expenses, any travel logs and your health fund details.

Don't chuck this stuff out, keep it organised and stored away for five years in case you're ever audited. Make sure you do whichever of these applies to you:

* **Chase receipts.** Track down receipts for tax-deductible expenses to maximise your tax return. If you know where you spent the money, go back to whoever you paid and see if they can provide a copy of the receipt or invoice. Bank and credit card statements showing details of purchases can be used in some cases.

    Use the ATO app or an app like Receipt Bank to photograph a receipt on your smartphone and store it away. The ATO app can pre-fill your tax return with the info you enter throughout the year.
* **Offset capital gains with losses.** As we just saw, profits on selling shares or investment properties will be charged CGT, but losses made on these types of investments can be offset against those profits. It's easy to make the most of this if you think about it early.

- **Delay income until next financial year.** Delay receiving income until next financial year if you're likely to earn less than this year and will be in a lower marginal rate.
- **Top up your super.** Pre-tax superannuation contributions reduce your taxable income, so less money goes to the ATO and more goes to your super savings. After-tax contributions are also worthwhile because returns are taxed at a maximum of 15 per cent, not your regular income tax rate.

NOTES

THE ATO IS WATCHING YOU

If you reckon you can cheat the ATO, don't even think about it. You can't, and it will only be a matter of time before you're caught. It's just not worth the effort and the risk.

How the tax office checks up on you

The tactics and resources the ATO has at its disposal are quite extraordinary. Around 450,000 tax reviews and audits are conducted each year, catching more than $1.1 billion in income tax that people were trying to dodge. A lot of the latest tax-enforcement techniques have come from the abundance of data they're analysing, as everything from booking a holiday to doing your banking has moved online. The ATO has the most powerful computers in the country, and many businesses are required to share their customer databases with the ATO.

This is how they do it.

1. Data matching

Your financial moves are being scrutinised very closely. Last tax year the ATO requested all credit and debit card payments received by merchants from 11 financial institutions. That's an incredible amount of information that was matched against ATO records (your tax return) for clues on what was missing. On top of that wide-ranging banking and retail data, you can add employers, health insurers, state and federal agencies and overseas tax offices to the list of data providers. And if you buy a car, boat, home or artwork, assume that the transaction will end up in the ATO computers.

The analysis of this data is increasingly sophisticated and specifically designed to look for income tax returns that might be missing information, contain wonky numbers or simply don't stack up. From there it's just a matter of the ATO asking, 'Can they really afford that much caviar . . . or a boat?'

2. Benchmarking

The ATO doesn't just look at your tax return by itself. Along with cross-referencing your claims with data from other businesses, websites and financial institutions, it also compares you to taxpayers in similar circumstances to see if your claims are significantly different.

Picture a flat line on a chart representing the average transport tax deduction for a person of your age in your profession in your city. If you've claimed too much, your dot will be out of place on the chart and stick out like a sore thumb. The computer will produce a red flag against you and, before you know it, an ATO officer with a calculator could be knocking at your door. A scary thought.

3. Whistleblowing

The ATO welcomes whistleblowers with open arms, encouraging people to come forward and report their suspicions in confidence. If the ATO thinks there's enough information to warrant a closer look, they'll follow it up.

While this seems like a long shot, just consider how many people you might have peeved off in the past few years – divorced partners, ex-employees, old work colleagues.

4. Special focus areas

Each year the ATO identifies key areas of tax law they think might be up for some 'clever accounting' and places a special focus on them. It's fair to assume that second jobs through the sharing economy are up for some extra scrutiny these days, as the ATO captures more income from sources like Airbnb, eBay and Uber. That said, you might as well assume a special focus on everything you do, just to be safe.

5. Serious detective work

Apart from computer power, the ATO can also collect information in rather unusual ways. I've heard a few impressive stories from tax accountants over the years, where people have been caught through more traditional detective efforts.

In one case I was told of tax officers sitting in football car parks and taking down car regos on utes to check private versus business use deductions. And, at the more sophisticated end of town, there was a smash-and-grab raid on a hotel room to seize evidence of offshore tax evasion. When you add that sort of endeavour to the giant computers cross-checking each taxpayer's every move, the game is up for tax cheats.

WHAT ARE RED FLAGS FOR THE ATO?

Apart from declaring a modest income but buying a flash car or boat, what will cause the ATO to take a close interest in you?

* **Work-related expenses.** An old chestnut where we try to claim even the most obscure expense. Check your expenses against the ATO list . . . any deviation will attract attention.
* **Capital gains tax.** How it's worked out, the costs claimed and any offsetting capital losses.
* **Tax losses from prior years.**
* **Rental property.** With so many Australians borrowing against the equity in their home to buy a rental property, this is a complex area the ATO is putting a lot of resources into. I advise getting some professional help.
* **Interest and dividend deductions.**
* **Foreign-sourced income.** From overseas investments or remuneration.
* **Losses from partnerships.**

When the 'taxman' comes knocking

Each year the ATO reveals its targets for this year's tax season. While the ATO computers analyse all tax returns against varying benchmarks, in recent times work-related expenses (especially laundry and clothing deductions) and investment property income and deductions have received closer than normal attention.

These are the most common tax mistakes we tend to make.

Missing income

Forgetting to report income is very easy to do and, thanks to the ATO's comprehensive data-matching systems, very easily detected. Think interest income, short-term contract or freelance work, government benefits, bonuses, dividends and any other passive income that might have come into your account.

In 2017 the ATO cross-referenced tax return information against almost a billion transactions provided to them by third parties to track down omitted income and incorrectly claimed offsets. Even the 'sharing' and digital economy is caught by the data-collection program. That resulted in a huge number of tax payers getting a call from the ATO for dicey discrepancies. Don't be one of the people caught this year.

Unclear expense claims

It's important to ensure you take advantage of all tax deductions you're eligible for, in order to avoid paying a dollar more in tax than necessary. But whatever you do, don't overstep the line. There's plenty of information on the ATO website and throughout the myTax program, so doing it yourself is no excuse for ignorance either. Be sure to check out any special deductions that are applicable to your circumstances, but don't go claiming things that push the envelope.

I recently read a suggestion from one 'expert' that women could buy a $2000 handbag and claim it as a work deduction if it carried their laptop. While claiming a computer bag is deductible, I reckon claiming a designer handbag pushes it a bit far and could get you into trouble. Don't take the risk.

Not lodging

This sounds a bit obvious, but lots of people get behind in lodging their tax returns and are then too scared to catch up. It's worth noting that tax agents have a bit longer to get returns in, so if you can't afford your tax bill or are really late it might be worth approaching a professional to lodge for you.

Remember, fines are applicable if you miss the end of October deadline each year, but the ATO is usually pretty lenient in applying these and really isn't the big bad guy it's made out to be. It's always willing to negotiate payment plans for outstanding tax and to provide help to those in need, so pick up the phone and get your tax filings back on track this year.

Reckless record keeping

The number of times I've had people say to me, 'I'm getting audited, what do I do?' followed by the revelation that their records are a mess, or even non-existent, astounds me. If you do one thing to stay safe at tax time, keep better records. Not only does good organisation make any audit a way easier process, but it helps you understand your financial position better, identify extra deductions that would have otherwise gone unclaimed, and it ultimately gets you in a better tax position.

So, while you're detecting deductions this year, also spend some time making sure you're doing the right thing by the ATO. It can save you a lot of time, trouble and money down the track.

WHAT HAVE WE LEARNT?

The federal government could be holding a big chunk of your money – because you haven't asked for it back. The way to get that cash is to focus on your tax, get it right and lodge a return. It's not that hard, but you do need to make sure you do it right and don't bend the rules.

In this chapter I've taken you through:

* how to pay the right amount of tax by following my Ten Tax Commandments
* how to get organised and prepared so that completing your tax return doesn't become a massive chore at the end of the financial year
* what could make the ATO scrutinise your return and audit you
* how to stay off the ATO's radar by being honest and well prepared.

HOMEWORK

KEY POINTS

- **Lodge your tax returns!**

- **Consider getting help from a registered tax agent**

- **Get your tax administration right throughout the year**

HOMEWORK

- ☐ **Do it now. Focus on completing any past overdue returns before the ATO catches up with you**

- ☐ **Talk to friends and family for recommendations on tax agents/ accountants they use and approve of**

- ☐ **Start a filing system, or use the ATO app or an app like Receipt Bank, to keep receipts for possible deductions as they come in**

NOTES

STEP 10: INVEST A THOUSAND BUCKS

Go on, do it. It will get you started on what's possibly the most beneficial financial activity available. If you're already an investor, read on for further tips.

> **DO THIS NOW**
>
> Pull out your latest superannuation statement and go to the 'Your current balance' section. The figure there is how much money you have in super and how much it's increased or decreased since the last balance date. See? You're an investor already!

ANYONE CAN BE AN INVESTOR

I know what you're thinking: 'Bloody hell, Kochie, I've got a bunch of kids, I'm trying to make ends meet and have a nice life. There's nothing left over to invest!' Believe me, I hear you.

But just think about it. While you might be cash-poor and find it hard to pay the bills, you're probably asset-rich when the family home and superannuation are taken into account. In fact, as we've just seen, you're already an investor – you just might not have realised it. If you have a home, you probably just think of it as a massive mortgage that chews up cash each month, forgetting that it has probably appreciated in value and your equity in it has followed. The fact is, in the five years leading up to the peak of the housing market in September 2017, national housing values rose 35 per cent.

Your superannuation is probably your second-biggest asset behind your home, but money is contributed without you knowing, almost by stealth. It just comes out of your salary automatically. If you didn't already do so in Step 6, check now how much that superannuation balance has grown – I think you'll be surprised.

Now you know you're a pretty big investor, don't you agree that it's worthwhile knowing the investment fundamentals and how to think about investing more, in the right way? Investing might seem completely out of reach for you right now, but let's demystify it and see if you change your mind. Obviously I don't want you to go crazy and invest money you can't really afford, but if you do happen to have some cash lying around, why not dip your toe in the water with a small investment and see how it goes. You might have more fun than you think!

In this chapter I want to provide some key tips on investing. We'll look at:

* which advice on investing is worth listening to
* how to approach investing with a good frame of mind
* how to evaluate your wealth
* how to dip your toe in the investing pool.

I understand you have a lot of pressures on your budget, but it's important to understand how small windfalls can make a huge difference to your financial future if you know what to do with them. It's all about starting small and getting comfortable with the process of investing.

WHICH ADVICE TO HEED OR IGNORE

We have an extended Koch family dinner every month at Mum's house. It's big (26 at a long table), and it's loud, but it's great fun.

Recently our grandkids were talking about their pocket money, asking for advice on what to do with it and on money generally. I automatically fell into grandparent mode, and then realised that I seemed to be channelling my own grandparents' advice. Spooky! Gee, I felt old. But it did remind me of the advice we received from those family financial sages, and lead me to question whether those pearls of wisdom are still relevant today.

Road-testing Granny's advice

Let's stress-test some of Granny's ageless advice and see whether it still stacks up today.

'Cut your coat according to your cloth'

Or 'Don't drink champagne on a beer income'. Both mean the same thing: don't live beyond your means. It's advice that's probably even more relevant now than in the past, because of the easy access to credit and cheap interest rates. So many people dig themselves into a financial hole because they want instant gratification and buy things they can't afford.

But I have to say, the decreasing use of credit cards and growing popularity of debit cards indicates that many people are getting the hint and following Grandma's advice.

'Watch the pennies and the pounds will follow'

Grandma was, of course (or at least for the sake of this saying), living before decimal currency. 'Watch the cents and the dollars will follow' just doesn't have the same ring to it. The basis of this advice is that, if you're careful with the little financial decisions, the benefits will add up. Great examples are things like making your own lunch instead of buying it – that $5 or more you save a day equals at least $25 a week or $1175 a year (factoring in annual leave and public holidays). The other money-saving tips in Step 4 will have the same effect.

So once again, Granny was right.

Thankfully, in our relationship, Libby not only gives this advice but lives it.

'Bricks and mortar never go down in value'

Obviously Granny hasn't lived in south-east Queensland, parts of Victoria, Perth or the US and Europe. Property goes through up-and-down cycles like any other investment, and needs to be approached with the same type of care and research. The big difference is that you know the value of your shares every day, but with property a sale is the only time you know its real value.

Sorry, Granny, times have changed.

'Borrowing money is evil'

Not always. As we saw in Step 3, there's good and bad debt.

Bad debt is when credit is used to buy a consumable item that disappears or rapidly depreciates. Borrowing for luxuries like fancy clothes, flash dinners out, a new upmarket boat or a fancy car is bad.

Good debt is borrowing to invest in an asset that appreciates in value to build wealth and a long-term investment portfolio. In this era of low interest rates, borrowing to invest in quality assets can be attractive.

So Granny is only half right.

'It's better to keep your money under the mattress'

Okay, banks aren't renowned for their generosity, and savings interest rates are really low, but they're still better than nothing, which is what that money would earn under the mattress.

As for security, Australia's banks are among the safest in the world and operate under strict regulations, with a government guarantee on deposits up to a limit. No investment is completely safe, but putting money in a major Australian bank can be one of the safest options.

I know the Banking Royal Commission has highlighted some pretty shonky practices from the banks, but these have now, hopefully, been rectified. And the reason I went into so much detail in Step 2 about how to get the most out of your bank was to make sure you can identify when you're being taken for a ride – and do something about it.

So, Granny, enough with scare mongering.

'Ignore it and it will go away'

When it comes to family finances, ignorance is not bliss. In the old days you could hide problems from the bank or be tardy in paying bills without anyone really knowing. But today every financial transaction is captured electronically. Sophisticated computers flag financial problems to banks, retailers, credit card companies and an array of other providers. Financial blemishes are recorded on your credit rating and can stalk you for years, so keep on top of things, particularly after recent changes to the *Privacy Act* that allow more of your financial history to be recorded on your credit file.

Road-testing modern advice

In this day and age everyone seems to have an opinion on everything. We're bombarded with advice on every element of our life. It may be well intentioned, but that doesn't mean it's always right. In fact, especially when it comes to money, some opinions can be downright dangerous.

Here are some of the most untrustworthy pieces of financial advice I hear regularly.

You're too young/busy/broke to invest

It's easy to think you'll put off investing until you're older, or when the kids have left home, or when you have more time or money. But, believe me, there'll always be competing interests for your money.

When you're younger it's hard to see long term – there are cars, mortgages and school expenses to pay for. But it's vital to save/invest first so you can spend later. Having an automatic system – such as bank account direct debits to an investment fund – makes it easier. The younger you start investing the better. Even small amounts added to an investment portfolio or super fund will multiply several times over many years because of compound interest (see page 219).

Better advice: it's all about discipline. Put a little away regularly and start as early as you can.

This hot tip will get you rich quick

We've all heard a hot tip from a friend, family member, Uber driver or even on social media. But, as I said at the beginning of this book, looking for a quick fix with any investment is dangerous and rarely successful. While it might be uncomfortable to hear, our desire for a quick fix is driven by greed. Usually these hot tips are based on hearsay and are speculative investments rather than a proven winner.

The people who lose the most money are those who rely too heavily on one thing to make them money. That's where your greatest risk is. Even if you have inside information about a share in a particular company, it can still go belly up. A lot of people who perpetuate these myths have a vested interest, so they can get out at a higher price – but you won't be able to.

You need to accept that achieving what you want rarely happens overnight. It's more likely to take a number of years, but it will be worth taking the slow road.

Better advice: slow, steady returns and the magic of compounding will always succeed.

You can't go wrong with bricks and mortar

Granny said this and people are still saying it. Property is arguably Australia's most popular type of investment, and many people swear it's the only way to build wealth effectively. Many factors, however – primarily falling house prices and rising interest rates – can turn real estate investments into a nightmare.

What people fail to take into account are the enormous holding costs of investing in property, or the fact that you never really know its value until you decide to sell it. With land tax, interest rates, council rates and other taxes, investment property is a very expensive asset. Some investors have purchased a property and later found that it had major structural issues, they couldn't rent it for what they expected, or they paid an over-inflated price and their asset has decreased in value to a more realistic price.

Better advice: property success is all about price, position and gearing. Buy in an attractive area, do your homework to establish the right price, and don't borrow too much.

Negative gearing is a smart strategy

As we saw in Step 7, negative gearing may give you a nice deduction at tax time, but it means you're still spending more than you get back. The 'negative' is in the term because you're paying more cash out (loan repayments, council rates, insurances, etc.) than the amount of cash coming in (rent from tenants). You can offset this income loss against personal income earned from elsewhere and so reduce your overall income and the tax on it. Investors need to be sure that the increase in the value of their negatively geared asset will offset the annual income losses they make on it.

If you're making a loss, how can it be good? High-income earners save some tax (they get bigger deductions because their marginal tax rates are higher), but it's not a good approach for most people to rely on to build wealth. Negative gearing can put the average family under huge financial pressure.

Rather than focusing on getting the ATO to help them pay for their property, investors should be buying property where the tenant is helping to pay for it.

Better advice: unless you're in the top tax bracket, negative gearing really isn't worth the risk. There's nothing wrong with positive gearing.

Buying your home is better than renting

As we saw in Step 7, there's a very good financial argument for renting and then investing the difference between the rent and the mortgage payment somewhere else. The key is having the discipline to invest the difference.

Remember, property can also go down in value. We're seeing that now.

Better advice: do the numbers and take in all the costs. If you don't have the discipline to invest the difference between owning a property and renting one, then own it and pay off the loan as a forced savings program.

It's a good idea to consolidate consumer debt into your mortgage

Using long-term borrowing, such as a mortgage, for short-term needs isn't necessarily a good mix: while the interest rates may be lower for a home loan, the amount repaid over the longer life of the mortgage will cost you much more.

Better advice: the only way to make this work is to pay the added debt off as quickly as you can. Don't make it part of your long-term home loan (see page 51).

GETTING YOUR HEAD RIGHT WITH INVESTING

Success or failure when it comes to investing often comes down to our personal psychological traits, and the way we make decisions, rather than the actual quality of the investments themselves. Just examine the way you 'think' about investing and I bet you'll be surprised by how influenced you are by a range of different emotions, biases and experiences. Some are good, but plenty are bad.

Bad approaches to investing

Trying to rectify some of your more damaging psychological traits can dramatically improve your financial decision-making and, hopefully, performance.

How many of these are you guilty of?

1. Giving in to fear and/or greed

Investing can be scary. Tensions can rise when markets unexpectedly gallop in either direction. Emotions cause you to flee a bear (falling) market or plunge headfirst into a bull (rising) market, acting directly counter to the investment adage of buying low and selling high.

Investment history shows that if we countered these emotions completely we'd be infinitely more successful investors. Counter-cyclical investing is buying a quality asset that's undervalued in falling markets and selling when it becomes overvalued in rising markets. It's not trying to pick the very top of a boom cycle, but rather it's being happy to bank good profits and leave something for the next investor. Those fear and greed emotions are very powerful, but can be so destructive, and often lead us into irrational decisions.

2. Being overconfident

Investing and making money need confidence, but there's a very fine line. People with an inflated sense of their own ability to make smart investments often take shortcuts and don't fully think decisions through. Having the discipline to do all the appropriate, thorough and objective research before committing, no matter how confident you are, is critical.

All the legendary investors have been renowned for their research and their ability to not go ahead with an investment if study showed its prospects weren't great. It takes courage to overturn a decision when the facts just don't stack up, but it can save a lot pain.

3. Looking backwards, not forwards

Investing is all about the future prospects of an asset – we want to know that it has a bright future and will provide good returns. As the future is hard to predict, we tend to look to the past for some guidance. That's fair enough, but many investors have a bad habit of dwelling on the past and talking about market developments as if it was obvious what was going to happen.

The reality is that it's never that obvious, and hindsight can be misleading. It's better to focus on the current environment and some of the lead indicators providing a glimpse of the future. The current residential property cycle is a classic case in point. A year ago historical data showed a booming market, particularly in Sydney, but leading indicators were strongly predicting a slowdown, which is happening as I write.

4. Not admitting a mistake

Whether it be through pride, hubris or stubbornness, there's nothing worse than 'marrying a dog'. This is an investment you were confident would succeed but that hasn't performed, one that's been a disaster but you simply hang onto hoping you'll eventually be right. As the losses mount you eventually sell, but the financial damage could have been significantly less if you'd admitted the mistake and cut your losses.

Objectivity – and understanding you won't be right all the time – are the keys to success. Make the hard calls and move on.

5. Doing mental accounting

Investors often fool themselves into thinking they're doing better than they are. It's human nature. So it's important to keep track of how you're doing on paper, not in your head.

It always amuses me, for example, when people talk about how much they've made on property deals. It's only when you gently ask them whether they've deducted stamp/transfer duties, legal fees, agent's commissions and council rates from the profit, that the penny drops that the transaction costs are substantial.

Yes, profit is the difference between a buying and selling price, but minus costs.

6. Not constantly adapting

We all have a natural aversion to change that can get in the way of successful investing. In order to be successful, you need to be able to recognise when things aren't working, and adapt accordingly.

Nothing ever stays the same. Investment cycles constantly change, as do politics, regulations, management and financial circumstances. These can all provide opportunities, but only to those who recognise the changes and are able to adapt.

We're not talking here about knee-jerk reactions to sudden changes. It's an ability to embrace an understanding of change, to think of it as an opportunity rather than a threat, and then to adapt your investment portfolio to suit.

My seven key concepts of investing

Building wealth is all about discipline: to set a strategy, to develop a plan, to implement it and to stick to it. The foundation of that strategy and plan is a clear understanding of the fundamental concepts of investing. It's about clear thinking – the right thinking.

Here are the basic financial concepts I think you need to understand before building your strategy.

1. Net worth

Net worth is your barometer of financial health. It's your total assets minus your total debt. It's the true litmus test of how successfully you're building wealth.

It often amuses me when people boast about the impressive value of their investment portfolio and how much it has appreciated. I usually follow up with, 'And how much debt do you have you against that?' If they stumble around, and come up with a vague answer, I know they've borrowed up to their eyeballs and it's not really wealth they're talking about but pure debt. It's a bit like the friend driving around in an impressive car when the finance company is the real owner.

We had a segment on *Sunrise* with a supposed property 'guru' and one of his clients, who had built an $8 million property portfolio in a short period of time. They were explaining how easy it was if you followed the guru's secret plan. I asked the client how much debt she had against the property portfolio. She didn't know and looked for guidance from the guru – who sheepishly answered, '$8.2 million.' I was shocked – and so was his client.

Obviously you're in good financial health if your net worth is well into the positives, and you have some work to do if your net worth is anywhere in the negatives.

> **DO THIS NOW**
>
> **Roughly calculate your net worth, using the table over the page and adding anything not listed here – e.g. musical instruments, valuable collections.**

CALCULATE YOUR NET WORTH

Assets (what you own)	
House	
Bank savings accounts	
Debts owed to you	
Car/s	
Superannuation	
Investments (shares, property, bonds, fixed interest)	
Jewellery/artwork	
Furniture	
Personal property	
Other	
TOTAL ASSETS	(A)
Liabilities (what you owe)	
Home loan	
Credit card outstanding balances	
Personal loans	
Debts you owe	
Taxes owed	
Other	
TOTAL LIABILITIES	(B)
NET WORTH (A − B)	

2. Real returns

Inflation occurs when the cost of living – the price of goods and services – goes up. As prices rise, the same amount of money will buy less – unless your income or investments are rising at a greater rate to compensate.

The current inflation rate (called the 'consumer price index' or CPI) is around 2.5 per cent. That means your income and investments need to grow in value by more than the CPI or you'll be standing still or going backwards.

The 'real return' is the actual return from your investments less the inflation rate. It's the only measure of how far you've actually got ahead.

KOCHIE CALCULATOR: YOUR REAL RETURN

Michelle makes 10% on an investment and the inflation rate is 4%. To calculate her real return, she:

* converts the percentages to decimals (0.10 and 0.04), adds 1 to both figures and divides the return by the inflation rate: (1.10 ÷ 1.04 = 1.0577), then
* multiplies that figure by 100 (1.0577 x 100 = $105.77).

So on a $100 investment that returns $10, Michelle's real return is $5.77.

---

3. Liquidity

Liquidity is simply how quickly you can get at your money – how accessible it is. Cash in your hand is the most liquid your money can be, while superannuation is probably at the other end of the liquidity scale because the government has regulated that you can't touch it until the defined retirement age. Shares and property are at different levels between cash and superannuation.

Liquidity is a big issue when it comes to investing. Access to your wealth is always an important consideration, depending on what you want your money to do for you. An emergency fund, for example, needs to be invested in liquid assets so it can be retrieved easily.

Libby and I rarely invest directly in property because it's such a big-ticket investment item that, depending on the state of the market, can take a long time to sell. Plus the transaction costs (stamp/transfer duty, agent's and lawyer's fees) can be really high.

If you want instant access to money then an online savings account is arguably the best option. If you're happy to wait up to three months, then a term deposit looks good. You can access money invested in a managed fund pretty quickly but, because of fees, you need to have had it invested for two or three years at least to make it work properly.

4. Investment cycles

When it comes to investing there's no guarantee – there are no 'sure things'. Economic and investment history tells us that every investment type moves in a cycle. There'll be times when values go up and times when values go down. As I said earlier, the key is knowing roughly where you are in the investment cycle and making sure you invest near the bottom of a cycle and sell near the top.

Stepping back and looking at the big-picture cycles is critical to investment decision-making.

5. Risk tolerance

Risk tolerance is how comfortable you are with the swings in the investment cycle – whether you understand the cycle and ride with it, or stress out about it. Your level of risk tolerance determines how aggressive you can be with your investing.

Risk tolerance isn't just emotional. It depends on a range of factors, such as how much time you have to commit to investing, your future earning potential, and the assets you have that aren't invested, such as your home.

6. Asset allocation and diversification

Asset allocation is basically the type of assets you invest in, which is determined by your investment strategy and goals. It's also the basis of diversification. The goal of diversification is reducing the risk of investing by spreading your wealth across a range of assets – not putting all your eggs in the one basket.

The idea is for this to smooth returns. An investment that's falling in value is ideally offset by another investment that's rising.

KOCHIE CALCULATOR: DIVERSIFICATION OF INVESTMENTS

If you have 100% of your investments in one listed company and its share price drops 10%, you've lost 10% of your money.

But if you have that same amount of money invested equally across five different stocks, property and fixed interest, that diversity may yield returns from the other four investments that make up for the one that loses.

Investment 1: −10%   Investment 2: +3%   Investment 3: +5%
Investment 4: +6%   Investment 5: +4%

Total return of portfolio (i.e. average return) = (−10 + 3 + 5 + 6 + 4)/5 = +1.6%

So, even though your one investment has lost 10% and your others provide only small returns, you still come out ahead.

7. Compound interest

Compound interest is interest you earn on a 'rolling balance' rather than on only the initial principal (the amount you invest to start with).

Here's an example: if you start off with $100 earning compound 5 per cent interest annually, after your first year you'll have $105. The next year, you'll be earning 5 per cent interest on *$105* rather than $100, which means you'll earn $5.25 instead of $5.

It doesn't sound so impressive when we're discussing $5 at a time, but the multiplier effect can absolutely supercharge returns.

KOCHIE CALCULATOR: THE MAGIC OF COMPOUNDING

Let's keep the $100 investment earning 5% interest (compounded monthly) and not add anything extra. After 10 years that $100 would be worth $165: a 65% total return after 10 years. Over 20 years that same $100 would be worth $271, almost triple the original investment just by letting it sit there. If the interest return was 10% instead of 5% that $100 would be worth $271 after 10 years and $733 after 20 years.

If you were to invest $2000 each year between the ages of 19–25, you will have invested $14,000 in total. Let's say the average return was 10% (5% interest plus 5% growth).

By the age of 65 that nest egg will have grown to $930,641, or 66 times what you put in. That's the magic of compounding, or earning a return on a return every year.

FUN FACT *The ASX Australian Investor Study in 2017 found that 60% of Australian adults (or 11.2 million people) hold investments outside of their institutional superannuation fund.*

INVEST A THOUSAND BUCKS

> **DO THIS NOW**
>
> Come up with a plan to source or raise $1000 you can earmark for investment. (I know, easier said than done, but it *can* be done: I've already given you loads of tips in Step 4!)

Okay, so you've sacrificed nights out with friends, you've worked hard on your side hustle, maybe received a share of an inheritance or saved up some nice work bonuses. Now you have $1000. There are plenty of options to start small with this amount and build a nest egg from there. And by starting small you can learn the fundamentals of investing and so be prepared for when more cash becomes available to invest.

It's a way better approach than saying, 'It's not worth investing such a small amount, so I'll spend it.' Don't.

What you do with an amount like this could change your life, so don't waste it. You can start investing in a term deposit, managed fund or exchange traded fund (ETF) with a minimum of $1000, and you can add to your investment regularly from then on. Apart from bank deposits up to $250,000 (which are guaranteed by the federal government), no investment is 100 per cent guaranteed. But earning a return from your money is a key ingredient to building wealth.

Let's look at your options in detail.

Pay off your debt

Doing this should be your priority when term deposits and savings account interest rates are only about 2 per cent. It's not as sexy as a new car, but paying down debt is one of the smartest things you can do with some of that extra cash. Paying off a chunk of the mortgage early, for example, can save you tens of thousands of dollars in interest payments over the life of the loan.

And while Australia seems to have an enduring love affair with credit cards, they're racking up interest at more than 18 per cent on outstanding balances, so it makes no sense to leave that debt sitting there. Pay off the credit card balance and you've made a guaranteed 16 per cent return – saving 18 per cent interest rather than earning 2 per cent on a term deposit.

Consumer debt is a drain on income, and the sooner the slate is wiped clean, the sooner you can start putting your money to work.

Top up your superannuation

Locking your windfalls away in long-term investments, like superannuation, is the key to building wealth. It's always hard to contemplate locking away spare cash until retirement, but it's still a terrific investment. Just make sure you understand the new rules and get good advice (see Step 6).

Start a share portfolio

Would you like to try investing in shares but don't know where to start? One approach would be to meet with a stockbroker and ask their advice on particular stocks to invest in, but I wouldn't recommend this as a first step. I think it's best to start cautiously. For those new to share investing, the first and safest step is to let professionals make all the decisions while you learn about how the market works.

The way to do this is via 'managed funds', which most banks offer to their customers. With these funds, hundreds of small investors pool their money into a unit trust, then professionals manage the portfolio and make all the investment decisions.

There is a huge number of different managed funds available that come with a variety of different investment focuses. These range from balanced funds that invest across shares, property and fixed interest, through to funds that specialise in US shares, or property, or Japanese shares . . . and a lot more.

Remember, most managed fund returns are measured in their unit/share price, which reflects how their investment portfolio has performed. So it's capital growth (or loss) on the unit price which investors receive. Over the last five years, the average balanced managed funds have returned about 6 per cent a year, while aggressively managed funds returned about 9 per cent a year. Compare that with five-year term deposit income returns of just over 3 per cent.

Try ETFs

Another alternative is exchange traded funds (or ETFs), which are great for diversification at a low cost and are an easy option. They're sort of like a managed fund but the money is invested in things listed on the share market, and their investment portfolio will mirror a share index like the All Ordinaries Index or even the Dow Jones Index in America. This means your returns will mirror the general market performance rather than an individual stock.

As I've said, ETFs are listed on the share market, so you buy and sell them like any share through any stockbroker: most banks own, or have a relationship with a stockbroker for their customers to use for share buying and selling. And because the ETF invests directly in a portfolio of shares, its value will rise and fall to reflect the share market.

For example, ETFs that mirror the portfolio of stocks which make up the ASX200 share index have returned about 8 per cent a year over the last five years – which is how the ASX200 index has performed.

MANAGED FUNDS AND ETFS: PROS AND CONS

	Managed funds	**ETFs**
Managed by	Professional funds manager	A computer admin system or algorithm
Invested in	Across all investment asset classes depending on the objective of the fund	Reflects the underlying assets of the sharemarket sector/index they represent
Pros	Diversity of being in a wide portfolio and, hopefully, out-performs the rest of the market if managed aggressively	Low cost
Cons	High-cost management fees	Performance will mirror the market and not outperform
How to begin	Invest through advisers/ brokers/banks or direct with fund manager	Invest through advisers/ brokers or direct through online platforms

Think about the next step

Bear in mind that you need to give investments time to perform. Long-term (four to seven years minimum) investors who invest in quality assets are the ones who generally make the most money. Once you've invested you have a couple of options:

* keep the money invested and watch it grow because the fund's portfolio continues to rise in value (hopefully, because investments can go down in value as well)

* sell the investment, receive the profit (hopefully) in cash, and then decide what you want to do with it: invest somewhere else, pay off debt, fund one of your financial goals (travel, deposit on a home, buy a car). It's your decision.

If you get hooked on investing, then I reckon your best option is to see a financial adviser and build a relationship with them. I covered how to find one on page 137.

Practise with a 'fantasy' portfolio

I reckon another great way to learn how to invest and have some fun is to start a 'fantasy' portfolio using imaginary money. Hypothetically invest, say, $10,000 in ten different shares you like. Follow everything about them for the next year and see how their share price goes.

Another option is the ASX Sharemarket Game, which is great fun. It's a bit like the AFL, NRL and BBL SuperCoach games, except instead of trading players you trade shares – you're the investor instead of the coach. They have two games a year which go for six months. Entry is free, you get fifty thousand virtual dollars to invest, and you can win actual cash prizes. What have you got to lose?

WHAT ARE THE TAX IMPLICATIONS OF INVESTING?

Basically there are only two types of return earned from investing:

* **Income:** where you invest your cash and receive an income return based on the cash the investment generates. For example, online savings accounts, term deposits, dividends from shares and rent from tenants of an investment property.
* **Capital growth:** where the value of the asset rises (or falls) and your return is based on the price of that asset at the time of sale. Capital growth/loss is simply the difference between what you paid for the asset and what you sell it for. Examples include share prices, property values and managed fund unit prices.

Income returns are added to your taxable income and subject to tax at your marginal rate.

Capital growth returns are subject to capital gains tax at the time of sale: the 'gain' is taxed at your marginal tax rate less a 50% discount.

WHAT HAVE WE LEARNT?

You're already an investor, so you need to have an understanding of how investment markets work when it comes to maximising the potential of your home and your superannuation.

It's not about the size of the investment, more about understanding the fundamentals of investing so that when an opportunity comes and you need to make a decision, you can do it comfortably.

In this chapter we've learnt:

* which advice is worth listening to
* how to get your head space right to invest
* the fundamentals of investing
* the magic of compounding interest
* some of the options available to invest as little as $1000.

Have a try and see where it leads you.

HOMEWORK

KEY POINTS

- **Investigate the magic of compound interest**

- **Understand your net worth**

- **Start practising**

- **You're probably more ready than you think**

HOMEWORK

- ☐ Google 'compounding calculator', plug in some figures and have fun seeing what compounding can do

- ☐ Calculate your own net worth using the template on page 216

- ☐ Have some fun and use 'pretend money' to invest in a variety of Australian shares and follow their fortunes. Get to know the business and read the reports on their performance

- ☐ Take the plunge and talk to your bank or financial adviser

NOTES

STEP 11: MAINTAIN GOOD HABITS

Get steps one to 10 in place and then it's just a matter of maintenance.

> **DO THIS NOW**
>
> Go back and look at the last page of every chapter, the one where I list the key points and homework (you'll find them on pages 22, 40, 61, 90, 120, 141, 160, 188, 204 and 224). How many of them have you done already? What do you have left? It doesn't look so bad, does it?

LET'S MAKE A PLAN

We've reached the final chapter of our journey to get your finances under control. Thanks for sticking with me. I hope you're feeling more confident and clearer now about your plan to get ahead. And my apologies if you're feeling a little overwhelmed – I know there's been a lot of information to take in.

This final step isn't about adding to that information overload. I now want you to clear your head and distil the other 10 steps into a plan to move forward from here. I find that a lot of practical books finish abruptly, which means, unfortunately, that readers often go, 'Phew, that's over', then get distracted by the other things in their life. That's fair enough – we're all busy. But it's a shame, because often we take things in and then move on without putting what we've learnt into action. I don't want that to happen to you.

So I've deliberately made this last step about how easy it is to take the next 100 steps forward. We're going to:

* review what you could save or earn by following the advice in this book
* organise your money calendar by diarising important financial events throughout the year
* develop a daily approach to money that will create healthy financial habits so instinctive that you don't even have to think about them consciously
* reinforce the importance of talking things though, with your partner, if you have one, and with others who can help – family, friends, a financial adviser, me.

WHAT YOU COULD HAVE SAVED/EARNED FROM THIS BOOK

It's really hard to make an exact calculation for everyone, but let's do the maths based on the average Australian household according to the ABS, which we used back at the start of the book. Let's go through each category and remind ourselves where the savings have come from.

HOW MUCH CAN I EARN/SAVE BY FOLLOWING KOCHIE'S 11-STEP MONEY PLAN?

AVERAGE HOUSEHOLD DEBT	
Mortgage	$165,000
Consumer	$17,000
Credit card balance	$3273
Credit card balance accruing interest	$2062
AVERAGE HOUSEHOLD INCOME	$110,000 a year
AVERAGE HOUSEHOLD NET WORTH	$929,000
AVERAGE HOUSE VALUE	$656,000
AVERAGE HOUSEHOLD CAR VALUE	$36,500

AVERAGE AUSTRALIAN HOUSEHOLD SPENDING PER YEAR

Category	Annual amount	Saving
Housing (rent and mortgage) On an average $165,000 home loan at a 4.5% interest rate, making the call and asking for a 0.5% discount will save $46 a month or $552 a year	$14,524	$552

AVERAGE AUSTRALIAN HOUSEHOLD SPENDING PER YEAR (CONT.)

Category	Annual amount	Saving
Food and non-alcoholic beverages Forming your own bulk-buying co-op for fruit and veg, and understanding how to avoid supermarket tactics to get you to pay more, will shave at least 10% off your bill	$12,301	$1200
Transport Replace the second (or only) car with a car-sharing service; buy a more fuel-efficient and low-maintenance car	$10,738	$600
Recreation Cut back on gym fees, reduce home-delivery food, scale back restaurant meals	$8966	$2000
Miscellaneous goods and services Cut bank fees, scrutinise service offerings	$5039	$500
Medical/health Check private health insurance	$4298	$500
Household furniture/equipment Negotiate on everything	$3038	$300
Communication If you're out of contract, ask your provider for the best data and mobile plan to suit your habits	$2445	$250
Household services/operations Don't renew insurance premiums automatically; go to comparative websites and ask for a better deal	$2371	$300
Clothing and footwear Buy non-designer brands, swap clothes with friends, etc.	$2297	$1000

AVERAGE AUSTRALIAN HOUSEHOLD SPENDING PER YEAR (CONT.)

Category	Annual amount	Saving
Education Buy uniforms from the second-hand shop, buy second-hand textbooks	$2297	$400
Domestic fuel and power Get rid of the second (or only) car, turn down the reverse-cycle thermostat, follow energy-saving strategies	$2149	$500
Alcohol Cut down your consumption, buy cheaper brands	$1630	$160
Personal care Buy from discount stores and use lesser known brands	$1482	$200
Tobacco We didn't talk about this before, because it's a no-brainer: commit to quitting, or at least cutting down drastically. It's good for your wallet and your health.	$667	$100
TOTAL SAVINGS (estimate)		$8562
PLUS SIDE HUSTLE INCOME (estimate) 10% of average income		$5500
TOTAL SAVINGS PLUS EARNINGS (estimate)		$14,062

You'll need to do your own calculations for your own situation, but the figures in the table above show that, by following the suggestions from the last 10 steps, you could save or earn as much as $14,000, which will go a long way towards paying off the average Australian family's outstanding credit card balance and personal loans.

That's not a bad return from the cost of this book and your time reading it.

YOUR ANNUAL MONEY CALENDAR

While I have you in a mood of enthusiasm, get out your calendar (paper or smartphone app, it doesn't matter) and let's diarise a year's worth of reminders right now. I'll go into more detail over the page, but here's what it looks like at a glance.

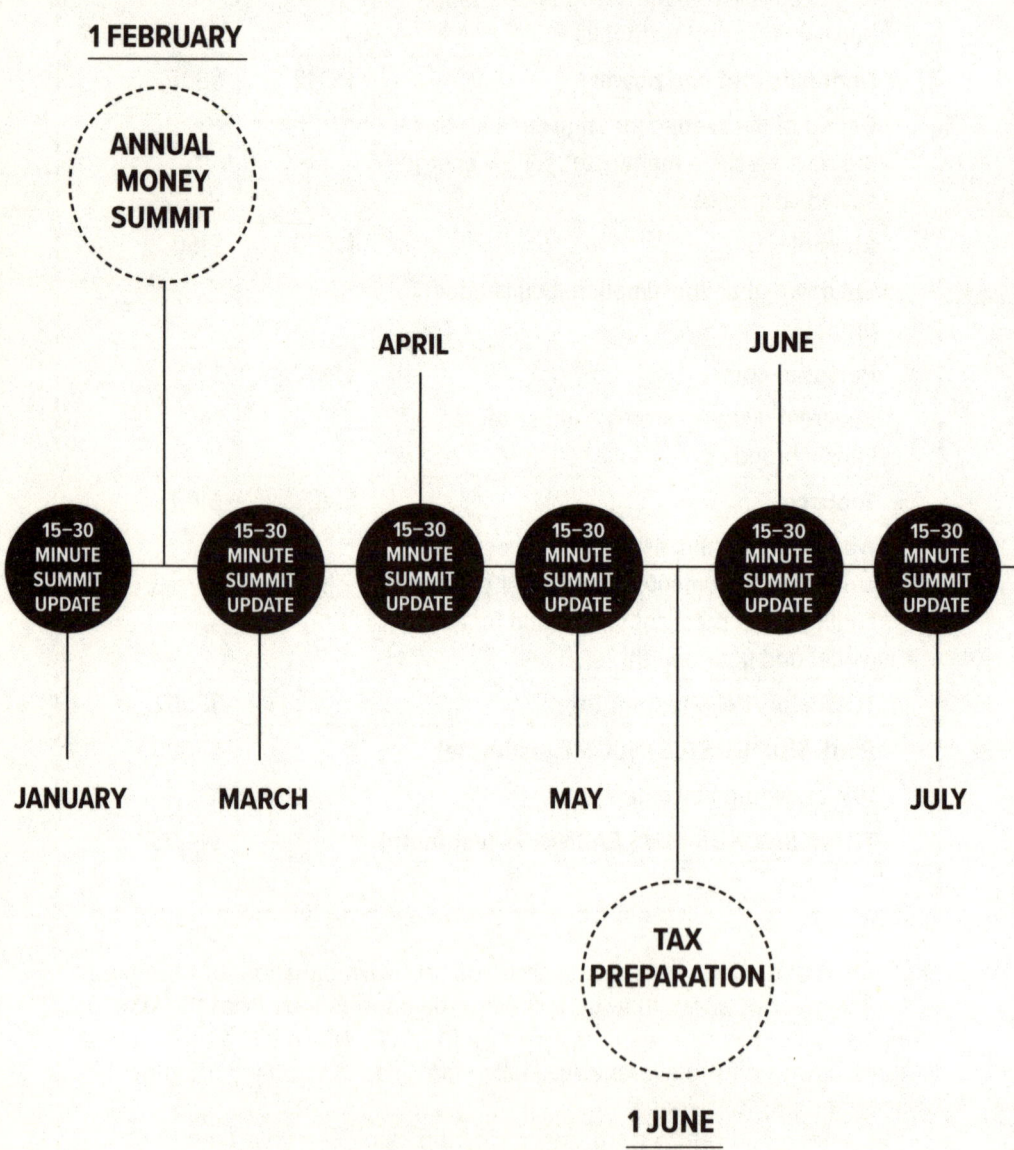

STEP 11: MAINTAIN GOOD HABITS

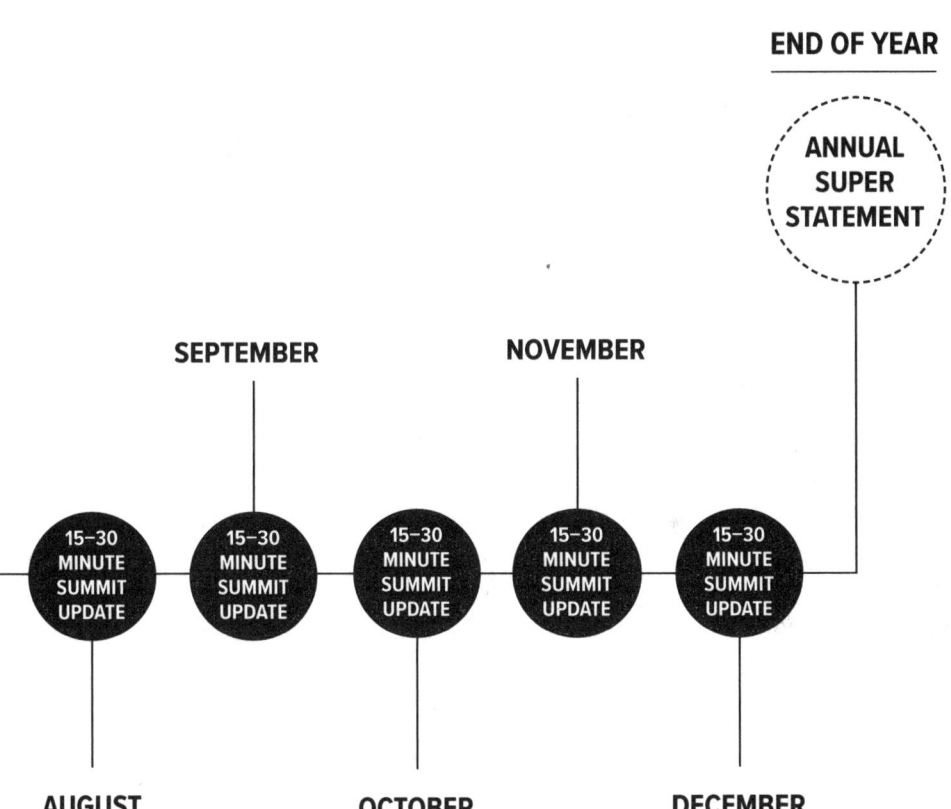

And don't forget: diarise major annual renewals

Get out all your major subscription (gym, magazine, TV) and insurance (life, income, car, home, contents) obligations, and diarise two weeks before their renewal dates. Check your bank and/or credit card statements for any you may have forgotten.

1 February: annual money summit

Christmas and summer holiday party time are over. It's back to work and the new year is ahead of us: perfect timing to review where you're at financially, see whether your goals are the same or have changed, and review any surprises.

Set aside a couple of hours for this – you may need some wine and snacks for sustenance. If you're in a relationship, this summit has to be a joint meeting where each of you speaks honestly and openly. It's also important to keep notes on what is decided, for reference throughout the year.

AGENDA FOR YOUR MONEY SUMMIT

A suggested agenda for your annual money summit would be something like this:

- Calculate our net worth. Has it changed from last year?
- Review the household budget and identify areas where we were over. (You'll need to refer to credit card and bank statements to analyse where those budget misses came from, so have all the necessary documents handy.)
- Set a new household budget for the upcoming year based on last year's results and learnings.
- Analyse whether our financial goals have stayed the same, changed or been achieved, and whether we need to agree to new goals. Discuss the situation and set the goals for the year.
- Review our individual financial responsibilities and assess whether each of us is happy to continue with those tasks, or maybe swap them to give one another greater insight into a different area of our finances.
- Make sure we're happy with our level of communication on money issues.
- Review our important documents – insurances, investments, superannuation. Organise and store them in a convenient place.
- Review our wills. Are they still current and do they represent our wishes?
- Assess our careers. Are we happy in our jobs? Are there opportunities for us to advance and earn more money? Are we confident in the strength of our employer and industry? Are there opportunities for us to improve our skills for advancement? In other words, will a change in job or career benefit us financially?
- Set an appointment with a financial planner for an annual review of our investment strategy and program.

Monthly catch-ups: 15–30-minute summit updates

These are quick meetings to track what was decided at the 1 February summit. Refer to your notes from the February summit to refresh your memory.

An agenda might address:

* assessing whether your household budget is going to plan
* examining your progress on achieving our goals
* doing a quick assessment of your career plans
* giving an update on your individual financial tasks to keep each other fully briefed on your areas of responsibility

Dates of major annual renewals, less two weeks

Get out all your major subscription (gym, magazine, TV) and insurance (life, income, car, home, contents) obligations, and diarise two weeks before their renewal dates. Check your bank and/or credit card statements for any you may have forgotten.

When the calendar note appears, go to the comparative websites and compare what you're paying with other similar products. Then, armed with that knowledge, ring your provider and ask whether they can offer you a better deal for the same service.

You have two weeks to do your research on finding and negotiating deal. If there's nothing better, great – pay the renewal if you still feel you need the service.

1 June: tax preparation

There are 30 days until the end of the financial year and you need to organise a lot of things to maximise any tax advantage:

* Collect your receipts for deductions (if you haven't been doing it all year).
* Follow up missing receipts from suppliers.
* Talk to your financial adviser to assess your investment portfolio (if you have one) and, where appropriate, how to offset any capital gains against losses.
* Make some extra charity donations.
* Take advantage of any incentives from the May federal budget.

Annual superannuation statement

Look at when your last annual statement from the superannuation fund came and diarise that week. The statements will come at pretty much the same time every year.

When the latest statement arrives, don't just file it with your important documents, but:

* read the results and commentary from the fund managers on how the fund has performed
* look at the investment performance and check that result on the comparison websites against the performance of similar funds
* check the fees you've paid and, again, compare them with other similar funds
* assess whether the investment options you've chosen within the super fund are still appropriate.

NOTES

TOP DAILY FINANCIAL HABITS TO DEVELOP

Now that your diary is organised with key dates and reminders for the year, here are some everyday habits that can save you big-time. I call them habits because they should become such a part of your daily life and routine that you do them almost subconsciously.

Ask, 'Is that your best price?'

This phrase should become part of your everyday language. Whatever you buy (apart from obvious things like groceries, of course), ask, 'Is that your best price?' It should be an automatic part of your purchase routine before actually paying for anything.

Most people will do it for big-ticket items like cars, whitegoods and electronics, but make sure you build it into the small stuff as well. It forces the salesperson to think about what they can offer you to get the sale across the line.

The barista might say, 'We have a coffee club where you get every fifth takeaway free' (that's a 20 per cent saving over five coffees), or the clothing store salesperson could say, 'We have a sale on next week and this dress will be 30 per cent off'. You just never know until you ask.

Be disciplined at the supermarket

The supermarket shop is your biggest regular weekly spend, so it deserves some planning before you get there to ensure every purchase counts. Always take a list of what you need after checking out the pantry at home and planning the meals for the week. Then stick to the list and don't be distracted by what else is on offer.

I know life is all about surprises and unexpected delights – you just don't want them to break the bank. If you do want to include some treats in the weekly supermarket shop, build it into the budget with a dollar limit.

Plug those expensive leaks

As we saw in Step 4, there are just so many stupid first-world financial leaks in a household budget. Having said that, I completely understand that one person's financial leak could be another's little reward that makes their day.

For example, I think paying for bottled water is silly when you can get it free from the tap and simply use your own water bottle. But a takeaway coffee every day is my little reward because I think it tastes soooo much better than instant coffee and I cherish that difference.

That's okay, though, because I *know* it's a financial leak: I've budgeted for it and I've made concessions elsewhere.

The key is just being aware of it.

Adopt a money mantra

'Ommmmmmm . . . Why am I buying this? Do I really need it?' Ask yourself these two very simple but frighteningly powerful questions before making any financial decision, no matter how big or small. Turn it into your money mantra.

It will break any emotional attachment to your buying cycle. You know those times when you're out shopping with a friend and you see something you like, your friend gets excited, you get even more excited, the fun is at fever pitch and you're swept along by the moment to buy it?

We all go through it. There are plenty of times when I've arrived home and wondered, 'Why the hell did I do that?' (You can re-read some of my confessions on pages 3 and 4.)

Your money mantra will snap you back to cold hard reality.

Look at a picture of your 'big goal' every day

 *Whatever your goal – a holiday, a car, visiting a child overseas, a new house, educating the kids, building a deck – put a photographic or drawn representation of it on the fridge as a constant reminder of why you're being financially disciplined.*

You have a wonderful dream to fulfil and you're going to absolutely cherish fulfilling it. Having worked hard to make the dream a reality will make it even sweeter.

TALK AGAIN SOON

Let's keep in touch. If you haven't done so already, a good start is to sign up to my weekly newsletter, which is free for everyone who's bought this book: check out the inside cover for how to subscribe. Each week I'll send you a short email (and I do mean short and sweet) that will not only tell you the latest important things I think you need to know, but also provide some reminders about good financial housekeeping. I'll also run some regular Facebook Live sessions and webcast events to answer your questions. I said at the start that I want us to build a lasting relationship with each other – and I mean it.

Life will continue to throw up financial curve balls, and I want to provide guidance on how to cope. I'm more than happy for you to reach out through the newsletter, Facebook Live sessions, webcasts or the forums on our Your Money and Your Life website (ymyl.com.au).

I'm not a working financial adviser; I see my role as breaking down financial problems into easy-to-manage solutions and pointing you in the right direction. And I'm a firm believer in sharing issues with others. Talking about problems can not only help you find solutions, but also stop you bottling up your emotions, which can often amplify the problem further in your mind. That's how panic steps in and clouds good decision-making. Libby and I talk things through all the time. It's how we cope with life's myriad little obstacles.

So do keep in touch.

ACKNOWLEDGEMENTS

For many years I've resisted writing another finance book because they date so quickly. As investment cycles, regulations and economies change so quickly, old information can be outdated and dangerous. Thanks to the team at Pan Macmillan for giving me the opportunity to match this book with a weekly email to readers highlighting the very latest information they need to know to manage their money. The book is the foundation and the email is the constant update. Special shout out to Pan Mac's Ingrid Ohlsson and Georgia Douglas for the support and encouragement.

My average week can be a bit of a juggle so I very much appreciate the understanding of Sunrise EP Michael Pell, AJ and Sam from Pinstripe Media, plus Katie. And to Sean Anderson for his wise counsel. Libby has been proofreader, critic, motivator and cheerleader: thanks and lots of love.

INDEX

A

accountants 191, 193, 198, 204
affording little luxuries 63, 82–9
  beauty 88–9
  celebrating Christmas without
    breaking the bank 85–6
  entertainment and dating 87–8
  fashion 88
  home 87
  simple tactics for 82
  travel without going broke 82–5
after-tax superannuation
  contributions 135, 136
Airbnb's
  ATO scrutiny of income from 201
  financial considerations 118
annual money calendar 232–6
  annual superannuation statement
    review 236
  dates of major annual renewals, less
    two weeks 235
  1 February – annual money
    summit 234
  1 June – tax preparation 235
  monthly catch-ups: 15–30-minute
    summit updates 12, 235
annual renewals 233, 235
annual superannuation statement 130–4, 236
apartment rental, vs hotel rooms 83–4
appliances (whitegoods) 70–1
asset allocation 218
assets
  buying 20
  selling your 59, 119
ASX Sharemarket Game 223
Australian Prudential Regulatory
  Authority (APRA) 34

Australian Securities and Investments
  Commission (ASIC) 34, 53
Australian Tax Office (ATO)
  Airbnb tax obligations 118
  asking for a withholding
    variation 195
  common tax mistakes 202–3
  how they check up on you 200–2
    benchmarking 200
    data matching 201
    serious detective work 201–2
    special focus areas 201
    whistleblowing 201
  and record keeping 195
  red flags for 202
  tax implications of part-time
    business 113
  top super tips 134–5
  work-related expenses 197–8
average Australian family budget 27
average Australian family
  finances xiii–xiv
  savings by following Kochie's
    11-step Money Plan 229–31

B

baby budget 168–71, 178
baby needs 170
babysitting club 177
bad approaches to investing 213–15
  being overconfident 213
  doing mental accounting 214
  giving in to fear and/or greed 213
  looking backwards, not forwards 214
  not admitting a mistake 214
  not constantly adapting 214–15
bad debt 39, 48, 210
balancing your budget 28–9

bank accounts
   comparing your accounts with the market 35–6
   culling unwanted 35
bank customers 38
   maximising the interest you receive 38
   minimising the interest you pay 39
   negotiating on everything 36, 38
   stop paying unnecessary fees 38
bank lenders 50
bank statements 3, 77
banking
   asking for a better deal from your existing bank 36, 38
   getting a lower home loan interest rate 33
   line up a new financial partner first before letting go of the old 36–7
   organising your 33–9
banking arrangements, analyse your existing 35
banking products, culling unwanted 37
Banking Royal Commission 34, 210
banks
   don't assume bigger banks are better 34
   how to find the right bank for you? 34–7
   safety of 210
basics, coverage of 5
be yourself (careers) 104
beauty care 88–9
being disorganised 79
being your own boss 109–10
benchmarking (by ATO) 200
beneficiary nomination (superannuation) 133
bill payment online 77–8
blogging 115
bottled water 78, 237
BPAY 78
brand, building your personal brand 101–2

brand names 78
budget 15, 25–40, 58
   average Australian family 27
   baby 168–71, 178
   for kids 185
   preparing your own 28–9, 46–7
   sticking to the 47
   template 30–1
building a home 71
building societies 50
building your brand 101–2
business documents 21
business vs hobby (as enterprise) 113, 114
buyer's agents 149
buying assets 20
buying your own home 143–60
   do your homework 148
   easing the financial pain of 148–51
   in a falling market 157
   find a guarantor 150–1
   find the right real estate agent 149
   first-home buyers schemes 148
   vs renting 143, 145–7, 212
   see also home loan

C

capital gains, offsetting with losses 196, 198
capital gains tax (CGT) 196, 198, 223
capital growth 223
car insurance 75, 125
car loan 75
car purchase 73–5
   be a smart buyer 74–5
   buying new or second hand 74
   getting the best loan 75
   timing it right 74
   understand your needs 74
career
   back your own instincts 103
   be yourself 104
   building your personal brand 101–2
   find a mentor 102–3

INDEX

getting the most out of your career 94–8
grab your opportunities 96
having a fallback position 99
look for a speciality, be unique 97–8
respect others 103–4
self-assessment 96
set yourself goals 98–9
slightly undervalue yourself 100–1
work on your self-confidence 97
working overseas 100
and your home loan 151
cars 72
  do you need a car? 72
  do you need a new car? 73
  owning or car-sharing 73
  running costs 75–6
  sharing the driving 76
  for your part-time business 117
cash 217
charitable donations 6, 187
checking your credit rating 54
cheque accounts 77
child care 173–5
  vs home care 174
Child Care Rebate 175
childcare subsidies 173, 175, 176
childcare facilities, important considerations 175
children
  deciding how to raise them 166
  deciding when to have them 165–6
  deciding whether to work or not 166–7, 170
  federal government benefits 173, 175–6
  financial steps once you have children 171
    costs of caring for children 173–7
    immediate steps to take 171–3
    ways to cut costs of having kids 177–8
  great joy but big cost 164
  part-time jobs 185
  pocket money rules 184–5
  preparing for children financially 168–70, 178
    financial pain 168
    financial plan 168–9
    talking with your partner 169–70
  supporting 6
  teaching them about money 179–87
  trust yourself to get it right 165–7
Christmas without breaking the bank 85
  holiday around home 86
  keep a price limit on gifts 85
  plan your meals 86
clothes 76
  budgeting 76–7
  buying less 77
  looking after 77
  planning 76
  pre-loved options 77, 88
  renting 88
  smart shopping 77, 88
clothes swapping parties 77, 177
coffins 79
community banks 50
compound interest 219
concessional superannuation contributions 135, 136, 195
consolidating debts 49–53, 212
consumer choices 186
consumer price index (CPI) 217
cooperative shopping 65–7
cosmetics 88
cost cutting to grow happiness 63–90
costume jewellery 88
couples
  annual money calendar 232–5
  avoiding sexually transmitted debt 19–21
  financial infidelity 17–19
  financial talk about having a baby 169–70
  healthy financial habits 12–15
  keeping your relationship solid in a crisis 16–21
  resolving your differences 16–17

couples *continued*
  talking about money 12–13
creative writing 115
creativity, as money making
  activity 116–17
credit card rewards 83, 86
credit card statements 3, 186
credit cards
  combining debt into a personal loan
    49–50
  consolidating debts 49–52
  don't fall in to the minimum payment
    trap 48–9
  interest 78
  paying off first 48
  transferring balances onto a zero rate
    transfer credit card 51
  transferring debt to a home loan 51–2,
    212
credit rating 54, 59, 210
  checking your 54
  importance of 54
  improving your 55
  using it to your advantage 55
credit unions 50
curtains 70, 72
cutting costs to grow happiness 63–90

D

Dad and Partner Pay 176
danger zones (sexually transmitted
  debt) 20–1
data matching (by ATO) 200
dating 87–8
debit cards 78, 187
debt
  concept of 187
  don't let it get you down 44
  paying off, versus savings 48, 49, 59
  paying off your most expensive debt
    first 48–9, 220
  seven-step debt diet 46–53
  taking control of your debt 45–6, 59
debt consolidation 49–53

combine your debts in a personal
  loan 49–50
consolidate all your debts into your
  mortgage 51–2, 212
  example 49
  how to choose a debt consolidation
    option? 52–3
  transfer all your credit card balances
    onto a zero rate transfer credit card 51
debt problem
  asking for help 46
  facing reality 46
  quiz 45–6
delaying income until next financial
  year 195, 199
delivered food services 78
details person 3
direct debits, forgotten 78–9
diversification of investments 218
dividing up financial
  responsibilities 13–14
documents
  business agreements 21
  read before signing 20–1
  sorting important 32
  see also tax records/receipts
doing your homework 8
draught stopping 70, 72
driving a hard bargain 9

E

earnings 187
emergency fund 60, 171–2, 217
energy costs and savings 69–72
energy-efficient homes 71
entertainment 87–8
entrepreneurs 109–10
  starting a part-time business 111–19
estate planning 14, 138–40, 171
exchange traded funds (ETFs) 221–22
executors 138–9, 187
exhibitions 87
expandable file for important
  documents 32

expenses, listing your (budget) 28
extended warranties 78

F

FaceTime 78
factory outlets 77
family, importance of 9
family budget *see* household budget
family business 21
family company 21
Family Tax Benefit (FTB) 176
federal government benefits to support Australian families 173, 175–6
15-minute monthly meeting 12, 235
finance lenders 50
financial advisers 136–7, 193, 222
financial counselling 58
financial decisions, based on economics not emotions 20
financial experiences, explaining to children 186–7
financial habits, healthy 12–15
financial infidelity 17–18
　how to fix 19
　quiz 18
　warning signs 18–19
financial plans, agreeing on 20
financial tasks, dividing up 13–14
financial values and goals 10–11, 13, 238
first impressions of your house (prospective buyers) 158–9
first-home buyers schemes 148
five-star energy rating 71
fixed-rate home loans, vs variable-rate home loans 149, 150
flexible working hours 108
forgotten direct debits 78–9
forward looking vs backward looking 4, 214
frugality 9, 119, 209
fruit and vegetables
　buying in bulk from markets 82
　cooperative shopping 65–7
funerals 79

future-proofing your earnings and assets 123–41

G

garage sales 77, 119
get rich quick schemes 211
gifts 85
goals
　career 98–9
　setting 10–11, 13, 238
good debt 48, 210
government benefits to support Australian families 173, 175–6
government co-contributions (superannuation) 134
grandparents, as child carers 173
graphic design 115
groceries 65
　buying in bulk from markets 82
　every little bit counts 68
　fruit and veg: cooperative shopping 65–7
　savings example 69
　tactics for beating the supermarket 67–8
　when on holiday 84
ground rules for spending 15
growing your income 60, 93–120
　get the most out of your career 94–8
　how to get more money coming in 94
　quick money earners 119
　side hustle (starting your own part-time business) 111–18
guarantor 20, 150–1
gym membership, 'freezing' your 119

H

having fun! 15
headspace, being in the right 2–4
health, investing in 6
health insurance 127–9, 168
healthy financial habits, couple approach to 12–15
heat loss through windows 70

heating 70
　and insulation 69–70
herbs, growing your own 82
hobbies (recreational) 4
hobby vs business (as enterprise) 113, 114
holidays 82–5, 86
　activities 84–5, 86, 177
　destinations 83
home and contents insurance 125
home care, vs child care 174
home energy and appliances 69–72
home improvement strategies 87
home loan
　asking for a lower interest rate 33, 37, 57
　budget for an extra $100 a month 57
　consolidate all your debts into your 51–2, 212
　increase the frequency of your repayments 56
　keep repayments constant when interest rates fall 56–7
　low interest rate loans 149–50
　paying off a chunk of your 220
　potential interest rate savings 37
　taming your 56–7
　and your career 151
　see also buying your own home
hot-water services 70, 72
hotel rooms 85
　vs apartments 83–4
house
　as asset 208
　renting out for holiday-makers 117
　selling your 157, 158–9
household budget 15, 25–32, 58
　important documents 32
　preparing 28–9, 46–7
　where's your money going? 27–32

I

ice cream 82
important documents, sorting 32

improving your credit rating 55
income
　from investing 221
　growing your 60, 93–120
　listing your (budget) 28
　starting a part-time business 111–19
income protection 136
income splitting 194
inflation rate 217
inside your home (prospective buyers' perspective) 159
instincts, listen to your own 103
insulation 69–70, 72
insurance 14, 124, 125–9, 171
　car 75, 125
　health 127–9, 168
　home and contents 125
　income protection 136
　life 126–7, 187
　superannuation 132
intangible benefits (flexible hours/working from home) 108
interest-rate savings, home loans 33, 37, 56–8
interest rates, home loans 148–9
interest you earn 186
　maximising 38–9
interest you pay, minimising 39
international banks 50
investing 205–22
　bad approaches to 213–15
　get rich quick schemes 209
　granny's advice 209–10
　modern advice 210–12
　one thousand dollars 220–22
　in property 209–10, 211–12
　seven key concepts of 215–19
　starting as early as you can 211
　tax implications 223
investment cycles 218
investment property 148, 152–4
　costs 154
　how to make it work 153–4
　pitfalls 152–3, 217

INDEX

investments 187
    for children 172–3
    shares or managed funds 172, 187, 209, 221
    superannuation funds 131
investors 208

J

Jessica's property example
    buying versus renting 147
    costs of an investment property 154
    fixed- versus variable-rate home loans 150
    negative equity 157
jobs (part-time businesses) 114–18
joint accounts 20

K

keeping your feet on the ground (importance of family) 9
key concepts of investing 215–19
Kochie
    financial weaknesses 3–4
    keeping in touch with 239
    weekly newsletter i, 36, 239

L

learning from failures/mistakes 4, 8
lenders, types of 50
Libby
    on child matters 100, 165, 166, 167, 177
    on financial matters 2–4, 29, 83, 88, 111, 209
    values and goals 10–11, 98
life events, affording 6
life insurance 126–7, 187
lighting 71
liquidity 217
living within your means 15, 209
lodging your tax return 194, 205
long-distance telephone calls 7
low interest rate home loans 149–50
luggage 85

luxuries, affording little 63, 82–9

M

maintaining good financial habits 227–39
making a list of your money values 1–22
making a will 14, 124, 138–40, 171, 187
managed funds 172, 221
meal planning 85
Medicare vs private health insurance 128
mentors 102–3
minimum credit card payment trap 48–9
missing income (tax returns) 204
money
    family and friends 9
    isn't everything 7
    knowing where it is coming from and going to 20
money mantra 238
money matters, keeping on top of 20
money secrets
    having no (between partners) 12
    quick money earners 119
    see also financial infidelity
money values, making a list of your 1–22
money wasters 78–9, 237
moonlighting a part-time venture 111–12
mortgage *see* home loan
mortgage offset account 39
mutual banks 50
myGov, to keep track of your super 134

N

negative equity 156, 157
negative gearing 153, 196, 212
negotiating
    pay rises 105–7
    purchases 80–1, 237
net worth 215–16
new car 73, 74
newborn payments 176
no-debt/low-debt pledge 43–61
no financial constraints, and richness 6
non-concessional superannuation contributions 135, 136

O

online banking 77–8
online coupons 82
organising your banking 33–9

P

paper coupons 82
Parental Leave Pay 176
parenting 165–7
part-time business, starting 111–19
part-time jobs, for kids 185
partners *see* couples
passions, as money makers 116–17
passive income, living off 6
pay rise
   if the boss says no 107–8
   mistakes when negotiating 106–7
   negotiating a 93, 105–6
paying attention to what your spend 64
paying bills 77–8, 186
paying off debt 220
   pay off your most expensive debt first 48–9, 220
   versus savings 48, 49, 59
peer-to-peer lenders 50
personal brand, building your 101–2
personal development 108
personal financial crisis (PFC), coping with 58
   don't go it alone 58
   focus on income generation 60
   planning for the next 60
   sell your assets 59
   set yourself a realistic deadline 58
   take control of your spending 59
   understand the big picture 58
personal loans
   combining debts into 49–50
   paying off 48
personal rewards 3, 17
personal shoppers 117
personal skills, as money making activities 114–15
petrol consumption and costs 76

philanthropic giving 6, 187
piggy banks 180
planning 228
   savings from following Kochie's 11-step Money Plan 229–31
   top daily financial habits to develop 237–8
   your annual money calendar 232–6
pocket money rules 184–5
   budgeting 185
   give them a sense of community 185
   savings plan 184
   value of money 185
positive gearing 212
power savings 72
pre-paying eligible expenses 196
pre-tax superannuation contributions 135, 136, 195
pregnancy insurance 168
preservation status (superannuation) 131
private health insurance 127–9
   choosing the right cover 128
   cutting costs 129
   do I need it? 127–8
   and pregnancy 168
product cycle 81
professional child care 173, 174
property crash, riding out a 155–7
   do you have too much debt against your home? 156–7
   do you want to live there for the next five years? 156
   early signs of 155
   never, ever buy before you sell 157
   set a realistic price when selling 157
property cycles 155–7, 209–10
property management (investment property) 153
property values 153
prospective buyers
   first impression of your home 158–9
   looking inside your home 159
purchasing, negotiating when 80–1, 237

INDEX

Q
quick money earners 119

R
reading 177
real estate agents 149
real returns 217
recycled clothing shops 77
refrigerator 70–1, 72
regional banks 50
relationships *see* couples
renting
   an apartment instead of a hotel room 83–4
   vs buying your own home 143, 145–7, 212
respecting others (careers) 103–4
respecting your partner's financial choices 15
restaurants 79, 87
rewards programs 83, 86
'rich', concept of 5–8
rich people, habits of 8–9
risk tolerance 8, 218

S
salary packaging 107
salary sacrificing into superannuation 134
savings
   from following Kochie's 11-step Money Plan 227–9
   versus paying off debt 48, 49, 59
savings accounts 180–1, 215
savings program (for your kids) 172, 181–2, 184
savings sprint (frugal living) 9, 119, 209
savings targets, setting 29
'scholarship' funds 172
school lunches 177
scrooge mentality 184
second hand, buying 82
second hand car 74
second hand clothes 77, 88
second hand textbooks 177

secured debt 51
self-confidence (careers) 97
self-education expenses 195
selling your assets 59, 119
selling your house
   in a falling market 157
   how to add value 158
      first impressions 158–9
      inside the home 159
setting savings targets 29
setting values and goals 10–11, 13, 98, 238
seven-step debt diet 46–53
sexually transmitted debt, avoiding 19–21
share portfolio, starting 221–22
shares 172, 187, 210
   'fantasy' portfolio 223
shoulder seasons (travel) 83
side hustle (starting a part-time business) 111–19
signing papers/documents, read before signing 20–1
Skype 78
smart risks 8
smartphones 78
specialty career 97–8
spending
   pay attention to what your spend 64
   spend less on the necessities 65–9
   take control of your 59
spending habits, be honest about 15, 22
spending leaks, plugging the 63, 64, 77–9, 237–8
spendthrift child 184–5
spoiling yourself *see* affording little luxuries
sports for kids 177
starting a part-time business 111–19
   considerations 112–13
   easing yourself in 111–12
   ideas 114
      use everything you have 118
      use your existing skills 114–15
      use your house 117

ideas *continued*
   use your labour 116–17
   use your passion and/or creativity 116–17
   use your vehicle 117
   tax implications 113
stay-at-home parents 165, 166–7
superannuation 124, 130–6, 208, 217
   ATO's top super tips 133–4
   government co-contributions 134
   salary sacrificing into 134
   supercharging your 134–6
   talk to a professional 136–7
   topping up 195, 199, 221
   will you have enough to retire on? 153
superannuation contributions
   after-tax (non-concessional) 135, 136
   pre-tax (concessional) 135, 136, 195
superannuation fund
   choosing the right fund 135
   consolidate your accounts into the one fund 135
   maximising your contributions 135–6
   switching to low-cost super fund 132, 134
superannuation statement, understanding your 130, 134, 236
   beneficiary nomination 133
   fees 132
   insurance (default cover) 132
   investments 131
   preservation status 131
   snapshot 130–1
   your details 130
supermarkets
   buying at 235
   buying ice cream at 82
   and consumer choices 186
   tactics for beating the 67–8

T

talking about money with your partner 12–13, 235

tax
   early tax preparation 198–9
   how the ATO checks up on you 200–2
   ignore it and it won't go away 192
   paying the right amount 193–7
   Ten Commandments 193–8
tax agents 193, 198, 203, 204
tax file number 134
tax implications, part-time business 113
tax records/receipts 195, 197, 198
   reckless record keeping 203
tax returns 191, 194
   common mistakes 202–3
teaching children good money habits 179–87
   how open should you be with your children about money? 186
   what not to share 187
   what to share 186–7
   what to teach and when
     ages two to four 180
     ages five to six 180–1
     ages seven to twelve 180–1
     ages thirteen and up 182–3
     big spender 184–5
     pocket money rules 184–5
     the scrooge 184
     starting off 179–80
teaching others online (money making activity) 115
teenagers and money 182–3
Ten Tax Commandments 193–8
   delay income until next financial year 195, 199
   have your tax adjusted 195
   income splitting 194
   keep accurate records 195
   negative gearing implications 196
   offset capital gains with losses 196, 198
   pre-pay eligible expenses 196
   self-education expenses 195
   superannuation top-up 195, 199
   work-related expenses 197–8

INDEX

tenants 153
term deposits 217, 221
textbooks, second hand 177
too embarrassed to say no 4
travel without going broke 82–5
trustee companies 139

U

undervaluing yourself (careers) 100–1
unexpected expenses (investment property) 152–3
unnecessary fees, stop paying 38

V

values and goals, setting 10–11, 13, 98, 238
variable-rate home loans, vs fixed-rate home loans 149, 150
virtual assistants 116–17

W

wage negotiations 93, 105–8
wants and needs 59
wasting money 77–9, 237

wealth creation 8
weather-stripping 70, 72
weekly newsletter (Kochie's) i, 36, 239
WhatsApp 78
where's your money going? 27–32
whistleblowing (to ATO) 201
whitegoods 70, 71
wills 14, 124, 138–40, 171, 187
   administration quiz 140
   checklist points 138–9
   events that can affect 139
windows 70, 72
withholding variation (tax) 195
work benefits, financial value of 108
work-related expenses 197–8
   unclear expense claims 202
working from home 108
working hard 9
working overseas 100
working parents 166–7

Z

zero debt 5
zero rate transfer credit card 49, 51, 53

NOTES

NOTES

NOTES

NOTES

NOTES